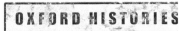

C000284276

DOMINION

SERIES ADVISORS
Geoff Eley, University of Michigan
Lyndal Roper, University of Oxford

Derek Hirst is William Eliot Smith Professor of History at Washington University, St Louis, and the author of a number of books on the history of early modern English history and literature, including *England in Conflict* (1999) and, as co-author, *Andrew Marvell, Orphan of the Hurricane* (forthcoming from Oxford University Press in 2012).

Dominion

ENGLAND AND ITS ISLAND
NEIGHBOURS 1500–1707

DEREK HIRST

OXFORD
UNIVERSITY PRESS

OXFORD

UNIVERSITY PRESS

Great Clarendon Street, Oxford OX2 6DP

Oxford University Press is a department of the University of Oxford.
It furthers the University's objective of excellence in research, scholarship,
and education by publishing worldwide in

Oxford New York

Auckland Cape Town Dar es Salaam Hong Kong Karachi
Kuala Lumpur Madrid Melbourne Mexico City Nairobi
New Delhi Shanghai Taipei Toronto

With offices in

Argentina Austria Brazil Chile Czech Republic France Greece
Guatemala Hungary Italy Japan Poland Portugal Singapore
South Korea Switzerland Thailand Turkey Ukraine Vietnam

Oxford is a registered trade mark of Oxford University Press
in the UK and in certain other countries

Published in the United States
by Oxford University Press Inc., New York

British Library Cataloguing in Publication Data

Data available

Library of Congress Cataloging in Publication Data
Library of Congress Control Number: 2011945241

Typeset by SPI Publisher Services, Pondicherry, India
Printed in Great Britain
on acid-free paper by
MPG Books Group, Bodmin and King's Lynn

ISBN: 978-0-19-953536-1 (hbk.)
      978-0-19-953537-8 (pbk.)

1 3 5 7 9 10 8 6 4 2

ACKNOWLEDGMENTS

All scholars are painfully conscious of their general condition of indebtedness, even if not always (such are human failings) of particular debts. An English historian who writes of English doings with the Irish, with the Scots, with the Welsh, is not only vulnerable to the charge of Anglocentrism; he is also more beholden than most to others' work. Forms of Anglocentrism are the subject of this book, so that charge needs no defence; but the book lacks citations, so the sense of obligation is as hard to express as it is to escape. The Bibliographic Essay only acknowledges a few of the monographs, and none of the journal articles, that have shaped this study. I would therefore like to state my gratitude to all colleagues in the profession whose labours and insights have helped me think and write about the motivations of English conduct, and its meanings whether in Ireland, Scotland, Wales, or indeed in England.

There are some particular debts I can express. I could not have completed this work without the *Oxford Dictionary of National Biography*: I did not realize when I began how invaluable I would find the ability to follow the turnings of individuals' careers, and like countless others I came to treasure online and immediate access. Less technologically based have been my encounters with John Morrill and Steve Zwicker, who between them read almost all of the manuscript: without John, the solecisms would be more frequent and the imbalances greater than they are; without Steve (and over many years), the argument and expression would be more ponderous. Matt Carlson executed the maps, and K.W. Nicholls gave me a valuable piece of last-minute advice. At Oxford

University Press, Christopher Wheeler and Matthew Cotton have been encouraging and helpful throughout—Christopher indeed from the beginning—as have Emma Barber, James Eaton, and Mary O'Neill more recently.

And members of my family have been as tolerant of my mental absences as they have been loving and supportive.

A Note on Dating

All dates are given Old-Style, with the year beginning on 1 January.

Since in this period the value of a pound differed substantially among the three kingdoms, sums have been given in English pounds; to make this clear after transactions or valuations in Scotland or Ireland, the word 'sterling' has been added.

CONTENTS

LIST OF MAPS

PART I
SEARCHING FOR MEANING
Empire and the Rat

England's assertion of its power over the subordinate kingdom of Ireland in the seventeenth century was costly, long-drawn-out, and often brutal (as indeed it had been in the sixteenth century). Encounters with Scotland were more tentative, as befitted dealings with an ancient and assertive kingdom, but in the middle of the seventeenth century (as in the sixteenth) they too involved costs and brutalities. Despite the costs, both series of engagements can appear merely opportunistic or even driven by circumstance. It would be going too far to say of this period, as it used to be said of the nineteenth century, that an empire was acquired in a fit of absence of mind. Nevertheless, there was a parallel with that later age of empire in the reluctance of early-moderns to acknowledge, still less to put a name to, what England seems incrementally to have been about.

The confidence of English assumptions of superiority was far more evident than the coherence of any arguments used in support. Defences were advanced not in modern terms of empire—reason of state, strategic need, regional hegemony—but in the characteristic early-modern frame of history and precedent. That lent them a certain piecemeal air. Memories of the twelfth-century Anglo-Norman conquest of Ireland made English domineering there almost second nature. Accordingly, the Chorus in Shakespeare's *Henry V*—or was it Shakespeare himself?—bluntly defined the enemy in the Earl of Essex's 1599 Irish campaign as mere 'rebellion', and the cartographer John Speed in 1601 presented his breathtakingly detailed map of the Irish wars under the heading *The Civill Warres of England*. Scotland was a trickier case. The king of

England's fortuitous and brief suzerainty over the northern kingdom in the late twelfth century bolstered Henry VIII's intermittent claims to overlordship, but the 1603 union of the Anglo-Scottish crowns began with a royal ride south from Edinburgh that might have challenged English assumptions of primacy: the subsequent residence in London of the king whom the kingdoms shared provided welcome reassurance. And when the monarchy fell in 1649 the centrality of the king's body was declared in reverse, for then the initial instinct of the English republic was to assume Scotland would go its own way (indeed, would go away, some journalists suggested). So, though in the 1650s Scotland and Ireland were forcibly incorporated with England, the cobbled-together title of the resulting union, 'The Commonwealth of England, Scotland, and Ireland', indicates some ideological haphazardness.

English power was manifestly projected; if the arguments were limp, how were the troops rallied, literally and metaphorically? That question may seem misplaced since this was not a time of democracy and an all-volunteer army; yet elections were held, and ease of recruiting always varied with circumstances and not only with prospects of pay. Anti-popish propaganda had provided a stiffening for English armies in Ireland at the end of the sixteenth century and again in 1649. When the soldiers marched into Scotland in 1650, the newsbooks accompanying them peddled eager reports of Scots' indecencies: the Commonwealth's journalists seem to have assumed that the soldiers and their supporters at home would find civility a legitimating argument. Then, at the end of the seventeenth century, England was drawn into intervention in Ireland and as well into an exercise in state-building that co-opted Scotland; in their ways, these were as demanding as the invasions of the 1650s, and certainly more definitive. How was popular support built up, when the newsbook sector was less active than it had been at mid-century?

Strange and Wonderful Prophecies and Predictions (1691) helps provide an answer. Within its small and physically vulnerable frame—broadsheets were designed to be displayed, and had a low survival rate—this prophetic extravaganza makes a striking attempt to join all three kingdoms in a single text. Most commentators were far happier addressing England-and-Ireland or England-and-Scotland. Whoever vented these prophecies did not quite escape that conceptual straitjacket: here, the

British empire, the English lion, and the Irish wolf all occupy the same space in the broadsheet without quite finding resolution or integration. But whoever set up the title was adventurous, according a rare prominence to a phrase that English panegyrists of the later Stuarts had used vaguely to attach added grandeur to the crown; here, the British empire seems expected to have wider and substantive appeal. We are not told explicitly what the empire is. Perhaps the 'new lands' to be added 'peradventure...to the British sovereignty' will be Irish rather than, say, American lands—in December 1690 when the broadsheet was licensed for publication, the campaign of King William III's forces in Ireland was in full swing and the need to bring Irish land firmly under his sovereignty would have been clear. But wherever they lay, the author expected them to fall under a British and not an English sovereignty—although in 1690–91 it was the English and not a British crown that was sovereign in Ireland and the American colonies alike.

What text and image do declare emphatically is the wartime context of this imagining of British unity and strength. Its most bucolic moment, the wonderful harvesting scene of women working beneath a summer sky, is secured by 'the noble resolution of the English for war'; the very peace of the countryside serves 'the glory of arms', since it enables the husbandmen to go off to fight, leaving their farms to the women. 'The rat of conspiracy', French and popish both, confronts the British empire at sea and in Ireland; indeed, that rat of Franco-popish conspiracy is what enables, or rather drives, the broadsheet's author to escape the usual discrete ways of thinking about the neighbours—as Irish, as Scots—and instead to think of a British empire comprehending all of them: it is surely as belligerent bloc that this empire achieves its composite character, its collectivity. *Strange and Wonderful Prophecies* thus provides a graphic instance of the way thinking about England's relations with its island neighbours was connected to European pressures. Indeed, at this beginning of the long engagement with France, the capacity of that engagement to shape 'Britain' and its empire was already clear.

Strange and Wonderful Prophecies and Predictions is scarcely an informed guide to the intricacies of late seventeenth-century history, nor a reasoned prompt to geopolitical analysis. It is an illustrated broadsheet, one furthermore whose title and its gothic black-lettering, whose

Figure 1 Bute broadside no. B 83, Houghton Library, Harvard.

ul Prophecies and Predictions.

&c. As to the Grand Affairs of *Christendom*: And what may in all
the Glory of the *British* Empire, and Confederate Princes; and to
sfusion of our Enemies, Abroad, and at Home: Lively portrayed in
ke never before made Publick to the World

Prophecy. 3. *Of Great Councils, and Success at Sea, &c.*

PRosperous Councils and Consultations amongst Princes, and Great Ones; for the tranquility of *Europe* are in Prospect, with Potent Fleets abroad; and we may expect to hear of some Famous Sea Victory, to the Honour of *England*, and the Advantages of all the Allies, to the opening and encreasing of Trade, &c.

Prophecy 4. *Of the Noble Resolution of the English for War, &c.*

FOR the Glory of Arms, and defying our Enemies perhaps in the Heart of their Strength; the Husband-men may leave their Harvest, to the Management of the Women; to Reap on in Victories more profitable to their Country, and Establish the Royal Diadem, beyond the Power of undeceiving by any Subtlety or Fraud, and the Rat of Conspiracy will be destroyed.

Prophecy 7. *Of Peace and Religion, &c.*

AFter many Victories Peace is gained, perhaps by the Sword; and New Lands, peradventure, added to the *British* Sovereignty; the Gospel shall spread its Beams as the Sun; Learning flourish, and be in its Ancient Esteem amongst Judicious Men.

Prophecy 8. *Of Plenty, Encrease, and Tranquility.*

THE Fields shall bring forth abundance, and the Pastures produce numerous Herds of Cattle; every man sit at ease, and in plenty, and a long Prosperity is promised, not only here, but many Neighbouring Kingdoms; the Grand Disturber being brought low and unable to rise.

Licensed, *December* 18.

Printed for *J. H.* 1691.

multiple small images and dramatic woodcuts, locate it in the almanac tradition. And there may lie a clue to its confident salute to a British empire, since the almanac-writers, more than any other group in the English printing industry, had been used to thinking in British terms for the best part of a century: whether for meteorological or astrological reasons, they were accustomed to casting their predictions over the island of Britain. And, again more than any other group, the almanac-writers were read by large and regular audiences.

The author and publisher of *Strange and Wonderful Prophecies and Predictions* certainly sought a popular audience, and with gestures and argument that may appear idiosyncratic. Since the eighteenth century, readers have been schooled to think of the revolution of 1688–89 not just as 'glorious' but as 'rational', 'sensible', even 'modern'; *Strange and Wonderful Prophecies* provides a corrective, for it suggests that there was no necessary and direct road from support of this revolution to a rational modernity. Of course, the broadsheet may be a quirk. The work 'J.H.', the publisher, produced in the 1680s and the 1690s includes plenty of material from the mainstream of the Church of England and the cause of William of Orange; *Strange and Wonderful Prophecies and Predictions* seems something of an outlier from such a press. Since the clothing styles and the natural hair of the figures in the illustrations are about thirty years out of date for a print from the bewigged world of 1690, it is tempting to think that 'J.H.' must have had some wood-block stock lying around from earlier decades, available for opportunist recycling. Yet the quality and thematic focus of the artwork and the crispness of the images do not suggest a worn-out piece of slipshod marketing— though haste is certainly apparent in the three-week turn-around from the issuing of the licence on 18 December to someone's acquisition of this copy on 7 January (or so the inscription at the top tells us). Furthermore, in ideological terms the broadsheet may not be quite so much an outlier. Others operated in the same territory: the Whig MP, admiral, and admiralty commissioner of the 1690s, Goodwin Wharton, was fully persuaded of his access to the Kingdom of the Fairies under Hounslow Heath. Perhaps more to the point—since one scholar has dismissed Wharton as a prime case-study for psychopathologists— William Atwood, Whig lawyer, polemicist, and future chief justice of the colony of New York, cast his own first defence of the revolution as the prophecies of Nostradamus. Indeed, as so often happened at times of early-modern upheaval—the Reformation, the Civil Wars—the press output of 1688 and the years that followed shows astrologers were in high demand. The Whig and Williamite causes thus crossed paths with the irrational.

The mis-shapen rat lurking in the fourth frame of *Strange and Wonderful Prophecies and Predictions* fixes the broadsheet in an older tradition than that of Nostradamus. A rat at the foot of an Edenic prospect of Englishness that is oriented north–south surely identifies a lurking and predatory France. But the true crown threatened there by what is, visually, very much a mole and not a rat conjures not just France but the Mouldwarp and with it the prophecies of Merlin; and then the Arthurian renewal of Britain cannot be far away. Britain, Great Britain, the British empire, resound in the almanacs of these years, not everywhere but loudly. *A Strange and Wonderful Prophecy, Pointing Out the Glorious Success of Great Britain* (1691) went as far as to predict that 'God in his good time shall see fit to spread, under the conduct and conquering arms of our conquering monarch, the prowess and glory of the British empire to the ends of the earth.' The almanacs as a whole were no more specific about the composition of this British empire than was *Strange and Wonderful Prophecies and Predictions*, and their writers were as ready as their intellectual betters to say Britain and mean England. They do nevertheless seem to have appreciated size, action, power, and the turn away from little England, and to have welcomed Scotland at least as a bit-player into King William's activist fold accordingly. The unification of the island kingdoms half-imagined in *Strange and Wonderful Prophecies and Predictions*, with its prophecies of the downfall of popery, the desolation of France, and a spreading plenty, carries with it a utopian promise that may redeem the strains and sufferings of war. But the traces of what would in a later age be known as jingoism in some of the almanacs' salutes to war and expansion, and the pejorative renaming some of them offered for Ireland—'Teagueland'—presume popular tastes that were far from utopian.

The conjunction of format with overt and implicit argument surely signals the persuasive purpose of *Strange and Wonderful Prophecies and*

Predictions. The almanac-style lay-out and title, the allegorical imagery and astrological figuring, the unfashionable hair and clothing, declare a popular appeal as much as does the utopian prophecy. And the technical quality suggests that this was not some piece of cast-off work but a new composition. Could it be a careful work of propaganda, whose utopianism, intimations of geopolitical grandeur, and predictions of inexorable triumph are designed to excite a popular audience, and to win it over to the support of a war that despite its expansionary appeal was not terribly popular?

PART II
ENGLAND'S ARCHIPELAGIC HISTORY
*c.*1500–1707

PROLOGUE

In the two centuries to 1707, England's relationships with its neighbours in Europe's north-western archipelago—conventionally called 'the British Isles'[1]—changed fundamentally. In 1500 a number of distinct polities and cultures, not to mention language-groups, occupied those islands; with some of these, England had at most only occasional and indirect dealings. By the end of the period a complex composite state firmly centred on England had formed.[2] Religious loyalties had fissured irreparably in the interim, but political configurations, cultural tastes, social practices, and economic fortunes, all increasingly overlapped in a way that they had not two centuries earlier. England's growing dominance in this changing regional order was multifaceted and by no means always formal; the political meaning of that dominance was, and is,

[1] The term has proven problematic, and not just because it was not much used in our period. It does not effectively denominate Ireland, which was never part of the Roman imperial province of Britannia; moreover, much of Ireland's history in the medieval and modern periods was formed in contested dealings among earlier inhabitants and incomers from the larger island that is more properly deemed British. There is precedent for careful distinctions, and the United Kingdom Interpretation Act of 1978 seeks to avoid confusion between 'the British islands' and 'the British Isles'. The last chapter of this book returns briefly to the matter of naming.

[2] It seems helpful to distinguish, if only along a spectrum, a composite state from the multiple kingdom that frames most discussion of the seventeenth century. In the composite state, linkages extend beyond the shared crown that is the primary characteristic of the multiple kingdom; in the composite state there is some coordination, if not yet centralization, of constituent regions whose distinct institutional and cultural heritages nevertheless remain clear.

resistant to easy generalization. 'Empire' in the early-modern meanings of the term does not fit very well until perhaps the end of the period, and 'hegemony' seems too fraught with modern theory. The 'dominion' of this book's title, extending figuratively from lordship or regality to mere control and even possession, acknowledges such imprecision.

England's dominance was shaped by economic and technological forces, but it rested as well on the decisions and prejudices, the triumphs, the compromises, and the sufferings, of countless individuals; it is the purpose of this book to trace some of these. The choice of 1500 as the starting-point may seem more arbitrary than many such exercises in periodization. It was a fairly uneventful year, but that quiet has its own appeal. At the other end, chronologically, the two decades after the revolution of 1688–89 were clearly a climacteric: for England and Wales, for Scotland, and for Ireland, individually and together. Two centuries earlier, no single moment or episode resonated equally across the archipelago. A starting-date that had obvious significance for one polity or for those along one axis, whether Anglo-Scottish, Anglo-Irish, or Anglo-Welsh—or, indeed, any other combination—might be taken to imply that it had meaning for the others, and thus that all the neighbouring polities, or other axes, were already aligned from a common point. Much better to choose a year with no obvious significance at all as a vantage from which to assess developments just as the tempo of interaction was beginning to change.

In 1500 England was no longer the expansionist polity it had been for much of the Middle Ages. The demographic recession brought by the Black Death put an end to the outward surge that had taken settlers from England into southern Wales, southern Scotland, southern and eastern Ireland. Concurrently, the Hundred Years War and then the Wars of the Roses drained military and political energies from the dynamic of conquest that had taken the knightly elites northwards and westwards from England's south-eastern heartland. Defeat in France and internal dissension generated a reverse dynamic, and England faced challenge at home. Early in the fifteenth century the Welsh leader Owen Glendower and his allies threatened English territorial integrity, while Scottish rulers soon pressed on the northern border. Then in 1487 the leading Anglo-Irish feudatory, Gerald Fitzgerald, 8th Earl of Kildare,

Henry VII's lord deputy in Ireland, in a supreme act of insubordination presided over the crowning of the pretender Lambert Simnel in Dublin, before dispatching him and his army of Irish kern and German mercenaries eastwards across the Irish Sea to battle, and disaster, at Stoke. Throughout the 1490s external backing from Burgundy, from Scotland, and from Ireland too, strengthened the next challenge, from Perkin Warbeck, the second pretender to the crown Henry VII had so recently seized from the Yorkist Richard III. Luckily for Henry, France—recovered now from the Hundred Years War—was distracted by its attempt to conquer north Italy.

In the aftermath of the Wars of the Roses, Henry Tudor famously practised retrenchment and consolidation at home, and nurtured England's trading ties to the Low Countries and Spain. But his strategic horizons were not bounded only by continental Europe, and it was not dynastic insecurity alone that led him to watch England's other neighbours to the north and west. Like all kings, he was subject to powerful ideological and cultural imperatives. More than other landowners, kings were expected to maintain their inheritance, their patrimony; they had therefore not only to protect frontiers but also to assert and defend past projections of royal power. Just as Tudor monarchs could not in honour forget that their forbears had ruled much of France—Mary Tudor was to die confessing her disgrace at losing Calais, the last relic of those ancient holdings—so they remembered all too easily Henry II's exploits in Ireland, and Edward I's in Scotland as well as Wales. When, at the beginning of his reign, Henry VII named his eldest son Arthur he did more than invoke the Tudors' own Welsh, or British, origins: he also gestured towards an ancient imperial myth. Such constructions of the past were repeatedly to disturb neighbourly relations.

More materially, Henry in the 1490s moved to contain Yorkist sympathies, the legacy of England's civil wars. His worries extended beyond the English nobility, for Lord Deputy Kildare's conduct had made a spectacle of disaffection in the shrunken medieval English Lordship of Ireland. Of course, Kildare had to go, but Henry did not stop there. In an unusual assertion of English power he announced in 1494 that he would reduce Ireland to 'order', and dispatched one of his English councillors, Sir Edward Poynings, along with 650 troops, to rule the troubled Lordship.

Poynings's brief sojourn exposed the complexity of the English presence in Ireland. However inconsequential most Englishmen thought the Lordship (if they thought about it at all), let alone the Gaelic lands beyond, there was a broader context. It was to the king of France that Henry in 1494 declared his intention of at last governing the Gael: prestige was involved. And like an imperialist of a later generation, Poynings—fresh from defending Calais—ran together the problems of holding overseas possessions: he it was who termed the fortified zones of both outliers 'the pale'. The arrival at last of English troops after decades of neglect excited some of the beleaguered Anglo-Irish to hope that the medieval conquest of Ireland would at last be completed.

The 'Irish enemies' beyond the Pale might threaten, but to the crown the most pressing problems lay with the supposedly loyal 'English of Ireland' themselves. They monopolized the Irish parliament in Dublin, and it was to their conviction of fundamental Englishness that Poynings appealed as he secured from that parliament a statute extending to Ireland, for the first time and at least as a theoretical claim, the whole body of English statute law to that date; he also confirmed the notorious Statutes of Kilkenny of 1366 that had declared the Gaelic population culturally alien, inferior, and dangerous. More famously, he persuaded parliament to pass the eponymous Poynings' Law that declared the subordination of the legislative process to the king's council in England. Although Poynings' Law was later to become central to struggles for Dublin's parliamentary autonomy, it was at the time not a statement of imperial intent but a practical response to Yorkist partisanship, an attempt to prevent Ireland's governor from using parliament for his own purposes. Ironically, under the Tudors it was to disable the Dublin parliament from serving on the Westminster model as a flexible instrument for building consensus around policy. Of far more immediate significance were the hard realities of direct English rule. Henry's revenues of just over £100,000 p.a. could ill support the Irish deficit of close to £7,000 p.a. sterling that Poynings's rather limp and painfully hard-pressed military adventure incurred. And for a king who ruled as well as reigned, and who famously read his state papers, the workload involved in actively governing Ireland probably provided its own disincentive.

Ruling Ireland through the local boss rather than from London had much to recommend it, and Henry quickly relinquished his dreams of order. In 1496 Kildare returned to Dublin with enhanced powers, firmer tenure, and firmer control over Ireland's administration, finances, and patronage. An equally significant mark of favour was the new bride he acquired from the fringes of Henry's royal family. Reformers, and there were some among the humanists who attended the King, might have questioned the wisdom of restoring magnate rule: despite Kildare's dominant position and web of alliances with bordering Gaelic chiefs, he had to deploy force continually—from his own retinue, mercenaries (usually Gaelic) raised with the royal revenues he controlled, and hostings summoned from the Englishry—in order to protect 'the king's subjects of Ireland' from raiders beyond the Pale. Nevertheless, in the all-important short term, Henry's decision to rely on Kildare paid off handsomely. It freed the Tudor throne from further dynastic mischief-making, and it protected Dublin itself from harassment by Kildare's own allies. The ambiguity of English policy is apparent. Henry's reaction at this point was not reluctant acquiescence to an outcome forced on him but considerable enthusiasm, since in 1504 he admitted Kildare to the great chivalric Order of the Garter after the lord deputy's victory at Knockdoe in Connacht—probably the largest battle fought to that point in Ireland—over Gaelic O'Briens and Gaelicized Clanricard Burkes, who had been pressing on the Anglo-Irish towns of Tipperary and Galway. Arguments for extending royal authority remained, and when two years later O'Brien struck back militarily at the Lord Deputy, Henry talked of taking an army of 6,000 to civilize the 'wild Irish'. But fortunately for the royal treasury, he continued to look to Kildare to hold Ireland's internal frontiers.

On the northern border, the auguries for major change looked if anything even less promising. England and Scotland had never formally made peace since the era of Robert the Bruce nearly two hundred years earlier, and they were locked in an unsteady cold war. In the fifteenth century insecure English and Scottish rulers repeatedly conspired with the disaffected across their common and contested border: it was by exploitation of Scottish faction that Edward IV secured one of the greatest coups of his reign, the recapture of the border fortress of Berwick in

1482. But such conspiracies were rarely—then or through much of our story—cast in a simple two-kingdom mould. Edward had briefly schemed with the McDonald Lord of the Isles to dismember Scotland; probably not coincidentally, the young Scottish king, James IV, declared that Lordship forfeit in 1493, just as Henry VII's distractions in Ireland, Brittany, and at home mounted. And it was in the aftermath of the forfeiture that Henry sent Poynings to Ireland. James exploited the presence of Warbeck by raiding northern England in 1496, in hope of regaining Berwick; Henry responded by preparing a major counterstrike, from which he was only deflected in 1497 by the outbreak of rebellion at his rear.

The 1497 rebellion exposed a weakness in the English body politic itself, for the rebels from Cornwall and Devon reached Blackheath, on the outskirts of London. Warbeck and his backers had not only been able to exploit Tudor dynastic weakness, but also perhaps a certain unfixedness in English nationhood. The inhabitants of the south-western peninsula proved no more eager to pay taxes for a war in distant Scotland than protesters in North Yorkshire had been to pay for a war in Brittany in 1489. Neither would have happily paid the bills that a final conquest of Ireland would have entailed.

Policy and pursuit then as now had multiple dimensions. The moves and counter-moves across the Anglo-Scottish border reveal not just two-kingdom tensions but three-nation convolutions and one-kingdom complications; they also disclose a further destabilizing context, in international rivalries. The Scottish polity, with its institutionally weak monarchy and assertive nobility, was perhaps unusually prone to faction. Scotland was also uncomfortably close to a powerful neighbour— England—which had long harboured dreams of overlordship or something more, and for that reason Scotland had long nurtured a friendship with England's other neighbour—France—on which England had also nourished designs. Scots, both nobles and commoners, served as soldiers of the French crown, and Scots attended French universities in droves. But in a world constituted of domestic faction as well as of international rivalries there could rarely be consistency. Although their public record in the fifteenth century was stormy, English and Scottish rulers could often see the advantages of peace even as they cultivated friends among their putative rivals' discontented subjects. And the more prominent among their subjects had to negotiate courses for themselves when there were genuine arguments to be made for both peace and war and when they were unsure which direction their own rivals would turn. There is perhaps no better measure of the complexity of Anglo-Scottish politics than in the doings of the two greatest noble houses in sixteenth-century Scotland, that of the Stewart earls of Lennox and the Hamilton earls of Arran, both of which had claims to be heirs to the Scottish throne; both houses yielded regents or governors of Scotland in the period, both gained French titles of nobility (Aubigny, Châtelherault), and their heads each spent years in close friendship with England. They were also at feud, sometimes deadly, with each other.

In these terms, England and Scotland might be thought of as magnetic poles: which way the magnetic charges aligned at any time might be a question. But as England's dynastic weakness grew throughout the sixteenth century, and as the potential consequences of the gesture of friendship towards which Henry VII of England and James IV of Scotland were turning at the end of the 1490s became more apparent, the intensity of those charges grew.

Map 1 England, Ireland, Scotland, and Wales 1500–1550

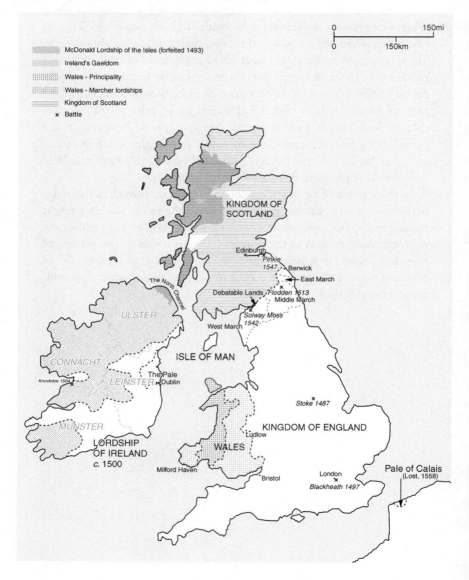

CHAPTER 1
THE OLD ORDER CHANGES 1500–1540

Henry VII was a king of his times, and his watchword was dynasty. The capture of Warbeck in 1497 and his execution two years later may not have constituted a watershed, but with two sons and a daughter approaching maturity, and with challengers removed, Henry and those he dealt with could now think beyond immediate survival. Nuptiality filled the air. By 1499 it was clear that Henry had beaten James IV of Scotland in the competition for a Spanish bride—Henry's potential help against France was more valuable than anything James could offer Spain—and in 1501 Katherine of Aragon arrived to marry Arthur, Henry's firstborn. No less momentous was the more drawn-out Anglo-Scottish saga of wary negotiation and threat that led in 1502 to the Treaty of Perpetual Friendship—the rarity of an Anglo-Scottish agreement almost warranting the grand title—and the marriage in 1503 of Henry's daughter Margaret to James IV. This was the marriage that eventually brought the succession of the Stewarts to the English throne, and in turn ensured the subordination of Scotland to England.

Royal marriages always mattered, but the scarcity of Tudor blood royal meant that the match between James and Margaret Tudor might prove decisive. Some of Henry's courtiers, calculating the reproductive odds, feared that the political dice would roll Scotland's way, and probably thought their king was whistling into the wind when he soothingly predicted that 'the greater [kingdom] would draw the less'. Their apprehensions surely grew when the death of Prince Arthur in 1502 brought renewed dynastic insecurity and gave Margaret added importance. Alarming signs of non-commitment to the Tudors emerged in the garrison of the cross-Channel dependency of Calais, and Henry turned to intensified, and resented, vigilance over the English nobility. The good feelings of the late 1490s fast evaporated.

The courtiers had reason to fear the consequences of linking Tudors and Stewarts. Hostilities between England and Scotland had spanned generations, and ill-feeling ran high. Scottish patriotism had been forged in the Wars of Independence against England, and as recently as the 1470s the old enmity had been reaffirmed in the hugely influential poem *Wallace* by the otherwise unknown Blind Harry. Around the same time, William Caxton was putting into English print a spate of works, including the *Chronicles of England* and Sir Thomas Malory's romance version of the Arthurian legends, that declared English sovereignty over all the islands and beyond, thanks to the legendary Brutus of Troy, founder of Britain, who left superiority to his eldest son Locrine of England, from whom empire over all descended eventually to Arthur...and so to Henry. Resentments were inevitable, and expansion of the Scottish navy coupled with assertions in 1506–08 of the old Franco-Scottish friendship—if not just yet the 'auld alliance' against England—prompted a suspicious Henry to forget Perpetual Friendship and arrest Scottish emissaries returning from France. Nevertheless, though anti-English sentiment in Edinburgh flared, there was another cultural pole in Scotland, largely across the Highland line, that inclined many Scots to moderate their distaste for the English: the greatest Scots poet of the generation, William Dunbar, damned Scottish Gaeldom to 'the deepest pot of hell', and celebrated 'our English' language and its luminary the poet Chaucer, 'a flower imperial'. With their own desires to cut costs by keeping the peace reinforced by some wider recognition that there were common interests, James and Henry managed to keep working together and with the regional nobles who served as wardens of the respective Marches on the Borders to reduce the raiding, reiving, and lawlessness endemic to medieval frontier zones. It was not the amity forecast in 1502, but it was not war.

Nor was it reform. Historians have traditionally cast Henry VII in his later years as a king who governed from the centre, carefully watching his accounts, building up his treasure chest, and, like some great spider, binding his noblemen to him by bonds of good behaviour. But in the north, in Ireland, and in Wales too, Henry showed himself quite comfortable with the powers of the land, and their distribution. The second largest proffer of troops for his abortive 1497 Scottish venture had come from the dominant figure in south-west Wales, Sir Rhys ap Thomas, on whom Henry relied throughout the reign. He reinforced that traditionalist approach to rule in 1501 when he dispatched the adolescent newly-weds, Arthur and Katherine, to take up residence in Ludlow Castle, and to preside—if briefly—as Prince and Princess over the administration of Wales and the Marches. Indeed, the celebration of Arthur as lord of the semi-autonomous Channel Islands of Jersey and Guernsey, his brief tenure as warden of all the Marches against Scotland, and the infant prince Henry's titular service in the 1490s as lord lieutenant of Ireland, suggest that the centralization for which the Tudor century is famous may have had something to do with the Tudors' infertility: otherwise, they might have settled royal princes in appanages on the frontiers. And there perhaps lies a longer-term tragedy. Historians properly resist the lure of counterfactual speculation, but any historian who deals with early-modern England's record in Ireland must find it hard to resist wondering how, given the powerful royal imperatives to hold and to keep, the painful future might have been mitigated. The Habsburgs in the mid sixteenth century managed to divide an empire. Perhaps if there had been more Tudor princes to go around, and one had been resident in Ireland, a partition whether voluntary or involuntary might have been achieved.

English political assumptions did not after all centre automatically on a unitary nation state. However impressive the tradition and rhetoric of a common law binding all Englishmen, there were seams in that fabric. The first Tudor king was, like his predecessors, accustomed to the corporate privileges and jurisdictions of the chartered towns, to the devolved and parcelled authorities of the northern Marches, still more to the fragmented structures of power in Wales, with its Marcher lordships, its Englishry in the south, and its mis-shapen royal Principality; and he was used everywhere to dealing with magnates: aristocrats who expected to have their way in their 'countries'—zones of influence centred on but by no means limited to the estates they owned. Henry VII was scarcely driven by thoughts of the programmatic extension of royal power, still less of the consolidation of an imperial monarchy.

Henry VIII's thoughts at the outset of his reign were no more structured, though they were more ambitious. He was 18 at his accession, and he aimed for glory, most of all in France. In his first campaign of 1513, and repeatedly thereafter, Henry sought to recover the English crown's medieval holdings across the Channel. There can be no doubt that he accorded much greater significance to his objectives in France, with or without glory, than he did to developments across England's other borders. Equally, there can be no doubt that throughout his reign his French ambitions determined developments elsewhere.

The old and threatening connection between France and Scotland emerged early in Henry VIII's reign, and it was not the work of Henry's imagination. Despite the 1502 treaty, James like many other Scots warmed more to the French than the English. His adaptation of French architectural styles for his massive building programme at Stirling Castle gave taste a competitive edge, while his warship programme—and his great ship the *Michael* was bigger than anything so far built by the English establishment—used French timber. The Scottish King seemed to hint at something more when he gave the potent name Arthur to the short-lived son born in 1508. He may not have realized just how competitive his young brother-in-law was. Henry lost no time in persuading his dashing friends among the nobility to help him spend his father's treasure in France. When he called his first parliament early in 1512 to request supply for war against France, he sensibly enough warned the Scots not to aid their old ally; but he went further, drawing on ancient accounts of feudal submission by Scottish kings to lecture a responsive parliament on the ingratitude of James IV, his 'very homager and obediencer', for refusing to join him in his designs on France. James, who had refused to break his friendship with France but had not, whatever Henry said, actively prepared for war, now had every reason to do so. Six months later he formally renewed the 'auld alliance': if Henry attacked France, Scotland would (with French aid) respond. Henry's assumption that he controlled events is nowhere clearer than in his outrage in 1513 when a Scottish herald turned up to declare war on him as he was settling down to siege-work outside Tournai. His surprise at what he insisted was an act of rebellion is itself surprising, since he had posited war on two fronts when he asked parliament for supply, and had accordingly assigned the elderly Thomas Howard, Earl of Surrey, to defend England's 'postern gate' on the northern border while he took his army royal off to France. Furious though he was—'I am the very owner of Scotland,' he insisted—he need not have worried, for Surrey outmanoeuvred and then devastated the invading Scottish force at Flodden on 9 September.

Were we to take the scale of carnage as evidence of hostility—not implausible in that age of low-technology warfare—we might assume the 1502 treaty had predicted an age of enmity rather than amity. James led his army in person, accompanied by the full weight of the Scottish nobility and Church, in the expectation of a glorious Border raid. But Surrey's young son, another Thomas Howard, who commanded the English vanguard, broke the usual conventions of restrained engagement—a quarter of Henry's 1544 regulations for war were to concern the taking of ransom—by proudly declaring that he was fighting to kill since, as the recent executioner of a celebrated Scottish privateer, he did not expect any mercy should he be captured. Estimates of Scottish fatalities by the end of the day reached 10,000, out of 20,000 Scots said to have been in the field; those left dead in the mud included James IV, nine earls, fourteen other leading lords, and two bishops, one of whom was the archbishop of St Andrews. That Thomas Howard may not have been alone in his dislike of the Scots is suggested by the poet John Skelton's gloating over corpses lying 'like drunken dranes', even that of 'Jocky' their king, which 'wretchedly…lay stark naked'.

The road to Edinburgh lay open after Flodden and Scotland lay leaderless—the Scottish King's son, now James V, was an infant—but Henry had scant interest once the northern kingdom no longer threatened. Little glory or gain was to be had there. Instead, he began to find, and not for the last time, that victory created bigger problems than war had been intended to solve. His sister Margaret, now Dowager Queen of Scots, was her son's protector, but the second in line for the throne was the head of the Lennox Stewarts, John Duke of Albany, born and brought up in France, a commander in the French king's Scots brigade, and the very embodiment of the French connection.

The surviving Scottish councillors were determined to call him home. Indeed, when Margaret quickly remarried—in this at least very like her brother—and thus compromised her position as royal guardian, Albany duly arrived (in 1515) with French troops at his back. Far from realizing whatever imperial dreams Henry might (or might not) have had, or at least—and a more likely aspiration—securing some token recognition of English superiority, Henry's Scottish policy for a decade or more after Flodden crumbled into a series of anxious attempts to prevent Albany tightening the 'auld alliance' still further and completing the encirclement of England.

Foresight is always in short supply, but Henry was even on a good day a less foresightful ruler than his father. The law of unintended consequences that doomed him to nervous watching of his northern frontier also largely determined Henry's increased attention to Ireland. For no more than England or Scotland was Ireland a self-contained political arena. Factions in Ireland had what proved to be significant extensions at the English court; Scotland was nearby; Gaeldom straddled national borders. Actions taken on one stage therefore reverberated on another, and often with mutually complicating echoes. Henry and his successors were to find it hard to maintain a coherent posture.

With the young king of England preoccupied with France and Scotland, the last years of Gerald, 8th and 'Great' Earl of Kildare, lord deputy of Ireland, can seem like the golden time of a Lordship left in local hands. Until his death in 1513, Kildare exploited to the full the resources of his position: his remarkable mandate from Henry VII guaranteed him the support of the English of the Pale, who prided themselves—at least in their imaginings—on their loyalty to the crown; his extensive Leinster territories allowed him both to protect and to dominate Dublin; his massive patronage of both English and Gaelic learning and culture earned him plaudits on all sides; and his multiple offspring allowed him to build marriage alliances—which he reinforced by selective use of force—with Gaelic and Gaelicized chieftains as far afield as Ulster (O'Neill) and Connacht (Clanricard Burke), as well as with Anglo-Irish magnates. Such was the Great Earl's power that his son, another Gerald, succeeded with little dispute to his pre-eminence in 1513. More tellingly, such was the political order the Great Earl established that the chief of the O'Donnells, the dominant clan in west Ulster but by no means free of challengers, felt secure enough in 1511 to go on pilgrimage to Rome and then spend several weeks at the English court on his return.

But there were those at the English court and in Ireland not satisfied with the Kildare peace. Gaeldom's competitive succession practices ensured constant background instability, and the geographic limits and political vulnerability of the Englishry's lands and law courts guaranteed background dissatisfaction. It was through coercion and accommodation that the 'Geraldines'—Fitzgerald followers—contained both instability and dissatisfaction, while regularized payments of 'black rents', or protection money, from Dublin and the other towns to assorted chiefs favoured by Kildare kept raiders away from their gates. Visiting London in 1515 to prepare bills for a new parliament under the terms of Poynings' Law, the young 9th Earl of Kildare may not have been surprised to find his administration of Ireland called into question. The coincidence of two local critiques alleging that Kildare's rule of Ireland was altogether Gaelicized in its arbitrary exactions, its private warfaring, and its favour to the 'wild Irish', suggests collusion with Whitehall. There, that assertive cleric Thomas Wolsey, emerging as the King's chief minister, was eager to reclaim lost Irish estates and revenues for the crown to help pay for the 1513 French adventure, and eager too to advance royal authority where he could.[1] When the English council moved to investigate the complaints, Kildare clashed openly with Wolsey, now a cardinal and, though a grazier's son, as self-confident as the mighty Earl. Kildare survived the encounter and returned to Ireland in 1516 with powers intact, but the episode proved to be the beginning of what was to be a long and fateful period of English governmental attention to Ireland.

The relative peace of the Lordship had hinged not only on the ageing Henry VII's benign inattention but on the dormancy of the Anglo-Irish magnate rivalry between the Fitzgeralds and the Butlers. The great earldom of Desmond in Munster in the south-west, one of the two branches of the house of Fitzgerald, had largely abandoned Lordship politics after the judicial murder of its then head and his sons in 1468; the other

---

[1] Such court concern may help explain why Thomas More, writing *Utopia* at just this moment, should have been interested in colonization of underused lands and also in mercenary warriors who appear suspiciously Irish.

branch—that of Kildare—had achieved hegemony. Meanwhile, successive Butler earls of Ormond, after participating enthusiastically in the Wars of the Roses, had settled in England as absentee Irish landlords. Leadership of Ireland's remaining Butler interest in the early sixteenth century devolved onto Piers Butler, head of a junior branch, who married one of the Great Earl's daughters and therewith gained Kildare patronage of his claims to the Ormond title and estate. The opportunity for Piers and for Kildare to cement a grand Anglo-Irish, indeed pan-Irish, alliance seemed to arrive in 1515, when the last of the absentee Ormonds died without sons, leaving the field clear for Piers. But though there were no Ormond sons, there were daughters. These had married Englishmen, and among their progeny was a leading courtier, Sir Thomas Boleyn. It was to prove a fateful, perhaps fatal, connection. But for the present, Henry had reason to protect the inheritances, and briskly ordered Kildare to switch his support from Piers Butler to the daughters. From Piers's sense of desertion grew a renewed Butler–Fitzgerald feud that was to threaten Ireland's very government, and against which Henry was to react with destructive finality.

The crucial interdependence of court and periphery, and the links to a wider world, are nowhere clearer than in these magnate quarrels. Since Butler felt betrayed by Kildare, and since Wolsey wanted to humble Kildare and increase the crown's independence in Ireland, what was more natural than for Butler to turn to Wolsey? Refortified as a Wolsey client, Butler was soon back on Kildare's borders, in the Ormond territories that he had quietly taken over, building an affinity among the Gaelic clans of the Irish midlands. One of these—the O'Mores of Leix—had been the death of the Great Earl, and his son the 9th Earl needed little encouragement to counter-violence. The outcry from these lordly broils broke at a sensitive time. In 1517 Albany increased Scottish pressure on Henry by contracting to marry the infant James V to a French princess, giving Henry extra incentive, if he needed any, to boost England's European standing and alliances. His brief pursuit of European pre-eminence that centred on the 1519 election for Holy Roman Emperor left him more sympathetic than ever to Wolsey's views on the nature of rule in a leading monarchy. The court cleric and diplomat Cuthbert Tunstal was soon to console him for the loss of the Imperial election by pointing out that he was after all true emperor—that is, in Roman law terms, without earthly superior—in his own dominions. From around this time too must date Henry's commission for the repainting of the already ancient, and prophetically if fancifully Arthurian, Round Table that still hangs in the Great Hall at Winchester Castle. These years also were to bring the magnificent and competitive chivalric display of the Field of Cloth of Gold, 'fought' with the new king of France, Francis I, in 1520. In 1519, Kildare was summoned to Whitehall to face conspiracy charges over his militarized following, and the following year Henry, determined more than ever to cut the proper figure of a king, resolved to displace him, and to end magnate government in Ireland. Accordingly, he dispatched the new Earl of Surrey—he who had led the vanguard at Flodden on England's other frontier—along with 500 troops and the more authoritative title of lord lieutenant.

Surrey's brief venture into Irish rule declared Henry's broad—if vague—ambition. It also exposed a dilemma that policy-makers in Whitehall had not previously had to face. English kings had long in practice divided Ireland between the Lordship and 'the King's Irish enemies' for whom the remedy in the statutes of Kilkenny had been exclusion. If Henry were to live up to his aspiration to be truly a king, he had to win acknowledgment of his rule from the Gaelic chieftains. This, he assured Surrey, would best be done 'by sober ways and persuasions, founded in law and reason, and not by violence'. Sober ways always come cheaper than large-scale violence, and Henry duly outlined a scheme of inducements, such as knighthoods for the compliant and recognition of their (English) legal title to the lands they occupied—but only if such lands had never, whether by conquest, forfeiture, or feudal escheat, been crown lands. Surrey and those he dealt with were to understand that Henry had vast rights by his 'absolute power', though he would, of his mere royal grace, rule benevolently. Surrey, who knew that much of what had once been the royal earldom of Ulster was occupied by the most powerful of the Irish clans, the O'Neills, was of another mind: 'this land will never be brought to due obedience but only with compulsion and conquest'. The tension between persuasion and coercion was to destabilize English approaches to Ireland for the rest of the century. Surrey soon appreciated the scale of the problem, and reported bleakly to the King that it would take years of work with at least

2,500 soldiers, and preferably 6,000, to reduce Ireland to order. Henry, with his eyes fixed on France, could ill afford that.

Surrey's uncertainty about conquest stemmed not just from his sense of the political but also from the strategic difficulties. He suspected outside troublemakers. Throughout their growing engagement with European foes—first France and then Spain—Tudor policy-makers watched nervously for contacts between a resentful Desmond in the far south-west and the meddlesome enemy. Surrey had identified something else: in revealingly obscure categories, he warned that 'the Irish can always be helped by the Irish and English Scots'. The 'Irish Scots' were the Gaels of the Highlands and islands just across the North Channel from Ulster, inhabitants of a Gaeldom that had little time for conventional state boundaries; the 'English Scots' were the Lowlanders, subjects of a Scottish monarchy aroused by Henry's other doings and surely looking to retaliate. Only conquest and thorough English control could ensure 'due obedience', Surrey warned, but that would be at a price.

Sadly for the King, no theatre of activity could be isolated. In 1521, Henry began planning with the Emperor Charles V a war to dismember France, their common foe, an exercise that Henry must have known would have repercussions in Scotland. In response to the small initial force Henry sent to France in 1522, Albany tightened the 'auld alliance'; by late summer of 1523 Henry's contingent in France was countered by the arrival of 5,000 French troops in Scotland and the beginnings of new fortifications, and by Albany's efforts to stir trouble along England's northern border. In the end, the episode proved an expensive charade: Henry was deserted by his Habsburg allies and had to bring his troops home, the French quickly exhausted Scotland's supplies and its welcome, and Albany was unable to persuade his fellow nobles to risk another disaster like Flodden once Surrey was known to be in the offing. Henry himself for once showed a certain moderation by declining to devastate the lands of any among his own far-northern subjects who showed signs of disaffection.

If England's northern borders in the early 1520s revealed the dangers in competition with a resurgent France, the disorders in Ireland showed the inadequacy of Henry's favoured strategy of divide-and-rule. The decision to replace Surrey with Wolsey's friend Piers Butler as deputy in

1522 proved a mistake. The greater distance of Butler territory from Dublin meant that the new deputy was less able to protect the Pale from Kildare's allies, particularly since English supplies were now diverted to French and Scottish causes. From London, Kildare instructed his followers to raid and harass, and by 1523 Butler himself was pleading for his rival to be allowed back. Kildare was duly restored to the deputyship in 1524, with his brother-in-law Conn O'Neill, the great Ulster chieftain, ostentatiously prominent at the ceremony. But Piers Butler was as reluctant as the King to accept a Geraldine status quo, and a proxy war between the Fitzgeralds and the Butlers simmered in the midlands, threatening the Pale. More alarmingly, the Earl of Desmond, not relishing a revived Butler presence with court support on his borders, shopped for foreign allies, first French and then Habsburg. In 1526, amid Butler charges of Lord Deputy Kildare's complicity in Desmond's treasonable activities, both Butler and Kildare were summoned to court.

Divisions at Henry's court soon compounded those in Ireland. To still the local broils, Wolsey fashioned a new deal: in 1528 Butler at last accepted the Ormond daughters' claims to the English side of the inheritance and accepted too Sir Thomas Boleyn's acquisition of the Ormond title; Butler himself was confirmed in the Irish lands, and returned to Ireland ennobled as Earl of Ossory and once again lord deputy. Kildare was detained at court. But some leading courtiers, including both Boleyn and his ally the Duke of Norfolk (formerly the Earl of Surrey) opposed Ossory's promotion to the deputyship, perhaps for reasons of jealousy; since the generally loyalist elite of the Pale needed a clear royal lead, the court's incoherence courted disaster. In Dublin's hinterland, violence returned to levels unknown for half a century as Kildare sought to show the King that he 'could not be served there, but only by him', as Henry put it angrily. Ossory, distracted by Desmond raids on his own lands from the west, could not protect the Pale from Kildare's Gaelic allies in the midlands. In this first Geraldine rebellion, Kildare's brother murdered the sheriff of Dublin while his Gaelic brother-in-law, Brian O'Connor, captured the vice-deputy, Lord Delvin. In 1530, Kildare was sent home under instructions to call off his followers and accompanied by a new lord deputy, Sir William Skeffington, an artillery specialist who had spent the last decade refurbishing the fortifications at England's

French outposts. Of course, Henry did not want to spend money, and sent only 250 ill-equipped soldiers with Skeffington; nevertheless, the appointment suggested Henry was rethinking his options. This was a crucial moment in the developing English presence in Ireland.

Henry did not trust Kildare, and he had doubts about other magnates too. The King's belief that noblemen existed to serve him only grew sharper as the escalating dispute with Rome strengthened his conviction of the imperial character of monarchy. The key statute declaring England's jurisdictional autonomy, the 1533 Act in Restraint of Appeals to Rome, based the claim to imperial kingship not just on theory but also on the 'old authentic histories and chronicles' that told of the glories of Brutus the Trojan and Arthur. Well schooled in these, Henry had little patience for subjects claiming autonomous—because ancient and inherited—privileges of their own. Wolsey's angry confrontation with Kildare in 1515–16 had been followed by a series of royal moves to correct or break the great territorial nobles. The Duke of Buckingham, foe of Wolsey, greatest of the Welsh Marcher lords, was fiercely admonished in 1518 for the disorder of his Welsh territories, only to end up on the block in 1521 for treasonous fascination with his own royal blood. On the northern frontier, where magnate independence had a dangerous dimension in these competitive times, Henry played the Marcher nobles off against each other even as he urged them to increase police action against the border 'names', or clans. The most decisive outcome was the humbling of the Percy Earls of Northumberland between 1525 and 1536. In 1531 another treason charge destroyed the turbulent Sir Rhys ap Gruffydd, whose south Welsh territories included Milford Haven, the port through which Henry VII had invaded in 1485. Lord Dacre, whose family had been the workhorses on the Scottish border for over a generation, narrowly escaped conviction on a similar charge in 1534.

Despite the painful meaning Henry's rule had for frontier nobles, he appointed Kildare deputy again in 1532—a fact that seems to confirm suspicions then and since of the unsteadiness of royal policy. There was a material rationale: the King's rivals were happy to exploit his Divorce woes, and he had to divert money and men from Skeffington's command as a precaution. A tight budget then allowed Norfolk to regain the deputyship for Kildare, who was cheaper because local. But Kildare was also vindictive, and now righteously indignant too. The view from Maynooth, his stronghold outside Dublin, must have been alarming: a panorama of royal action not only against Fitzgerald interests but against the customary governance of the whole Lordship. Cardinal Wolsey had, in his drive to dominate the Church and bind it to himself, in 1528 appointed as archbishop of Dublin as well as lord chancellor an aggressive ecclesiastical lawyer, John Alen, who promptly clashed with Kildare and local Church interests alike. Local suspicions that the crown was a dangerous innovator strengthened when Thomas Cromwell, newly settled in power by the end of 1532 as Henry's chief minister, made several non-Geraldine appointments to the Dublin administration. From Henry's Whitehall, of course, the view was of a turbulent Irish frontier run by unruly and sometimes centrifugal magnates, beyond them a wild hinterland whose relationship with the king was nominal at best. Further beyond—though geographically and politically much closer—stood a Europe turned hostile by the royal divorce.

Henry was boxed in. The geopolitical complications of the Divorce crisis diverted his resources from his unsteady Lordship, but those complications also compelled him to look to his frontiers. The capacity of the new politics of the 1530s to create unconventional alliances was also becoming apparent. Approaches by Henry's nephew, Scotland's young and ambitious James V—conventional in his religion, eager to embarrass Henry—to Katherine of Aragon's Habsburg relatives weakened the usual Franco-Scottish alignment; Henry's assiduous courting of François I of France ensured there would be no frontal response from that quarter. But when James in 1532 invited the McDonalds to make trouble for Henry in Ulster, Henry countered by instructing the Earl of Northumberland to initiate a border war as a distraction. The flux, but also the high stakes, of Anglo-Scottish relations appears in Henry's 1535 conferral of the supreme chivalric honour of the Order of the Garter on James—who had just begun his personal rule in Scotland—along with a proposal for a meeting to restore the Amity (and to divert him from thoughts of a French marriage alliance). Henry's nervousness about his frontiers appeared brutally in the treason charge he suddenly brought in 1534 against the Warden of the West March, Lord Dacre, a known friend of Katherine of Aragon: Dacre was ageing and surely loyal, though he

had—like lords on every medieval frontier—developed working relationships on the other side. Meanwhile, in Ireland, Kildare countered
Henry in kind. He was reported to be seeking Habsburg goodwill, and
he failed to take action against his cousin Desmond, who had certainly
had treasonable contacts of his own with Habsburg agents. More
provocatively, he transferred royal cannon from Dublin Castle to
Maynooth.

Feudal defiance was no longer a viable card to play. Transferring the
cannon was a gambit the 8th Earl might have tried, but now it quickly
spun out of control. Late in 1533 Kildare was once again summoned to
court, and as he left, he instructed his son, Thomas Lord Offaly, whom
he appointed his deputy in his absence, to disregard any summons from
London. Obedient in that at least, Offaly—who succeeded as 10th Earl
when his father died in the Tower in September 1534—protested in feudal terms against his father's arrest, and as he rallied his partisans and
much of the Pale elite he clearly intended the familiar Fitzgerald ploy of
negotiating from strength. But even if his killings of Butler supporters,
the siege of Dublin Castle, and the dismembering of Archbishop Alen
were intended as reminders of the centrality of the house of Kildare,
these were not reminders that the King would any longer accept. Still
more troubling were the reports that the young Kildare ordered the killing of anyone of English birth. The 9th Earl's conduct through the 1520s
had been violent enough, but the 10th Earl's in 1534–35 confirmed that
the government of Ireland could not be left a Kildare preserve.

Did displacement of the Kildare interest mean its destruction? The
ailing Skeffington's carefully staged butchery of Maynooth's defenders
after quarter had been given seemed to declare as much, and to declare
too a hard-pressed government's determination to establish itself by terror. Kildare raised the stakes further when he briefly raised the banner of
the Catholic faith against a heretic King of England and contemplated
flight to the Habsburgs, but others did not yet think in polarized terms.
The Thomond chieftain Murrough O'Brien persuaded him to surrender
in August 1535 to Skeffington's successor as deputy, Lord Leonard Grey—
and with some reason, since Grey (Kildare's maternal step-uncle) duly
promised him his life. Closer to the heart of the court Kildare had
another supporter in Norfolk, that stalwart of old nobility. Such affinities

and complicated loyalties did not make the final decision easy, and perhaps even Henry Tudor found the implications of breaking the Fitzgeralds daunting. Although the campaign against the rebels had cost him £40,000 sterling, not until early 1537 did the executioner's axe cut through the King's uncertainties along with the necks of Kildare and his five paternal uncles. These fell victim, like so many others, to the imperial monarchy that was being fashioned in these years out of Roman law and ancient lore; still more, they fell to the political pressures of the Divorce crisis that buffeted a wilful and now fearful king.

What the Fitzgeralds did not fall prey to was religious contention. Neither in Dublin nor at Whitehall did factions have clear religious identifications. The 9th Earl of Kildare's supporters at court, Norfolk and his Boleyn brother-in-law, differed markedly in religion; and while both the 9th and the 10th earls certainly tried to raise the banner of religion, Ireland's instabilities did not yet follow confessional lines. The overriding concern of Henry and of Thomas Cromwell at this point was to establish the crown's jurisdictional hold over the Church in Ireland, rather than to advance protestant reformation there. In England between 1536 and 1538, King, parliament, and leading bishops not only established royal control over the Church and dissolved some monasteries but took the first steps to confessional change, promulgating for the new Church of England that great engine of Reformation, the vernacular English Bible. But the parliament that Lord Deputy Grey summoned to Dublin in 1536 confronted only the first two of these tasks.

The cause of religion was soon to give the Anglo-Irish community who filled the benches in Dublin's parliaments a painful education in the ambiguity of being English in Ireland. But not yet, and they found it fairly easy to do what Lord Grey asked of them. They attainted, or declared forfeit, Kildare and his inheritance readily enough, for they were subjects of the crown and treason had been involved; anyway, many of them hoped for governmental reform and 'civility' English-style. They were also instructed—'forasmuch as this land of Ireland is depending and belonging justly and rightfully to the imperial crown of England'— to follow their Westminster counterparts by abolishing the pope's jurisdiction, to declare instead the King's supreme headship of the Irish Church, and to dissolve lesser monasteries in the Anglo-Irish areas.

These proposals occasioned signs of foot-dragging—though less than at Westminster—requiring fiscal concessions from the crown. There were signs of resistance from clergy of the Pale too, a number of whom had supported Offaly, but the government made a few examples and also abolished the clerical third house of the Dublin parliament, thus conforming Irish institutions more nearly to English. For the rest, parliament did as it was asked and made the King head of a generally patchwork and threadbare Irish Church, or at least that part of it which was the preserve of the English of Ireland. The Church in the Gaelic areas, poorer still and more fragmented, felt little of these developments.

Wales, the other great patchwork of the King's dominions, came under many of the same royal pressures in the 1520s and 1530s, though to very different effect. One pressure was the drive of the legal reformers and the humanists to regularize, to improve. Like Ireland, Wales had never been unified; its English speakers were probably even fewer, proportionately, than Ireland's, and the legal practices within its various jurisdictions were far from the ways of the Westminster courts. But it was contiguous with England. Trade and people could flow more easily, at least in the lowland areas; maritime traffic between the Irish ports and Bristol was easy and frequent enough, but foot traffic along the coastal roads into south and north Wales was still more commonplace. By 1541 about 2.5% of householders in some London parishes had Welsh surnames. But malefactors could travel too, and brigands from the hills who preyed on English border counties— habits alleged in the English nursery rhyme, 'Taffy was a Welshman, Taffy was a thief'—were more troubling to a king thinking imperial thoughts than those far away who preyed on the Irish Pale, as Buckingham had found to his discomfort in 1518.

There were political consequences to contiguity too, for English nobles were readier to seek Welsh estates and to use those estates in their English political adventures. When they lost, as many did in the wars and rebellions of the fifteenth century, their estates and titles fell to the crown. By Henry VIII's time, there were few Marcher lords left. But though Wales's political geography as a result looked very different from Ireland's, Wales was far from uniform, and the separate jurisdictions of the various Marcher lordships, each with its distinct legal practices, provided havens for criminals and fugitives. Several minor statutes of the early 1530s reduced Welsh legal immunities, and these were given a sharper point by the appointment in 1534 of Cromwell's friend Bishop Rowland Lee, a fierce disciplinarian, as president of the executive Council of Wales and the Marches. Lee saw his mission as hanging thieves, and if possible some of their gentry supporters too, as examples.

Wales was of course not immune to the crisis spawned by Henry's divorce. There were fears of French intervention, while allegations of conspiracy with James V of Scotland constituted the 1531 treason charge against Sir Rhys ap Gruffydd, the one remaining magnate in the region and one who, like Buckingham before him, was unlucky enough to have some royal blood in his veins. More certainly, Sir Rhys had been ill-timed in his friendships with Katherine of Aragon and Cardinal Wolsey. But Henry had been doing his own work of subversion, building up the courtier Walter Devereux, Lord Ferrers, as regional competition for Sir Rhys in the 1520s, just as he fostered challengers to Kildare in Ireland, to the Percy interest in the East March against Scotland, and to the Dacre interest in the West March. The King may simply have distrusted the old nobility and sought to promote his friends, but in the context of the increasing talk around the court of imperial monarchy, his jealousies suggest something more.

The Divorce crisis formed the context in a much deeper way for the great statutes of 1536 and 1543 that united the patchwork that was Wales with England, its law, and its parliament. As Cromwell steered Henry through the dangerous waters of the early and mid 1530s he recognized the value of statute in legitimating the break with Rome and declaring and enforcing the King's supremacy in the Church. Ireland had its own parliament through which the key measures could be pushed, but Wales did not and needed to be brought within Westminster's orbit (as indeed did the palatine county of Chester and the enclave of Calais, which were admitted to parliament along with Wales). There is therefore an element of contingency to Wales's union with England, and that is underscored by the way the 1536 statute left intact the old quasi-legislative powers of the prince of Wales within the Principality—just in case Henry ever wanted to create an appanage in Wales for a son.

But there is also in the 1536 statute a cultural and ideological fabric that stretches beyond the Divorce crisis. The text made few concessions to complexity as it generalized from the old dependency of the Principality of Wales on the English crown after its 1284 conquest: Wales 'is, and ever hath been incorporated, annexed, united and subject to and under the Imperial Crown' of England—no recognition there of the separate histories of Wales's variegated parts. The 1536 act resounds with the momentous claim to an eternal and royal *imperium,* a classical doctrine of autonomy and self-sufficiency officially framed three years earlier in the Act in Restraint of Appeals to Rome, but one here fused with ideas of territorial extent and domination. The proximity of the union with Wales to the Divorce crisis is apparent in the reminder that in disunity lies the potential for 'division, murmur and sedition', but the political claim of union rests on cultural and social assumptions too. Welsh language is 'nothing like, ne [nor] consonant to the natural mother tongue used within this realm'; Welsh customs are different from English customs; and it is only out of the entire benevolence of the King, his 'singular zeal, love and favour', that the act seeks 'utterly to extirp[ate] all and singular the sinister usages and customs' of the Welsh.

The Henrician claim to benevolence appears particularly in the 1543 statute's extension of English legal procedures so that the Welsh 'may grow and arise to more wealth and prosperity'. The claim had some validity, for Welsh gentry and farmers with access to the English market had long chafed at the restrictions on enterprise implicit in Welsh practices of partible inheritance and of lineage claims to land. In his later years, Henry VII had allowed scattered Welsh communities access (for a price: the privilege had to be bought) to the English property law, primogenitive inheritance, and rights to hold land across the border that were now to be extended throughout Wales. Such consonance of governmental aspirations with those of local interest groups was to prove sadly lacking in Ireland.

Taking shape in the Welsh union statutes was an ideology of empire. This underwrote main force and economic dominance with assertions of the cultural superiority of the rulers, and of the benefit they generously conferred on the ruled. That had been Rome's claim, and it was revived by Tudor humanists—Thomas More had imagined the Utopians' rule over willing neighbours in such terms. Myth too played its part, in the prophecies of England's primacy contained in the legends of Britain's founder Brutus of Troy. Thomas Cromwell clearly subscribed to these, and though the debunking scholarship of Polydore Vergil's *Anglica Historia* was published (in Latin) in 1534, it was widely execrated, most influentially by the antiquarian-poet, John Leland. Leland in fact played a considerable role in what was to prove a seminal moment of English self-affirmation. As he hurried around England and Wales, saving what he could of the past's written remains while the monastic libraries disappeared around him, he voiced growing scorn—widely circulated through his manuscript 'Itineraries'—for the laziness and credulity of those who lived outside England's arable heartland. And from the heart of the establishment, Sir Thomas Elyot, clerk to the King's council, gave learned grounding to that claim to superiority. In his influential *Boke Named The Governour* (1531), Elyot advised the Henrician gentleman who wished to understand the contemporary Scots and Irish to read Caesar's account of the no less savage Germans and Gauls. It is noticeable that Elyot did not add the Welsh to his target list. Presumably he was himself familiar with well-placed Welshmen like Cromwell's nephew by marriage, the administrator Sir John Price (Sion ap Rhys ap Gwilym). Such cultural amphibians must have helped ease the absorption of the Welsh into the world of parliaments and the central courts.

The points of contact that helped integrate Wales into an increasingly assertive English polity were lacking in the case of more distant Ireland. The migrants who might have built bridges were few, and so were such patronage resources as those that drew in the Welsh elite. The crown controlled a large pool of jobs in England (and Wales) to which ambitious and mobile Welshmen had access, and the crown was after Buckingham's fall by far the largest landowner in Wales. In Ireland, the crown's resources were few, and its lands in the early 1530s brought in a mere £350 p.a. The impoverished monasteries plundered in 1536–37 added little to the stock, while the new lord deputy, Grey, lacked the independent local patronage and connections that Kildare the magnate deputy had possessed.

But what Lord Deputy Grey did possess was a willingness to use force. An experienced soldier who had served on England's northern borders,

Grey followed Skeffington in going beyond the customary practices—killing swordsmen, taking hostages, seizing cattle—of war in Ireland. While Henry in England insisted to his northern Wardens that house burnings and scorched earth were strictly a matter of royal prerogative, appropriate to foreign wars but not to be used against disorderly clans within the kingdom, Grey burned Irish crops and dwellings with determination. After devastating the midlands strongholds of the O'Connor Faly, perhaps the greatest threat to the Pale, he led expeditions deep and destructively into Connacht and Ulster. His successors in office declared by their practice a similar conviction that Ireland was not England.

Innovation bred response. Such was Grey's energy and violence, such the apprehension sparked by the corridors for the royal siege artillery he cut through the woodlands, and such the swingeing submissions and levies of tribute he extracted, that in 1539 there emerged an unprecedentedly broad Gaelic coalition against him in the so-called Geraldine League. O'Donnell and O'Neill from Ulster, O'Connor from Sligo and O'Brien from Connacht, O'Connor Faly from Leinster, and many lesser chiefs, came together with the avowed aim of protecting Offaly's young nephew, the fugitive heir to the Kildare interest. The cooperation of some habitual foes in what was almost a pan-Gaelic movement testified to unease, and not just over the nature and extent of Grey's assaults on customary ways in the Lordship. Now too the King seemed to threaten the Church, for 1539 brought orders from a revenue-hungry crown for the suppression of all monasteries and friaries, and also of the pilgrimage sites that were the centres of considerable local devotion. The injunctions were scarcely implemented outside the Anglo-Irish areas—in all, about 55% of Ireland's monasteries went down, and about 40% of the friaries—but they attracted notice. So the chiefs challenged Grey in a massive raid from Ulster in 1539 deep into the heart of the Pale. And the crisis extended onto a larger stage, for in 1539 the pope revoked the 1155 bull *Laudabiliter* that had conferred the Lordship of Ireland on Henry II, and instead styled Conn O'Neill 'King of Our Realm of Ireland'. That gesture may, ironically, have helped spur his Ulster rival Manus O'Donnell to offer an Irish crown to James V of Scotland in 1540. There can be no mistaking the concern that reports of these initiatives triggered in Whitehall. At just this moment, Henry in England began the religious reaction associated with the Six Articles of 1539 that was to bring the fall of Thomas Cromwell the following year.

The moment was an extraordinary one in Ireland, as the Geraldine League suspected. Cromwell himself sensed it, and when he asked, after the 10th Earl's surrender in 1535, 'whether it shall be expedient to begin a conquest or a reformation', he articulated what was to become the central Tudor dilemma in Ireland. He never answered his own question, but in 1537–38, like a good bureaucrat, he dispatched an investigatory commission. Cromwell's correspondence with the Irish commission fills more than half of his extant papers for those busy months, and suggests the indirect costs of direct rule over an empire. There were direct costs too. In the heyday of the Great Earl the semi-autonomous government of Ireland had largely escaped the king's will, but at least it had been self-sustaining. The suppression of Offaly's revolt had cost £40,000, and while the confiscated Kildare estates boosted the crown's landed revenues significantly between 1533 and 1537—with the prospect of more to come as monastic lands were absorbed—expenditures more than kept pace. The King needed some way out. By 1537 the 2,500 troops sent from England against Offaly had been reduced to 340, and their pay cut. Whatever Cromwell's hopes may have been, Henry would only agree to a conquest if Ireland would pay for it, and Grey's 1536–37 Dublin parliament had shown no inclination to do that.

Henry's reluctance to spend left the Lord Deputy dangerously compromised. Without adequate forces of his own, Grey could not risk deepening the distaste for the royal supremacy within the Pale by emphasizing Church reform. Although he came from one of the most prominent protestant families in England, he made little attempt to wean the Englishry from the pope, and his unease showed in repeated squabbles with the loyally Henrician archbishop of Dublin, George Browne. Grey's lack of resources affected his warfaring too. Amid the upheavals of the mid 1530s—the fragility of peace was underscored by the Pilgrimage of Grace in England's north in 1536–37—a lord deputy needed troops. The old Kildare interest was leaderless and available, and Grey duly picked up some of Kildare's Gaelic allies, including inveterate troublers of the Pale from the clans of the midlands. With such aid, not only was he able to lead impressive military hostings beyond the Pale's edge, he also made progresses as far afield as Limerick and Galway, manifesting the royal authority and enforcing in the towns the oath of supremacy to the King as head of the Church.

There were risks in Grey's strategy, especially when it was his house in England that provided refuge for his sister, the 9th Earl of Kildare's widow, and her younger son. By 1538 members of the Butler family were denouncing the Lord Deputy as 'the Earl of Kildare newly born again'. Aided by an impressive victory at Bellahoe in 1539 over the Geraldine League, Grey was able to withstand such complaints. But he was powerless against the court faction that in 1540 brought down his patron and friend, Cromwell. Cromwell's execution coincided with the embarrassing escape to France of Grey's nephew, the young Geraldine heir; Grey's enemies—Butlers and resentful palesmen alike—seized their opportunity. Doubtless in order to protect the rest of his family, Grey quickly confessed to reconstituting the Fitzgerald affinity and to treasonous dealings with the King's Irish enemies.

Like so many of that decade's sacrifices to majesty and obedience, Grey's death was driven by the murderous uncertainties of the royal court. If Henry did not premeditate the palace coup against Cromwell, still less does he seem to have planned to displace Grey, who was in good standing when he arrived at court for consultations in the spring of 1540. But while mere faction may account for the rivalries of Butlers and Fitzgeralds, at a court that confronted momentous policy decisions faction was increasingly twinned with advocacy, even ideology. And that was to be the story of the Stewarts' court too. The negotiations between such riven courts, and among those courts and their hinterlands, were to become more complex and more costly.

CHAPTER 2
TITLES IN QUESTION 1540–1551

The years after the break with Rome were pivotal for a monarchy that had survived isolation and acquired from the English Church a massive treasure. Henry briefly felt freedom of action like that he had enjoyed at the start of his reign, when he had also had a sizeable treasure chest. This time, he and his subjects were to discover that the consequences of grand gestures in France—Boulogne, his acquisition in the 1540s, was worth little more than Tournai had been thirty years earlier—were massive. Just as at the start of his reign, he found he shared the stage with a Scottish king determined on alliance with France. This time, the war into which Henry blundered was to recast the English monarchy; paradoxically, it was also to go some way to reduce the old animosities between the two British kingdoms. And of course, the consequences of an Anglo-Scottish war were felt beyond the two kingdoms. Henry's policies and his distractions allowed the recasting of English rule in Ireland that had begun in the confrontation with Kildare to proceed further and faster than those at Whitehall had imagined. These proved years of unexpected possibilities—years that saw both crowns and landscapes laid open to remodelling.

Freedom of action was of course only relative. Henry knew all too well the interconnectedness of the diplomatic world. But the worst pressures did seem to have eased, and particularly the fears that France and the Empire would unite in a grand crusade against schismatic England. But though the falling-out of the Empire and France gave Henry hope of making European gains once more, the good relations of France and Scotland were troubling. If only Henry could persuade his young nephew James V of Scotland to meet him face to face: he could surely alert him to the errors of the Roman Catholic churchmen who beguiled him into foolish courses; he might convince him as well to extradite Henry's own annoying domestic critics who had taken refuge in Scotland. James demurred: his clerical councillors warned him of the dangers of kidnap if he crossed the border, his conscience would not allow him to yield up religious refugees. James assured France that he preferred the French alliance, but he gave Henry only a series of misleading signals in order to stall English military pressure on the refugee matter. Henry's long wait at York in September 1541 for a king—his ungrateful nephew, no less—who never came left him furious. His discovery on returning to London that his fifth bride, Katherine Howard, had been serially unchaste did not ease his temper, particularly since James, whose wife had been producing (short-lived) sons, had had the temerity to name each of these Arthur. James's reluctance to meet and talk friendship left Henry more than ever suspicious of Scotland's alignment in the coming war with France in which the royal cuckold hoped to revive his tattered name. Self-esteem after the public snub needed to be recovered too: 'We be indeed so injured, contemned and despised, as we ought not with sufferance to pretermit and pass over,' protested the King in his declaration of war.

The raids on the Scottish borders Henry unleashed were dwarfed by their theoretical framing. Henry's *Declaration* (1542) supplemented the usual English claims to feudal suzerainty over Scotland with an extension of the argument of the 1533 Act of Appeals: from Brutus the Trojan, empire over Britain had descended to the kings of England. In Edinburgh such arguments were probably thought more provocative than the raids, and James had little option but to retaliate. Few Scots died in the resulting encounter at Solway Moss in November 1542, though over 1,200, including two earls, five other lords, and five hundred lairds, were captured. James himself died—many said of shock—shortly afterwards, leaving the crown to his week-old daughter Mary Stewart. The fact that her heir presumptive, who was quickly appointed governor of Scotland, was the youthful James Hamilton, Earl of Arran—who equally quickly declared his own protestantism and accordingly his friendship with England and his interest in an English marriage for Mary—dramatically reconfigured the politics of north-west Europe. Not least, it allowed Henry to concentrate on his war plans for France untroubled by what the Scots might do, either on his northern border or in Ireland.

The breathing-space secured by Solway Moss was felt most of all in Ireland, where the lord deputyship of Sir Anthony St Leger constituted one of the most remarkable episodes of early-modern English rule there. St Leger had been the leading member of Cromwell's 1537–38 Irish commission, and had come to his own conclusion about what needed to be done. It would take time, not Grey's campaigning, to win the Gael to English ways.

What is so remarkable about St Leger's administration is the degree to which he initiated policies with little consultation at Whitehall, beyond accepting Henry's injunctions to keep costs down. Granted, control over policy after Cromwell's fall was unstable, and Norfolk—now the dominant figure at court—was scarcely the man of business Wolsey and Cromwell had been; St Leger therefore had more room to move. Nevertheless, the amount of room he made for himself tells us something of Ireland's political distance from England. Provided the lord deputy could produce results at little cost, Henry seems to have been ready to let him do so—as he had been ready to let Grey up to the end, albeit on a very different trajectory. We might wonder how much had changed since the days of the 'Great Earl' of Kildare, who had similarly been left to achieve results with the resources at his disposal.

St Leger's first moves on arriving in Ireland in the late summer of 1540 were military. Much as Grey had done before him, he struck at clans in the Wicklow mountains of Leinster who threatened the Pale from the south. But instead of contenting himself with extracting submissions, hostages, tribute—or, as Henry himself intended, extirpating the trouble-makers—he adopted a version of Cromwell's approach to Wales, indeed, a version of the approach Henry himself had toyed with for Ireland in 1520. He sought by institutional reform to turn Gaels into loyal subjects, even Englishmen. He hoped to persuade the clan chiefs to surrender Gaelic headships that rested on force and informal authority—the mere clan name, with its instrumental definite article, as title—and to receive instead English titles of lordship: thus, 'the McGillapatrick' on Leinster's western edge became Baron of Upper Ossory, holding his lands by knight's service to the king and passing those lands by primogeniture to his heir. Compliant chiefs were to use their best endeavours to speak English, to educate their sons in English, and to become settled, practising agriculture and building houses instead of following Gaelic transhumance cattle-herding practices and living in temporary huts. As important, they were to take rents rather than billet swordsmen arbitrarily on the peasantry. And those social practices would be set in the same framing of counties that had been exported to Wales, and that was the prerequisite for the rooting of English law and justice.

The programme, known to historians as 'surrender and regrant', was ad hoc, but it amounted to an attempt at cultural and social transformation. Versions of it were to remain the cornerstone of Tudor policy towards Gaelic Ireland for most of the century. Over the following months St Leger progressed into the midlands, and then westwards into Munster where he reached an accommodation with the long-disaffected and now divided house of Desmond. Throwing his support to one of the claimants to the earldom, St Leger persuaded him to acknowledge the King's supremacy in the Church and to abandon the violent methods required for survival beyond the Pale. In the summer of 1541, St Leger moved on to Ulster; there, though Conn O'Neill, the O'Neill, resisted, Manus O'Donnell agreed to the terms of surrender and regrant, gaining ownership over the lands of his lordship of Tyrconnell in return for agreeing to tenancy-in-chief under the king. Here lies the measure of St Leger's brilliance. A significant section of Gaelic Ireland had in 1539–40 in the Geraldine League drawn together against English policy and even against the English crown. By conciliation backed with that opening demonstration of force, St Leger convinced most of those involved—including, after some instructive campaigning, O'Neill as well in 1542—to come to a settlement. And in 1543 he persuaded the greatest Connacht lords, the Gaelic O'Brien and the Gaelicized Anglo-Irish chief of the Clanricard Burkes, to surrender their Gaelic identities and become Earl of Thomond and Earl of Clanricard respectively. The Lord Deputy had an opportunist's sense of the instruments of persuasion available to him in the confiscated resources of the Church, but he was also unusually willing to listen and to talk, and to go back to the drawing board if once rebuffed.

The vexed problem of inheritance and land-use taxed St Leger's flexibility most. Succession to the chieftainship in the Gaelic world was in principle competitive, with the strongest member of the lineage within (usually) three descents gaining recognition as tanist, or heir, within the lifetime of the previous chief. Claims to land centred on use rights rather than the individual property rights favoured in most west European law, and fundamental entitlements remained in the lineage; members of a sept, or kin-group, might readjust such entitlements each generation or at each change in leadership. Furthermore, use-rights overlapped, and chiefs claimed rights to services or dues from lands that in other respects 'belonged' to inferior septs or collateral lines of their own sept. Translating the fluidity of the Gaelic world to the more stratified language and practice of English common law was a massive undertaking.

The most intractable problem, as St Leger recognized, lay in the subordinate lines of the warrior elite. Kin and affines who had once possessed use rights and entitlements and now found themselves excluded by primogeniture would turn violent. St Leger therefore worked hard, especially in sensitive areas around the Pale such as the Kavanagh territories in the Wicklow mountains, to secure some provision for the sept's junior lines and for the sub-clans too. There was certainly an anglicizing aesthetic in his drive to balance the lordship of the newly conformist chiefs with groupings that approximated to the gentry and freeholders of the English social structure, but there was a security concern too. And security too led him to labour to adjudicate the competing claims and interests—O'Neill, collateral O'Neill septs, O'Donnell—in the key province of Ulster, adjacent as it was not just to the Pale, but more importantly to mobile Scots across the North Channel. On the chiefs' side, motives for cooperating were various. St Leger had incentives available. He generally recognized the western Gaelic chiefs' control over Church appointments and ex-monastic lands in their territories, and—optimistically presuming on continuing royal goodwill and solvency—he offered the Kavanaghs government loans to help them transform local farming practices, in a visionary attempt at consensual plantation on former Church lands in the region. A readiness to see their own sons established in a secured descent surely played a part in some chiefs' submissions. But so did the unease triggered by Lord Grey's ability to move artillery through the woodland passes, and by the persistence of English attentions in the twenty years since Surrey's lieutenancy.

The other achievement of St Leger's first year was the Act for the Kingly Title passed by the 1541 Dublin parliament. This declared Henry king of Ireland, and asserted his rule over all the people, not merely the Anglo-Irish of the Lordship. It thus put a constitutional frame around the Lord Deputy's effort to integrate the Gaelic Irish into the (English) political community of Ireland; in so doing, it had the potential to erode the special status of the Anglo-Irish. Although Henry himself had had no doubt of the validity of English rule in Ireland, the council in Dublin clearly judged that freeing his title from the embarrassing papal warrant of 1155 would be advisable.[1] It was indeed in the ecclesiastical arena that the drive to an Irish kingdom originated. The bishops of the Pale instructed by the King to establish the Church anew had met some questioning of the royal supremacy since Henry was not in fact royal in Ireland: 'The common voice in the Irishry is that the King's supremacy is maintained only by power,' one lamented in 1538. It would be interesting to know if he was merely exculpating his fellow Anglo-Irish by blaming the native Irish, or if there was such targeted opposition in Gaeldom. St Leger, less focused on the supremacy, was happy to keep the preamble to the 1541 Act general: it extolled the eminence of kingship, and blamed disrespect and disorder in Ireland on the 'lack of naming' of the kings of England as kings of Ireland. Henry's later complaint that he had been granted the crown of a kingdom which lacked the resources to sustain the dignity provides a reminder that kings did not always make policy. It points too to the weakness of the English position in Ireland.

The Reformation crisis thus changed the constitutional status of Ireland as well as Wales. For the Welsh, of course, the solution was their absorption into the English kingdom and, it was hoped, English ways and speech. St Leger's hope for the Irish Gaels was certainly absorption and anglicization; but because not only the geographies but also the medieval constitutional structures of Ireland and Wales were so different,

---

[1] Henry's advisers had no such qualms about the 1483 papal bull warranting the status of the semi-autonomous, but 'English' Channel Islands; indeed, the crown quietly accepted the bull until 1689.

the Irish could not be similarly absorbed. There was a further difference, one that was to prove crucially important in the seventeenth century. Henry's abiding conviction of his imperial kingship underlay Welsh unification and Irish kingly title alike. But whereas Wales was formally subordinated to statute and the crown-in-parliament formula of English sovereignty (of which, once it gained representation, it became a part), Ireland's new crown was 'united and knit to the imperial crown of the realm of England'. What that might mean in practice when, as Tudor theorists delighted in observing, the crown was most fully articulated when it was in parliament, nobody seems to have asked. Perhaps if Cromwell had been alive to shape the Act, someone would have. Henry himself let it be known that he was not responsible. Happy enough to receive the succession of Irish chiefs who made their way to court in the 1540s to declare their submissions and their acceptance of the royal supremacy, he may not have given much thought to what came next.

And in his campaign of accommodation, St Leger achieved much. The first of the Gaels to be ennobled—the Baron of Upper Ossory—sat in the upper house of St Leger's 1541 parliament, while other chiefs visited as spectators. To that parliament also came Desmond and several Anglo-Irish notables from the south-west who had been estranged during the generations-long primacy of Kildare and Ormond. The Ulster leader Conn O'Neill went to Whitehall in 1542 and became Earl of Tyrone. There were more surprising marks of St Leger's achievement. Although the royal supremacy had been a matter of occasional unease in the Englishry, and the Geraldine League had cited the 1539 order for the dissolution of monasteries and shrines when it sought foreign support, the Church issue now seemed defanged. The ageing Henry was by this time engaged in a religious reaction in England, and St Leger's concession to the local chiefs of effective control over Church lands and local Church appointments provided them further welcome reassurance. Although by 1546, the end of St Leger's first term in office, few of the monasteries and even fewer of the friaries in Gaelic Ireland had been dissolved, he was not pushing for action against those that remained. Accordingly, the two Jesuit priests Rome sent to Ulster in 1542 to reclaim the Gaelic heartland for orthodoxy met such a cool reception that after six months they sailed for Scotland.

Perhaps acknowledging St Leger's achievements, Henry's assorted enemies in his last years made no effort to trouble Ireland. The traffic in fact ran the other way. In 1544 O'Neill—now Tyrone—and Desmond were sufficiently reassured of the peaceableness of Ireland and the acceptability of the King's purposes that each dispatched a thousand of their own kern, or Gaelic foot-soldiers, to assist in Henry's French and Scottish campaigns; the following year Ormond followed suit with a larger number. The French and the Scots were distressed by the kern's readiness to fight to the death. For their part, their employers were ready enough to sacrifice assets they seem to have thought now redundant.

Ireland under St Leger appeared set on the familiar West European road to state formation. The King's authority was on its way to acceptance across the land; not even in long-settled south-east England was his will always done, so scattered Irish acts of disregard, even defiance, could be tolerated if submission was forthcoming. Some of the greatest lords of Munster and Connacht far beyond the Pale, not just Desmond but the new earls, Clanricard and Thomond, now participated in orderly local government, in local commissions, and in the appointment of county sheriffs; and the Anglo-Irish towns of the south and west were beginning to emerge from their long history of harassment and intimidation. We can think of this as anglicization, and note that Upper Ossory sent his eldest son off to Henry's court to be educated. Most importantly, by using the estates of the monasteries and of forfeited Kildare partisans, St Leger was creating a vested interest in a new order that centred on the crown and the royal supremacy. True, the ancient tendency of the Gaelic lordships to absorb all resources, including those of the Church, into the septs' local patrimony meant that in practice the crown had fewer resources to distribute here at the Reformation than in its other territories; as the event was to show, it meant too that the lords tended to see in ecclesiastical reform a threat to their interests. Nevertheless, St Leger's success in working with the Kavanaghs to plant English settlers on former monastic lands contrasts with the upheavals surrounding later ventures in plantation, in colonization.

St Leger's first term as lord deputy offers one of the most poignant counterfactual questions of early-modern Irish history, and surely of English history too: what if he had had more time and support? Conn

O'Neill confessed to tears when 'so just a governor' was recalled. Could the transformation of Ireland to which circumstances, and increasingly their own conscious choices, were pulling the English crown and its advisors have been peaceful? In his ability to rule with few English troops and without building a local interest of the kind that had undermined Grey, above all in his grasp of the graduated structures of the Gaelic world, and in his willingness to work with and through them even while he sought to reshape them, St Leger was without doubt the most perceptive and skilled of those who held power in Ireland.

But Ireland was never a self-contained field for action, and signs of strain appeared even before St Leger's successors began to distort his work. His success depended on the systematic deployment of royal patronage: at its crudest, to buy support; more generously, to inculcate habits of obedience. And patronage cost the King money, for the Church lands and Kildare lands were quickly followed by royal estates and royal manors, at below-market leases. Henry like his father believed that English rule in Ireland should be self-sustaining. He often hectored St Leger for giving away royal claims or royal rights, and sometimes carefully vetted what the deputy allowed him to see of the details of grants. For a king whose watchword for his Irish administration was economy, St Leger's practices were alarming. Grey's administration had run at a deficit of about £4,000 p.a.; St Leger's, with reduced military activity but also dwindling revenues, roughly doubled that shortfall. St Leger might have achieved long-term success in Ireland had he served a king who intended the confiscated Church wealth not for war but for reform; but that king would not have been Henry, and the Dissolution might not then have happened. The growing unease was to lead to St Leger's recall in Henry's last year for investigation.

As St Leger was not to be allowed to forget, the context of English rule in Ireland was formed of France and Scotland, and by the mid 1540s Henry's outlays there were soaring, along with his frustrations. The Anglo-Scottish breathing-space that opened at Solway Moss had been a luxurious moment. Governor Arran looked to a protestant future in both British kingdoms, and surely with some reason, since there must be something providential in the dynastic conjuncture represented by a child queen in one and a young boy heir to the other. Furthermore, protestantism and William Tyndale's vernacular English Bible were spreading slowly not just in the Scottish Lowlands but at court, and building some rare goodwill towards England. Henry, father of the young Edward, saw only dazzling possibilities in the presence in Edinburgh of the infant Mary as queen: a new Anglo-Scottish royal marriage might second the dynastic dice Henry VII had rolled in 1503. The disappointment, when it came, was aggravated by the scale of the hopes that were dashed.

Arran quickly discovered he had insufficient power to reverse Scotland's politics and alliances. In the summer of 1543 Matthew Stewart, Earl of Lennox—Arran's rival for the title of heir presumptive—returned from military service in France and as French ambassador made common cause with the Catholic and anti-English groups at court. After some little English pressure–particularly by way of the 'assured Scots', captives from Solway Moss who were freed in return for swearing to advance Henry's cause–the Treaty of Greenwich was signed that July, contracting the young queen and prince in marriage. But Henry's hand grew heavy on what he considered a vassal kingdom that was already showing signs of restiveness. His demand that Mary be brought to London for safety, that all treaties with France be broken, and that Scottish shipping and castles be ceded as security, convinced even well-disposed Scots that it was not even an Irish but a Welsh future that lay ahead: Scotland would be swallowed. In December 1543 the Scottish parliament rejected the Treaty of Greenwich, and Arran–who had already returned to the Catholic fold—renewed the 'auld alliance'.

Henry responded as furiously to what he insisted was rank betrayal as he had to the public snub by James V in 1541. Edinburgh was to be destroyed, along with the ecclesiastical centre of St Andrews and the port of Leith, for a 'perpetual memory of the vengeance of God...for their falsehood and disloyalty'. So began the 'rough wooing', the campaign of devastation that aimed to chastise the Scots and, almost incidentally, unite Mary and Edward, and with them their crowns.

The King's faith in the efficacy of such courtship methods was as striking as his vision of whatever united kingdom might develop. It would be an English-speaking kingdom, centred on England. In 1543 Henry's diplomats tried to bribe Arran to support the union by offering him the kingship of the Highlands (Gaeldom was not limited to the Highlands, but there was considerable overlap). And Henry played the Gaelic card again in 1545: in return for financial support, the McDonald chiefs who attempted to revive the Lordship of the Isles made their submission to Henry as overlord and promised aid in his campaign against the Edinburgh government. James V's 1532 invitation to the McDonalds to make trouble for Henry in Ulster pales in comparison. Only Donald Dubh McDonald's death in 1545 foreclosed the instructive spectacle of a king of England helping to re-establish a semi-autonomous Gaelic power that possessed major military capacity in Ulster as well as in Scotland's Western Isles. It is easy to see the tactical reasons why Henry should have contemplated such an option. Nevertheless, his eagerness to hive off the Gaelic strongholds from an English-dominated Scotland suggests that St Leger's assimilationist approach in Ireland did not represent a concerted English policy towards the Gael. At the very moment that Henry was trying to create new Gaelic enclaves, the Lord Deputy was striving to eliminate old ones, including those of the McDonalds in Ulster.

Consistency was not the only casualty of the straitened circumstances of the mid 1540s, as ruinous war in France merged with escalating campaigning in Scotland. When the King heaved his ailing body across the Channel in July 1544 at the head of a truly massive force of 42,000 men for one more adventure, the budgetary consequences were inescapable. St Leger's approach to accommodation in Ireland had been built on an open-handedness that was proving unsustainable. The Lord Deputy survived investigation in 1546, but the questions would not disappear.

Whitehall's doubts about St Leger were fed from Dublin. The good feelings St Leger had worked hard to create could never be universal, and support from the centre was needed to quieten the jealous. Such support was fast disappearing, even as the jealous grew in number and confidence. The beneficiaries of tacit royal largesse in Ireland had not been limited to the Gaelic chiefs: indeed, the largest gainers from dissolved monastic estates, with some 40% of the total, were English-born. The officials and captains Cromwell had sent over in the 1530s, and St Leger himself and his entourage, had done well for themselves out of confiscated Kildare estates. As they set themselves up on their new lands—in and around Dublin if they were senior officials like St Leger and the key financial administrator Sir William Brabazon, in the more unstable marches if they were junior captains—these came to constitute a novel interest group in Ireland, 'the New English'. The Anglo-Irish, long the 'English of Ireland', had no difficulty distinguishing themselves from these often abrasive newcomers, and in Elizabeth's reign they began to call themselves 'the Old English'. In 1546, Ormond was among those who levelled charges of corruption against St Leger's administration, and with some justice, for Brabazon's self-help was massive. Royal largesse could not be limitless, new sectional tensions were developing, and the involvement of Ormond in the politics of jealousy gave those tensions a dangerous charge.

Divisions within Gaeldom exceeded those that were appearing among the 'English of Ireland'. St Leger had had no illusions about the task facing him. Claims of lordship overlapped since chiefs and sub-chiefs alike drew resources from the same lands and people; possession of land depended on the ability to exercise effective power over it; and the working out of inherently flexible inheritance and succession practices also depended on power relationships within a warrior society. The greatest problem was the affront offered to competing lines within the sept when the crown awarded title—to land and lordship both—to the current chief and thus fixed his line in possession and superiority. The very first participant in surrender and regrant, Turlough O'Toole from Wicklow in Leinster, was immediately assassinated by his cousin. Just as promptly, St Leger went back to work trying to rescue what he could of the agreement.

It is hard to identify any guiding principle in St Leger's proceedings: he was learning on the job as he tried to accommodate the interests in the Gaelic lordships. But though he worked hard and had an unusual awareness of the risks involved in leaving subordinate kin-groups unprovided for, without more resources than Henry was willing to commit St Leger could not resolve the discrepancies between English and Gaelic ways. He was attempting social engineering with a handful of clerks posting along muddy ways, and it is no wonder that inattention and inconsistencies sapped the trust that was crucial to his schemes. Unable to devote constant care to the region, he could do no more in southern

Leinster than secure a truce among and within leading septs. There was no attempt to anglicize land-use, even—despite the promises—in Kavanagh territory. And some disputes proved too big to contain: when Conn O'Neill, Earl of Tyrone, exploited surrender and regrant to declare as his heir and Baron Dungannon his illegitimate eldest son Matthew, he breached not only the principles of English law but of Irish tanistry too. The resulting struggles within clan O'Neill were to tear Ulster apart for two generations, and disastrously to shift English policy.

Equally beyond easy control were the midlands. There, the O'Mores and O'Connors had been more or less contained in their woodland fast-nesses of Leix and Offaly by their neighbour and sometime patron Kildare. His fall left a regional power vacuum, intensified in 1546 when the Earl of Ormond succumbed, with his entourage, to food poisoning during his London visit to lobby against St Leger. With no one to restrain them locally and the Lord Deputy in London, the destabilized clans seized the opportunity to strike back against the Butler interests that had turned on them since Kildare's fall, and as well to raid deep into the Pale. St Leger showed his recognition of the seriousness of the chal-lenge by proclaiming the O'Connor and the O'More traitors; in his absence at court his deputy Brabazon mounted a raid of his own. Not content with scorching the local earth, the punitive method Grey had established as appropriate beyond the Pale, Brabazon took a step further by leaving troops in the main O'Connor stronghold. The following year, the fort was expanded and improved on orders from London; and when in 1548 St Leger was replaced as lord deputy, the incoming Sir Edward Bellingham established additional garrisons in Leix and Offaly, another on the edge of the Wicklow mountains fifteen miles south of Dublin, and two on the approaches from Ulster to the north. The process was driven by Whitehall's fears of Scots to the north and of French interven-tion into the south, but the Pale was being progressively expanded as well as strengthened. An expanded Pale might be to some a means to further anglicization, but lines of defence were scarcely compatible with assimilation.

Surrender and regrant did not therefore have a clear field, and nor did St Leger have a free hand. The clans were competitive aristocracies, and inherently unstable. The transition from raiding and pastoralism to settled agriculture could not be achieved overnight, nor without compensation—and the royal budget was rapidly tightening. Transforming Gaeldom was bound to be difficult. But there were equal difficulties on the other side. As the English court involved itself more with Irish government, its rivalries intersected—usually uncomfortably—with those of Ireland. Service to the king was no less competitive than Gaelic chieftaincy, it was no less predicated on warfaring—in youth and in old age alike Henry VIII was eager for the field—and courtiers were coming to recognize, as they had not during Kildare's last years, that there were now gains to be had in Ireland. Although Brabazon and St Leger had collaborated for years to their mutual benefit, the Lord Deputy was vulnerable when Brabazon—closer to the elite of the Pale and accordingly less than wholehearted in his support of surrender and regrant—fed information to a courtier who wanted the Deputy's job. And the new man, Bellingham, was like so many of his contemporaries a soldier as well as a courtier. The shift from St Leger's programme of accommodation towards Bellingham's garrison-work exemplified a major new element in English thinking and English rule.

The generation that came to power in the 1540s had preoccupations that marked it off from its Wolseian/Cromwellian predecessor. Not only was it shaped by its experience of resurgent French power and the anxieties and isolation of the Reformation years, it was also witness to the late arrival in England of the artillery revolution that was transforming European warfare. Fortification grew into fashion. Bellingham had commanded the defences of the Isle of Wight when French raiders tested them in 1545, but the most important convert to the new defensive mood and mode was Edward Seymour, uncle to the boy king Edward VI, who took over government as Lord Protector and Duke of Somerset on Henry VIII's death in 1547. Whatever St Leger's hopes of political and cultural assimilation, the raids on the Pale showed that Ireland still constituted a frontier; best military practices dictated the response. Unfortunately for the histories of Ireland and England, fortifications were both expensive and disruptive.

It was in Scotland after Henry's death that the growing English preoccupation with fortifications manifested itself most dramatically. The old King sought to harry southern Scotland into obedience, and in that cause Seymour, commanding in the north in 1544, inflicted two days of pillaging on Edinburgh for its refusal to surrender unconditionally, and burned the Border towns in 1545. When he himself gained control over policy, the newly elevated Somerset attributed the Scots' failure to abide by the Treaty of Greenwich to Henry's reliance on raiding and harrying. So, after smashing another Scottish army at Pinkie in September 1547, he proceeded for the next two years on a more systematic strategy of intimidation. Taking 16,000 troops with him, he established twenty-four garrisons in the southern lowlands as an English pale. Somerset's aim was to persuade Scots to support the royal marriage: the persuasion was to be in the form of protection for the willing, the fostering of the protestantism now established in Edwardian England, and the intimidation of the recalcitrant. But, inadequately funded as they were—by taxation on the English, it should be noted, not the Scots—the English garrisons failed to deliver much in the way of protection to the 'assured Scots'. Instead, as they contemplated the increasing numbers who refused to become or to stay 'assured' once French reinforcements arrived after Pinkie, they accentuated the negative side of their mission. It was not that the English commanders were necessarily hardened professional warriors, though many of their men were. Somerset, 'the good Duke', was one of the more devout and socially concerned of England's soldier-rulers, and some of his subordinates were otherwise paragons of Renaissance humanism. But they came to see the Scottish problem as one of obedience and betrayal, with predictable consequences as conditions worsened. Thus, Sir John Luttrell, the subject of a superb allegorical exercise in elevation by the painter Hans Eworth, having concluded after the French landings that there was 'no hope for any practice for friendship', urged 'an extreme plague with fire and sword which shall reduce them to poverty and submission'. Edinburgh, Leith, Haddington, Dunbar, Musselburgh, Buccleuch, Craigmillar, Hume, the villages around the Clyde, the great Border abbeys, all were burned, and scarcely a roof left on in Dundee.

The campaign to sway Scottish opinion by terror proved as ineffectual as the military strategy that prepared the way. Up to a point, Henry had been right. Military action could be persuasive: in south-eastern Scotland sheer weariness, and a recognition that wars would continue if the

French gained Scotland, did win converts to the English cause. For most Scots, though, the destruction and bloodletting at Pinkie and beyond consummated national identity in anger and resentment. There was no little relief when in 1548 the young Mary Stewart was spirited to France away from the iron fist of England.

Scotland's patriotic consensus nevertheless showed some signs of fraying. Surely the most remarkable mid-century unravelling is the career of the Earl of Lennox: when Arran held onto power by rejoining the Catholic Church and breaking with England in late 1543, Lennox promptly turned the other way. As the reward for his defection to England he gained lands in Yorkshire confiscated from the Pilgrims of Grace and a Scottish bride who, as the daughter of Henry's sister Margaret by her second marriage, had claims to the English throne; since Lennox had a good claim to the Scottish throne the couple featured in many dynastic calculations. And there were those who tried to build less personal bridges. Even before the Reformation broke, the great Scottish philosopher-theologian John Mair, in his *Historia maioris Britanniae* (1521), had condemned the competitive historical fictions of both English and Scots, and urged a common civility (against the barbarian Highlanders). Mair's call gained some support in the 1540s as protestantism spread in Scotland. From some of the Scots who fled to Berwick—the great reformer John Knox was one of these once he was released from French galley-slavery—to Newcastle, even to London, to escape religious persecution at home came enthusiastic calls to Anglo-Scottish union under 'one Empire and governance...then should we have this common weal of ours, being now...in most miserable state and condition to be most happy and most flourishing', as the Edinburgh merchant Robert Henrison put it in his *Exhortacion to the Scottes* (1547). Somerset's apologists reciprocated, pointing to the divine providence that set a boy and a girl on the neighbour thrones. Somerset himself sought to undo generations of English triumphalism with a 1547 proclamation of the necessity for union under 'the indifferent old name of Britons again', and with the assurance that Scottish laws and institutions would be left intact. As he reflected on the English taste for Arthurian myths, the anonymous author of *The Complaynt of Scotland* (1548) could be forgiven for his scepticism about Somerset's intentions.

Somerset managed to achieve not only near-bankruptcy but also what English rulers had for centuries sought to avoid, the cementing of a Franco-Scottish dynastic union as the foundation for a new French empire. In 1548 the French, still trying to regain Henry's conquest of Boulogne and not wishing to see England swallow southern Scotland, made a massive commitment to their old ally, sending eventually 10,000 troops and the equivalent of nearly £250,000 as part of a package deal that wafted Mary to France and betrothal to the dauphin, the heir to the throne. The English forces were soon driven from Scotland as the French dug in militarily and politically. And while the seizure of Church wealth had briefly made the English crown the richest in Europe, these years of highly professionalized warfaring in France and Scotland left it all but bankrupt. The crown's regular revenues were running at around £170,000 p.a., but the Scottish adventure in 1547–49 cost nearly £600,000, out of total military expenditures of just over twice that sum. The government just kept itself afloat, though taxes played small part in its survival: much more important were further land sales and above all further massive debasements of the currency. The government thus increased its unpopularity even as it saw its freedom of action lost. Meanwhile, Henri II staged a great festival of monarchy at Rouen in 1550, celebrating not only the imminent acquisition of Scotland—and eventually perhaps England— but also French expansion into the Americas. The self-confident imperialism of the French crown's triumphings offered a chastening comment on English achievement and English uncertainties.

However unsettling the mid-century dynastic crisis might feel in England, it was in strategic terms a moment of significant reorientation. The fundamental ambiguity of English garrison policy—aggressive purpose behind defensive walls—unfolded with consequences as massive in Ireland as in Scotland. Somerset had found that getting supplies through to his Scottish garrisons, particularly those away from the coasts, required what were in effect separate military campaigns. The forts in the Irish midlands were still more inaccessible. To support them, Bellingham turned first to the traditional royal prerogative of purveyance, compulsorily levying supplies from the Pale at fixed prices in that inflationary age; for the 300 men of the new Fort Protector in Leix and for the hostings he mounted in 1549, he levied enough for 1,000 men—3,442 cubic feet of grain and malt, and 2,120 head of cattle. The resentments provoked within the Pale community were matched by the logistical nightmare. The supply problem could be eased if the soldiers of Fort Protector, and of Fort Governor in Offaly, were given land close by, on the model of Roman military colonies. The palesmen had long urged not just further conquest but also the expansion of English settlement in order to protect Dublin's environs and extend civility; growing population pressure in England indicated that this might at last be possible. There were other considerations. In northern France in the 1540s too, Henry VIII's government had contemplated establishing colonies as part of a strengthened garrison—as so often, advanced military thinking was exploring options across several frontiers. And, of course, a deputy's friends and followers might hope for landed estates.

It was now that land began to play a disruptive role in the Tudor politics of Ireland, as the new context of the 'kingly title' provided justification, even an imperative, for action. If disorderly Gaels were no longer merely 'the Irish enemy' preying on the Lordship but rebels and therefore traitors against their king, they must suffer the consequences: not just execution but the forfeiture of their lands. St Leger's proclamation of O'More and O'Connor as traitors allowed Brabazon to begin the disposal of their territories, and as Thomas More had noted in *Utopia*, if those beyond the frontier did not till the soil, improve the land, they had no rights in it anyway—still less if they had no written titles of individual ownership. The political, the ideological, and the demographic now began their fateful colonial intersection in the woodlands of Leinster. English immigration to Ireland, English colonization, had ceased with the Black Death, if not earlier. Its resumption in the mid-Tudor period presented an insidious threat to clans who feared that their lands would form the next targets of new arrivals.

And as in Scotland, the garrison approach developed a momentum of its own in a time of French expansion. Troop numbers in government pay in Ireland rose from around 600 in the early 1540s to 2,500 in 1551–52, and costs rose accordingly. Indeed, costs far outstripped Irish revenues that had been crimped by St Leger's largesse and by widespread corruption. A deficit that ran at around £4,000 p.a. in 1540 was by 1550 close to £20,000, and £40,000 p.a. the following year as the Deputy fortified the south coast against French invasion. The wars in France and Scotland proved to have major policy-making consequences. No longer cushioned financially by confiscated Church endowments, the government was left vulnerable to events and to interest groups, and these could drag it further than it had intended. The government's first survey of Leix and Offaly in 1549 anticipated that most of the region would continue in Gaelic hands; by 1552 officials were assuming that most Gaels would be replaced by new English proprietors. The association of ethnicity and loyalty was—like the penalty of expropriation for the traitor—hardly novel. When Edward III captured Calais in 1347 he had much of its French population replaced by English settlers, and English policy in the Lordship of Ireland in the later Middle Ages had been premised on the separation of English from Gaels. But material pressures were central in the decision to eject the midlands septs from their lands. By 1552, consortia had formed that were willing to undertake colonization as a paying proposition, while the crown found it increasingly difficult to reject solicitations from officials and soldiers whom it could not pay adequately.

Nor could the crown restrain its servants adequately. Indeed, the character of some of the new personnel in Ireland helps to explain the English tendency in these years towards what would now be called 'mission creep'. Nicholas Bagenal became marshal of the army in Ireland in 1547, and was established by Bellingham on former Church lands at Newry on the edge of Ulster, with instructions to use them to maintain a garrison and contain the 'Scots', the McDonalds of the Isles, who were encroaching in the north-east. A tailor's son from Staffordshire, Bagenal had fled a murder charge to the relative safety of Conn O'Neill's Ulster; armed with the pardon the new Earl of Tyrone secured for him, Bagenal gained further military experience in France in 1544—presumably in Tyrone's contingent for that campaign. At one level, the decision to appoint such a man to such a command speaks well of the imagination of mid-Tudor planners: here surely was someone well suited to border warfare. But such an appointment could only undermine St Leger's hopes of assimilating Gaeldom. Commanders of pre-modern forts left without adequate support had few options other than private enterprise, and many of them relished their fate. As Bagenal took his own war into O'Neill territory, the frontier element in English conduct loomed large.

The incoherence of English rule in Ireland around the mid century stemmed not only from the crystallization of divergent policy options—assimilation, colonization, garrisons—but also from the mounting pressure of events. Henry VIII may have felt beleaguered during the Reformation crisis, but the governments of Edward VI's minority—first Somerset's, then from 1550 that of his rival, John Dudley, Duke of Northumberland—were far more seriously beset. Some problems they inflicted on themselves: not just the military adventure in Scotland that brought financial exhaustion, but also a new burst of religious innovation that triggered major unrest in south-western England in 1549. But they could not be blamed for the harvest failures at the end of the 1540s that intensified the effects of the currency debasements and provoked rebellion in East Anglia and unrest elsewhere.

Nor could English governors have anticipated the effects of the McDonald collapse of 1545 in Scotland's Western Isles. A destabilized Scottish Gaeldom then loosed a flood of swordsmen—the so-called 'redshanks', or short-contract fighters, as distinguished from the longer-term and more settled 'galloglass' contingents—down the sea lanes in search of other employment. Demand met supply in Ulster and in Gaelic Ireland more broadly. The reassurances given by St Leger began to crumble under the pressure of mercenary-fuelled intra- and inter-sept competition even before the appearance of the new English settlements in the midlands. Ireland's Gaelic world faced not only towards the Pale and the English garrisons, but also and always towards Scotland's Highlands and islands, and increasingly towards a wider Europe too. In 1549 the French crown explored the use of Scottish Gaels to stir their Ulster kin to attack the English. The following year, an English diplomat in Paris reported that Gaelic agents from the midlands were seeking French support and protesting that unless they resisted they might all 'be driven out of their ancient possessions', as the O'Mores and O'Connors had been. The reverberations from Leix and Offaly threatened to resurrect the alignments of a decade earlier, the time of the Geraldine League.

The Pale too was becoming querulous, for both religious and material reasons. Somerset's regime energetically manufactured money to pay its bills, and covered the shortfall between Dublin's incomings and outgoings by sending over coins whose bullion content had by 1550 fallen to about one-third that of their already-debased English equivalents, which were themselves dramatically debased. Economic confidence in the market-oriented Englishry plunged accordingly. The timing could not have been worse for religious change and the issue of injunctions to the Pale in 1550 to observe England's protestant 1549 Prayer Book. With the local economy battered by bad harvests as well as governmental misdoings, many prices in the Pale rose five-fold in 1551, and the lord deputy, Sir James Croft, warned that only the large army presence averted rebellion. Though a firm protestant himself, the overburdened Croft made little attempt to enforce the Prayer Book's venture towards doctrinal change, or to check the many bishops who told him they could do nothing with it on their own because of the local opposition to new ways.

Not for the last time, instability in Ireland elicited contradictory responses from Whitehall. Fears that the French would exploit Gaeldom's discontents prompted Northumberland to soft-pedal, and he briefly dispatched St Leger for a second term as lord deputy in 1550–51. But though the latter secured the cooperation of Thomond, of Desmond, of O'Donnell, and of O'Neill in his efforts to discourage the deployment of redshanks and to push on with surrender and regrant, the English council read events in more polarized terms and quickly recalled him. It saw the redshanks as simply Scots, allies of the French, enemy aliens rather than clansmen from the stateless reaches of Gaeldom, and pushed for more forts on Ulster's perimeter to protect the Pale. And when Croft reported from far southwestern Munster in the summer of 1551 that he had cajoled the leading McCarthy chief, the McCarthy Mor, into surrender and regrant, the council retorted sourly, in terms that as surely drew on growing impatience with the uncivil as it did on the new language of sovereignty, 'We win them not by their wills, but by our power...then shall they obey because they cannot choose.' But that same month, Northumberland swore in as gentleman of the King's privy chamber young Barnaby Fitzpatrick, heir to Upper Ossory (formerly the McGillapatrick), and whipping boy for his friend and fellow student, the unwhippable Edward VI. The choice between coercion and conciliation still lay before those in power, if they had leisure to make it.

Map 2 Ireland, 16th Century

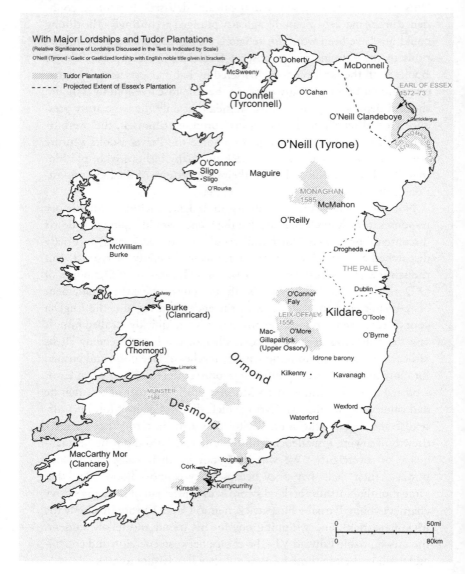

With Major Lordships and Tudor Plantations
(Relative Significance of Lordships Discussed in the Text is Indicated by Scale)
O'Neill (Tyrone) - Gaelic or Gaelicized lordship with English noble title given in brackets

Tudor Plantation
Projected Extent of Essex's Plantation

O'Doherty
McDonnell
McSweeny
EARL OF ESSEX
1572–73
O'Donnell
(Tyrconnell)
O'Cahan
O'Neill Clandeboye
Carrickfergus
O'Neill (Tyrone)
SIR THOMAS SMITH'S 1570
O'Connor
Sligo
Sligo
Maguire
O'Rourke
MONAGHAN
1585
McMahon
O'Reilly
Drogheda
McWilliam
Burke
THE PALE
Dublin
Galway
O'Connor
Faly
Burke
(Clanricard)
LEIX-OFFALY
1556
Kildare
O'Toole
O'Brien
(Thomond)
Mac-
Gillapatrick
(Upper Ossory)
O'More
O'Byrne
Limerick
Idrone barony
Ormond
Kilkenny
Kavanagh
MUNSTER
1584
Desmond
Wexford
Waterford
MacCarthy Mor
(Clancare)
Youghal
Cork
Kinsale
Kerrycurrihy

0   50mi
0   80km

CHAPTER 3
STATE FORMATIONS 1551–1568

The catastrophe to English hopes of Scotland announced by the 1550 festival at Rouen ushered in something worse: for a decade, England was to experience what had for so long been its nightmare, encirclement by France. French soldiers and officials ruled Scotland, Scots flooded into northern Ireland, and indeed the French in 1550 announced Mary Queen of Scots as their candidate for the throne of England. French domination of Scotland was thorough, and there was little in political or military terms that an exhausted England could do directly beyond modernizing the defensive fortifications at Berwick. Yet in what was left of that third quarter of the century, English forces were to march into Scotland five times. That they did so reflected not just the intensity of English fears of the French threat, present or future, but also the fact that the English had acquired Scottish friends whom they hoped to protect or advance. They found most of these friends in the years of adversity at the end of the 1540s and in the 1550s, when Scottish protestants like John Knox sought refuge in England, and then with English protestants sought a deeper refuge in Geneva, and when the far larger number of Scots who stayed at home learned what the French alliance could mean. With few thanks to England, the 1550s proved terminal for the auld alliance and the old enmity alike.

The 1550s and 1560s also have claims to being a pivotal moment for the English in Ireland. Although official thinking was overwhelmingly defensive, something recognizably like an English state emerged there, a veritable Tudor revolution in government. Of course, English governors would have said that they had no wish to dig English officialdom more deeply into Ireland: they sought to make that kingdom 'civil' and conformable, no longer a drain on the English exchequer, no longer an invitation to England's enemies in an increasingly divided world. And such hopes still seemed feasible: returned from a brave judicial foray into southern Connacht in 1552, lord chancellor Sir Thomas Cusack reported that he had found the number of ploughs multiplied fivefold in the decade since the piecemeal implementation there of surrender and regrant—a heartening sign, since elimination of the Gaelic pattern of cattle-raising and raiding hinged on the extension of arable.

But dig themselves in the English did: in to the first 'plantations', or colonies, of the period, and in as a governing interest. They did so with more or less gusto because to successive English governors the threats to stability in Ireland's provinces more than offset the occasional signs of economic advance. The rapid militarization of Ulster was particularly unnerving. The contests among Conn O'Neill's heirs generated a powerful market for Scottish mercenaries, and the clans of the Isles were happy to supply these. The Scots quickly became the wild card in Ulster's politics, as well as in English thinking about Ireland. That thinking grew grim after Croft and his enlarged army of 2,000 were humiliated in an attempt to eject the McDonalds—McDonnells in their Irish extension—from Antrim in 1552. Defeated in direct action, Croft then turned to divide-and-rule, and to Tyrone, in the hope that he would help expel the Scots. East and central Ulster soon saw endemic violence as Tyrone with Dungannon in tow and intermittently backed by the English confronted an alliance of McDonnells and of Tyrone's youngest son Shane, son-in-law to James McDonnell. Those who had urged primogeniture as the civilizing alternative to tanistry had not foreseen how bloody the transition might be.

It was not only Ulster that shook patterns of English rule around mid century. In Edward's later years, the arrival in Ireland of elements of the protestant reform agenda had caused dismay in the Anglo-Irish areas that felt them. The Anglo-Irish primate, Archbishop George Dowdall of Armagh, had conformed readily to the Henrician supremacy, but he could not abide the 1552 Prayer Book's attack on the traditional mass and the regime's acceptance of married clergy. In Kilkenny, Ormond's town, Mary's accession prompted enthusiastic declarations of loyalty to the

Queen as well as to old ways, for there the arrival of the brilliant evangelist and polemicist John Bale in 1552 as protestant bishop of Ossory had sparked something of a generational divide between supporters of the old and the new. The succession of Mary put an end to whatever dreams reformers may have had, but the degree to which religious division determined the discontinuities in policy can be exaggerated. Mary certainly appreciated St Leger's conservative religious views when she sent him back to Ireland in 1553 for a third term as lord deputy, but the protestant advisors of the ailing Edward had themselves been about to return to him the previous year since Lord Deputy Croft's budget deficit of about £40,000 p.a. had bought only military failure. Indeed, nothing shows better the dilemma of English rule around mid century than the alternation of deputies and emphases: Grey – St Leger – Bellingham – St Leger – Croft – St Leger, and then on to another militarizing man, the Earl of Sussex.

In practice, therefore, there was considerable continuity in Edwardian and Marian government in Ireland outside the field of religion. The problems confronting chief governors were intractable, they endured, and St Leger no longer had a magic wand. Hopes that he could substantially reduce the crown's military commitment, get government off its treadmill, crumbled as English initiatives disrupted Gaelic society. Several surrender-and-regrant agreements were falling apart—the O'Briens, like the O'Neills, suffered the consequences of Gaelic serial marriages and competing progeny; the seizure of O'More and O'Connor lands for plantation sparked wide resentment; and the material resources with which St Leger once bought peace had evaporated. Indeed, his earlier success now haunted him, for in the straitened circumstances of Whitehall in the 1550s the old charges of financial corruption had more purchase. From 1554 until his final unhappy recall in 1556, St Leger was under constant investigation as courtiers jostled for his place, while in Ireland New English suspicions of his cost-cutting turn towards the Old English only fed the accusations.

Marian conservatism brought its own problems to a partially reshaped Ireland, for destabilization, once begun, was hard to reverse. The return to Catholicism was welcome enough to those who mattered, but Marian government had other dimensions too. Perhaps because she clung to the old nobility, more certainly because she hoped to hold the frontiers more cheaply, Mary looked again to the nobles whom Henry VIII had removed. In northern England, the Percy earldom of Northumberland was restored and the Dacres returned to the West March; and in 1554, Gerald Fitzgerald, nephew of the 10th Earl of Kildare, returned to Ireland as 11th Earl. He brought a new potential for conflict as well as for service, for New English 'planters', or settlers, now occupied not just former monastic lands but former Fitzgerald estates. To complicate matters further, another Marian returnee, Thomas Butler, 10th Earl of Ormond—resident at court throughout Edward's reign—soon plunged into the old magnate quarrels with Desmond, his neighbour to the south-west; the latter was quickly seconded by his cousin Kildare. No lord deputy could have much freedom of movement.

The new lord deputy was ill-suited to the delicate balancing of interest groups. Thomas Radcliffe, Lord Fitzwalter (who succeeded to the earldom of Sussex in 1557), was the first major English nobleman to serve in Ireland since Surrey a generation earlier, and his appointment in 1556 suggests the determination of an English regime involved in a major war against France to secure Ireland. Energetic and ambitious, Sussex came with an impressive programme. Ireland was to be made defensible against the French by the expulsion of the Scots and the defeat of Shane O'Neill, while the Pale would be protected by the completion of the Leix–Offaly plantation. All this would be expensive: he would need, he insisted, nearly twice the number of troops with which St Leger had worked, though he promised to improve the government's finances in Ireland within three years, primarily through the elimination of St Leger's corruption. To that end, he would need new officials in Dublin. But despite the detailed agenda, Ireland was for Sussex, as for the crown, merely a part of a larger drama. The prize for which Sussex, like all deputies, played was office at court, and—like the court—he was convinced of Ireland's subordination to England's needs. When his policies were already far adrift in 1560, Sussex insisted that he offered new proposals solely with an eye to the Franco-Scottish threat and 'not so much for the care I have of Ireland, which I have often wished to be sunk in the sea'. He may have been the first of many English administrators to voice that wish, but his protest was not simply that of a frustrated Englishman.

He was a seasoned politician; the conjunction of France and Scotland, not the condition of Ireland, was the card to play when seeking support at court. The tragedy was that Tudor governments perennially saw Ireland in the context of an embattled Europe. That context required ever-increasing attention to Ireland, but it also diverted the resources that might have ensured English objectives there.

Sussex embodied the contradictions of the English position. No mere soldier (indeed, he was not very good at that, though he led over 2,000 troops), he did not oppose St Leger's political goals. He certainly interpreted primogeniture more rigidly, but he supported surrender and regrant, and he was capable of reforming initiatives. It was his parliament in 1557 that took English law to Leix and Offaly, shiring them as King's and Queen's Counties in honour of Philip of Spain and Mary Tudor, to stand as models of civility; and his eventual recommendation of provincial presidencies and councils for Connacht and Munster, on the Welsh model, shows him contemplating the slower work of cultural transformation. But he had a taste for polarizing rhetoric, conspiracy theories, and the language of power–all of which found a ready audience at Whitehall in 1556. When Sussex encountered recalcitrance – as he quickly did not just in Antrim but in Leix and Offaly where he oversaw a plantation that appropriated two-thirds of the area of the new counties–he demonized it: *unless* the Scots were expelled, *unless* the O'Mores and O'Connors were uprooted, Ireland was lost. His determination to exclude those whom he claimed might become allies of the French was reflected in the leases of confiscated lands he made, largely to his New English supporters: these barred future sale or grant to 'mere' Irish. Faced with continuing regional turbulence during an international crisis, Sussex was building policy on ethnic distinction. Of course, not even St Leger had abandoned the old and normative characterization of the Gaels as 'the wild Irish'; but St Leger insisted that the Gael could be won to civility, whereas Sussex was as interested in coercion as persuasion. Nothing was fundamentally new in this: Northumberland's regime had celebrated coercion rather than conciliation when the McCarthy Mor accepted surrender and regrant in 1551, and Bellingham had established his garrison settlements in the midlands. But Bellingham's work had been essentially ad hoc; Sussex presented conquest—albeit incremental, regional—as the key to the kingdom. The irony is that such a shift came under a lord deputy appointed by a Catholic regime, and one who proved under Elizabeth fairly detached in his protestantism. Frustration at the failure of past initiatives and fear of foreign intervention were driving policy; they were also cementing old definitions of ethnicity.

And at court the mood of crisis was gathering. The French held Scotland, the Scots in Antrim were proliferating, and Spain's war with France might prompt the French to intervene in Ireland against Philip II's queen. In that bleak mid century, the crisis mood had a domestic origin too. The English elite had responded viciously as harvest failures drove popular revolts in 1549, and they inflicted thousands of casualties in the field and hundreds, perhaps thousands, more by martial law afterwards: 300 were executed peremptorily in Norwich alone. Mary's government showed restraint in face of the eminently respectable Wyatt's Revolt of 1554, but—in a sign of fear—it proclaimed martial law in 1557 against spreaders of discouraging rumours. Sussex's accelerating grants in 1557–58 of martial law commissions to captains whom he set to keep the peace in the border areas of Leix–Offaly and southern Leinster had an English as well as an Irish context.

Brutal punishment was certainly inflicted in England, but it became a hallmark of English practice in Ireland. There were general ideological as well as particular cultural reasons for this. Throughout Europe, claims to obedience were being more clearly articulated as classical precepts of rule were absorbed in a time of religious division. The imposition of kingship and English law, keystones of the assimilationist programme in Ireland as well as of imperial monarchy in England, made traitors out of rebels or enemies, be they English peasants or 'mere Irish'. This was the other face of civility. But there was another and older context—that of ethnic and cultural difference—for the scorched-earth tactics that Grey and Brabazon had applied *in extremis* and that Sussex's agents now incrementally explored. Burnings were not confined to Ireland, it should be stressed. The Scottish crown granted commissions of fire and the sword repeatedly to the Campbells against the McDonalds and their allies. From the articulation in the twelfth century of a sense of what Christian and Roman Europe meant, the Normanized kingdoms of England and

Scotland had held the north-western frontiers of the civilized world against peoples whose difference exercised priests and academics. Whether conventional standards should prevail beyond those frontiers was and remained a question.

The crisis mood that encouraged the slippage of standards grew out of material constraints too. Sussex's misfortune—and Ireland's, and indeed England's—was that the late 1550s were not the best time for advocates of decisive action, since decisive action is usually expensive. Mary's government struggled vainly with the financial consequences of the wars of Henry and of Somerset, and the pressures were felt in higher-priority sectors than Ireland. Even before war began with France, English commanders had noted Calais' weakness; lacking resources, they lost the city and the war. As the devastating influenza of 1557 took its toll, as harvests failed again, as Mary's government grew distracted by religious divisions and dynastic crisis, the wonder is that Sussex was able to mount campaigns at all. That he did so owed little to royal largesse—what there was of that was tainted, for though Mary's government had called a halt to English debasements it had no qualms about sending particularly debased stock to Ireland. Much more important to the Lord Deputy was what he and his commanders could extract from those they ruled, within and without the Pale.

The Lord Deputy's arbitrary levy of 'the cess' was not novel, though that did not make it any more popular. Medieval practice had accepted that kings were entitled to aid from their subjects, particularly for defence; it accepted too that royal households were entitled to purveyance, that is, guaranteed access to cheap supplies and transport. Previous deputies had used purveyance eagerly for their hostings and for general maintenance. But Sussex's campaigning soon focused on distant Ulster rather than on districts bordering the Pale, and his army was large in Irish terms. Its food and maintenance costs averaged close to £30,000 p.a., and the burden of billeting was far heavier. The Dublin lord chancellor, a second John Alen, advised Sussex on his arrival to cess the people early to acclimatize them, and Sussex needed little encouragement. Beyond the Pale, the regularized demands of the garrisons may slowly have helped to transform and commercialize agriculture in their Gaelicized hinterlands, but more immediately they fed resentments as well as soldiers. Old English protests against the cess were heard in the 1557 Dublin parliament, and they were apparently supported by the attorney general, who was dismissed, along with the complaints. There were protests too, and sometimes bloodshed in the streets, over the behaviour of Sussex's soldiers, who when their pay failed took what they needed from those around them, Old English and Gaelic alike.

Polarization under Sussex was therefore not just a matter of the Lord Deputy's rhetoric. In the winter of 1557–58 the archbishop of Dublin and the old Earl of Desmond protested at Mary's court about growing insecurity as well as about undue exactions. Sussex blamed the complaints on supporters of Kildare who, he insisted, were promoting the latter's designs on the deputyship. He thus lumped together in the devil's party both Gaeldom and the palesmen. Meanwhile, in Dublin, the Deputy put his own following into office. The casualties included Anglo-Irish hold-overs as well as St Leger's appointees, and the Lord Deputy's political isolation grew even as Anglo-Irish assumptions of political entitlement diminished. In the localities, the captains and seneschals whom he established in strong points on the Pale's edge with martial law powers to intervene in and to extract from the territories of the Kavanaghs, the O'Byrnes, the O'Tooles, introduced a disruptively acquisitive element. And as the captains looked to their own interests as well as the crown's, the English cause gained an unstable dynamic.

The political costs might have mattered less had Sussex been successful militarily. Here, he was at a strategic disadvantage. He had too few troops for campaigns against the mobile Ulster Scots; he also had the wrong troops, ill-supplied and, as usual, ill-equipped for the wooded and hilly terrain from which their foes drew strength. The McDonnells of Antrim and Shane O'Neill simply withdrew into their fastnesses in Sussex's campaigns of 1557–58, and their cousins the McDonalds of Islay were no more forthcoming when the Lord Deputy, exploiting the Franco-Spanish war, practised hot pursuit across the North Channel in 1558. Furthermore, the 'Irish enemy' were becoming more numerous and aggressive. For a decade or more the inflow of redshanks, seasonal mercenaries from the Isles and the nearby Highlands, had intensified, and not just because of the final failure of the Lordship of the Isles; the worsening climate made life for those on poor soils more marginal, and pushed them to look elsewhere. The market for their services held strong as Ulster's politics fragmented.

Elizabeth's accession coincided with a transformative moment in Ulster. In 1558–59 the O'Neill lordship of Tyrone regained much of its unity and Sussex acquired a charismatic foe when Shane succeeded his father Conn as the O'Neill and eliminated the English-sponsored competition by assassinating his half-brother, Dungannon. Shane saw opportunity in the pressure from the new English garrisons, since it created instabilities. Here was the chance, he believed, to consolidate his hegemony not only over Tyrone but even—the ancient O'Neill dream—over all Ulster. McDonald manpower, to which his McDonnell marriage gave him access, would be the means. The collateral O'Neill lordship of Clandeboye, battered by McDonnell expansion in Antrim to its north-east, was weakening; lesser Ulster lordships like the O'Reillys, McMahons, and Maguires, which it had been the purpose of surrender and regrant to enfranchise and detach, and which were now indeed dealing with the lord deputy, could be brought back to a proper subordination; and superiority might yet be established over neighbouring Tyrconnell, where the O'Donnells were badly divided. Defeated in his attempt on Tyrconnell in 1557, Shane only became more convinced of the importance of gaining the Tyrone earldom as an additional resource. And he had every hope that the irresolute English government of an untested young queen would concede. There is no way to tell whether the earldom and the trappings of civility he evidently appreciated would have satisfied him, but to Sussex's dismay Elizabeth saw Shane's claim on the earldom as negotiable.

Ulster was not the only site of transformation that season, for the not unexpected marriage of the young Mary Queen of Scots to François the French dauphin in the Paris spring of 1558 triggered a geopolitical revolution in Scotland. England's entry into Spain's war against France in 1555 had prompted the French to tighten their hold on Scotland, and to replace Arran as Regent with the queen mother, Mary of Guise. An ill-kept secret of the marriage treaty signed by the teenaged Mary Queen of Scots at French prompting was the promise to the dauphin of the 'crown matrimonial' of Scotland—the right to rule in his own name—should Mary predecease him. With 5,000 French troops garrisoning the country and the French ambassador joining the Regent in key decisions, the French now threatened Scottish independence even more than the English had a decade earlier: France's absorption of Brittany in 1532 showed what happened to marital spoils. Present sufferings as well as future prospects fuelled Scottish anger: Scotland's taxes soared to support the French occupiers and a European war in France's interest, even as the harvests of the late 1550s dwindled and hunger grew.

Patriotic revolution began to break in Scotland in the spring of 1559, spearheaded by an alliance of protestant nobles, the Lords of the Congregation. The Regent and her well-entrenched French troops might have faced it down, but she fell victim to dynastic overreach. The succession of young François II to the French crown that summer of 1559 emboldened his Guise in-laws to celebrate by publicly flaunting the claims (through her grandmother Margaret Tudor) of his wife, Mary Queen of Scots—legitimate and Catholic—to an English throne so recently mounted by the protestant, and allegedly bastard, Elizabeth. With Lennox and his Catholic wife in Yorkshire also making no secret of her claims on the English throne, Elizabeth was under pressure to defend her standing. When the hard-pressed Lords of the Congregation begged aid from their English co-religionists they found a willing audience.

Elizabeth herself, a congenital conservative, was a reluctant partner in a geopolitical revolution. But her new secretary of state, William Cecil, had been with Somerset in Scotland in the late 1540s, and had an unusual sense—for an Englishman—of union as security for a beleaguered protestant Britain: 'one isle divided from the rest of the world', as he put it. Under his prompting and in this crisis, the Queen overcame her deep dislike of rebels. In March 1560 her troops—woefully equipped and ineffectual, though their cost drove the Queen to sell land worth nearly £100,000—re-entered the northern kingdom England had left ten years earlier. They were enough to make a statement both to the Congregation and the French of English commitment. And this time, the accidents of mortality spared Cecil a painful re-education in the difficulties of conquest and Elizabeth some difficult choices. The death of the Regent, Mary of Guise, combined with the outbreak of religious war in France to open the way that summer to the Treaty of Edinburgh, a triumph of circumstance. The previously unimaginable agreement that both French and English forces would quit Scotland established the Lords of the Congregation in power and marked the beginning of the Scottish Reformation. It also freed Elizabeth from financial disaster, and opened the way to an Anglo-Scottish rapprochement of which few could have dreamed during the previous centuries of English claims to lordship.

Dynastic instabilities shaped the strange history of the Anglo-Scottish 'Amity' as they had the catastrophes of the 1540s and 1550s. Another death, that of François II in December 1560, put a sudden stop to Guise aspirations and marked the young royal widow for return to Scotland. But it did not set England and Scotland back onto their separate paths. The returning widow of France wanted to be recognized as Elizabeth's heir, and while Elizabeth prevaricated on that question she did make clear her hope that Mary would favour protestants in her kingdom. Since the Congregation held power and since that policy seemed the price of recognition, Mary was ready to comply. While fully French in her sympathies she was moderate in her Catholicism, and she enjoyed good relations with her half-brother, the Earl of Moray, leader of the Congregation lords. To the dismay of the great reformer John Knox, Moray collaborated with Mary in moderate courses: Mary did not try to displace him, while he allowed her private Catholic worship and did not seek a full-blown Calvinist settlement for the nation. Such stability and moderation in Scotland seemed to Moray essential if Elizabeth were to recognize Mary's claims and thus ensure her eventual succession: and only the peaceful union of England and Scotland could secure protestantism and, not incidentally, the Congregation's members too. Elizabeth's psychologically strange readiness to offer her favourite, Dudley, to Mary as husband in 1564 suggests that the Virgin Queen may also have reconciled herself to a Stewart successor, but she would make no pronouncement. As the royal cousins watched each other nervously, personal attachments developed among some of the committed protestants around them; the most important were Cecil's with Mary's secretary, William Maitland of Lethington, and with another of the Congregation's leading figures, the remarkable Gaelic protestant, Archibald Campbell, 5th Earl of Argyll. But the larger relationship was not quite one of friendship, for the embrace into which the two kingdoms were drawn was both guarded and turbulent. The growing fractures—religious, factional—in the Scottish polity made protestants there dependent on English support, while the fears that helped Elizabeth overcome her intensely conservative instincts made her responses unpredictable.

To Elizabeth's consternation, the first real fruit of the Amity hung over Ulster. The young queen was pulled between those who advocated winning over Shane O'Neill by offering him the earldom he coveted and those who wanted to get rid of him fast. For once, the means were available for decisive action. As a grateful return on English assistance to the Scottish protestant cause and as a step towards the Reformation of Gaeldom, in 1560 Argyll—the biggest lord of men in all Britain—offered Elizabeth 3,000 of his followers. Well used to fighting Gaelic foes, these would deal with Shane. True, Argyll's clansmen would have added to the number of Scots in Ulster, but at least they would have been under protestant command. Cecil jumped at the proposal, and reciprocated with an offer of English heavy weaponry for Argyll to use against his own local enemies. But though English forces had floundered through Ulster's bogs repeatedly since 1552 in their attempts to curb the O'Neills and their redshanks, Elizabeth rejected the deal. Cecil saw it as the best chance to stabilize Ulster, and at no cost to the Queen; her disagreement marks one of England's lost opportunities in Ireland, perhaps on a scale with the first recall of St Leger. Argyll's decision to cast into common Gaelic rather than its Scottish variant the protestant liturgy he sponsored in 1567—the first book printed in Gaelic—suggests his real commitment to evangelizing the whole Gaelic world.

The failure of the Argyll option provides a case-study in the complications of an activist policy in Ireland. Elizabeth naturally had a stronger sense of the dignity of monarchy than did her advisers. She had been reluctant to intervene in Scotland in 1559–60, and she had no wish to see Scots intervene in Ireland, particularly since Scots in Ulster had a history of outstaying their welcome. Elizabeth well knew that Ulster had a British and now, because of Mary Stewart's French connections, a European dimension, and she had no wish indulge these. The Irish dimension was complex enough. Educated by Argyll, Cecil could see England's problem in Ulster as transnational, and capable of solution in

Gaelic terms. For his part, Lord Deputy Sussex saw everywhere a challenge to the expanding English interest in Ireland, and to himself. In
September 1560, the very moment he wished Ireland sunk into the sea,
Sussex advised the Queen that Shane—whom he loathed—was actually
a second-order difficulty, thrown in England's way by Kildare who
sought to regain the deputyship for his family. Since Kildare also backed
his cousin the Earl of Desmond in the old Fitzgerald feud against the
house of Ormond, alignments in Ireland seemed—and certainly to
Sussex—to be reverting to type. But there was a new wrinkle to the pattern, a new—though soon all too familiar—overlay of interest and ideology. Sussex's advocacy of the New English interest against Kildare
entailed a covert effort to build a position for his brother in and around
the Pale, the old Kildare preserve. Kildare retaliated by backing Shane;
he had a plausible case too, since the burden of the cess occasioned by
Sussex's campaigning was so high in these years that farmers and tenants
were migrating from the Pale to O'Neill lands. Responses to Gaeldom
in Ulster and beyond thus merged inexorably with the developing conflict between Old and New English interests.

The intersection in the 1560s of court rivalries, magnate jealousies,
international tensions, Anglo-Irish resentments, and the structural pressures reshaping Gaeldom made it hard for the Queen to decide what to
do. In June 1560 she buttressed the self-proclaiming Sussex by promoting him to the lord lieutenancy, a title not seen since Surrey in 1520–21,
but then he was humiliated in the 1561 campaigning season. His enemies
seized their opportunity: in particular, Lord Robert Dudley saw a chance
to harass Sussex at court in support for Kildare in the midlands. The
Fitzgerald–O'Neill association was an old one, and it now returned to
confront Sussex when Dudley gained permission for Kildare to negotiate with the victorious Shane and then to arrange his visit to court.
Sussex could only protest helplessly, 'If Shane be overthrown all is settled, if Shane be settled all is overthrown.'

Shane's submission to Elizabeth in January 1562 was, in its dramatiza-
tion of cultural estrangement and accommodation, one of the most
remarkable Tudor episodes. Though he had protested his eagerness to
reduce Ulster to civility, Shane appeared with a retinue of Gaelic galloglass clad Gaelic-style in shirts the colour of stale urine, and threw

himself at the Queen's feet declaiming in Gaelic. The display, and the political argument, had shifted in the twenty years since his father had appeared before Henry VIII clad at all points courtier-style. In this more divided world, Shane presumably sought to claim that even the most Gaelic of the Gaels could be gained if he were made the broker of royal authority in Ulster. To emphasize the point, he stressed in the talks the distance of tanistry and Gaelic chieftaincy from primogeniture and English lordship. But that difficulty was one Elizabeth and her advisers would not face: this was not the time. Nervous of the French Queen of Scots enthroned now to the north, and fearful too for the survival of the Congregation's government to which Mary was yoked if the French crown recovered strength, activists among Elizabeth's councillors were urging her to exploit the continuing religious disorders in France. In the autumn of 1562 she hesitantly committed herself to what proved a disastrous English military intervention across the Channel. Innovation in Ireland could wait. The Queen shelved a decision on the earldom; but she went further, and exasperated Shane by endorsing the official position that underlay Tudor anglicizing attempts: the lesser Ulster lords— Maguire, O'Cahan, O'Reilly—were not vassals to the great. The rebuff to the O'Neill did little to help Sussex, since Elizabeth would not commit more of her scant resources to war.

Sussex's enemies found it easier than the Queen to innovate. Under pressure from the English garrisons to the south and challenged by the Scots in Antrim to the north-east, Shane abandoned the traditional Gaelic insistence that only the elite fought while the labouring 'churls' existed to be exploited and despised. He turned the entire male population of Tyrone into a military resource, and by 1565 he could put 5,000 men in the field. That major social and ideological shift reflected the stakes involved. Sussex now found himself caught in a trap that was political as well as military. Its three prongs were Dudley, the resentful Old English of the Pale, and Shane O'Neill. Dudley, determined both to build his following and do down his rivals, responded to the failure of the accommodation he had tried to broker in 1562 by securing council hearings for protests against the arbitrariness, the illegality, the un-Englishness, as well as the intolerable burden, of the cess—the essential support for Sussex's army. First came Old English law students at

London's Inns of Court, who were briefly gaoled for their outspokenness but scarcely rebuffed; Dudley then helped the Pale gentry extract from Elizabeth a commission of inquiry into misgovernment and corruption in Ireland, to be headed by a long-term Dudley client, Sir Nicholas Arnold. Sussex's counter-proposal for provincial executive councils in Connacht and Munster on the lines of the Queen's council in Wales— the fashionable model for those pondering the integration of the outlying regions—was obliterated in the failure of his 1563 campaign against Shane. That miserable outcome allowed the alliance of old and new a moment of triumph when, at Dudley's prompting, Elizabeth empowered Kildare to broker negotiations with Shane. The remarkable agreement at Drumcree that followed—recognition of Shane as the O'Neill, recognition of O'Neill predominance in Ulster, withdrawal of the key English garrison at Armagh, and the promise of an Irish parliament that would give a favourable hearing to Shane's claims on the earldom— registered Sussex's failure.

The Drumcree agreement might have signalled a new direction for England's government of Ireland, since the arguments for accommodation were strong. The direct costs to Elizabeth of subjugating the kingdom averaged above £25,000 p.a. into the mid 1560s, or over 10% of her regular, non-parliamentary, revenues of c.£200,000 p.a. at that point. Ireland's troubles also ate up time and attention, as Cecil pored over the maps he steadily commissioned and the Queen dealt with formal encounters: in 1562—a year eaten up by intervention in France and the royal encounter with smallpox—both Shane O'Neill and the Earl of Desmond came calling in some state. Not surprisingly, Elizabeth considered her options: early in 1564 she recalled Sussex and listened to grievances. The hopes of the palesmen rose when Arnold was appointed chief governor, with a smaller army, the promise of further investigation of abuses, and a powerful friend at court in Dudley, now promoted Earl of Leicester.

Good feelings might have grown. Protestant Reformation had not yet accelerated in England, still less in Ireland. Early in 1560 Sussex had easily secured the passage through the Irish parliament of legislation paralleling the 1559 measures in England: an Act of Supremacy requiring office-holders to swear to Elizabeth's governorship of the Church, and an Act of

Uniformity requiring a modified and Latin version of England's 1552 Prayer Book that left aspects of the liturgy appearing curiously unreformed. It remained entirely possible for palesmen to hold a 'church papist' position, accepting Elizabeth's supremacy while convincing themselves that fundamentals of worship had not changed. Beyond the Pale, there might be occasional suppressions of friaries and dispersals of their occupants, but there was little sign yet of a new ecclesiastical regime. And in Ulster, Shane now made a show of conciliatoriness in hope of his earldom, releasing the O'Donnell chief whom he had captured (though holding on to O'Donnell's wife, who had become his mistress), and cooperating when in 1564 Leicester urged him into action against his now cast-off in-laws, the Antrim Scots. In the southwest, Desmond and Ormond maintained an uneasy truce, and there were hopes of something more. Elizabeth had shown Desmond signs of favour when he and she had both come into their inheritances in 1558; Ormond—confident of his Boleyn affinity with the Queen, confident of his connections to Norfolk and Sussex at court, and eager to bring his sprawling family under his control and improve his own income—was working hard to establish the cess locally in place of coign and livery, the semi-arbitrary billeting of fighting men on tenants. In the midlands, too, some subordinate septs were participating in the plantation of Leix and Offaly at the expense of old overlords, the O'Mores and O'Connors.

But however good the intentions, and however sweeping the claims of kingship, the crown was dangerously weak in Ireland. It could neither communicate its will to the localities nor enforce it. Arnold's investigations into corruption were thwarted when the commander of the army, Sussex's brother-in-law Fitzwilliam, urged his officers not to cooperate; Arnold's subsequent inquiries among the soldiers outraged the officers as an affront to hierarchy and honour. Administration quickly frayed among mutual recriminations. And in the regions there were upsets aplenty. The assertiveness of the officers Sussex had planted around the Wicklow mountains, and the resentments created by the attempts to foster common-law tenure and succession, condemned parts of the O'Byrne and Kavanagh countries to endemic low-level conflict. Meanwhile, dispossessed O'Mores harassed English settlers in King's and Queen's Counties in the midlands.

The unreliability of the crown as a reforming force was still more painfully exposed in south-west Ireland. There Desmond—whose responses to the opposed pulls of anglicization and Gaeldom to which he was subject in his remote fastness were sometimes unfairly read by contemporaries as insanity—countered Ormond's preferential access to Elizabeth by abandoning his promises of civility. Late in 1564 he raided and killed in Ormond's lands, and the following February the two magnates' armies met at Affane, near Waterford. The last private battle of the medieval English nobility left a wounded Desmond marching in chains as Ormond's captive; it also infuriated Elizabeth. Not for the first time, the two magnates made their way to court in disfavour, and entered massive bonds for their good behaviour. Their challenge to sovereignty was remarkable enough; as ominous was Ormond's return to local ways of warfaring. Although he had banished coign and livery from his Munster territories, he rapidly readopted them when he confronted a threat that distant English troops and the cess could not deter. The disarray in Ulster and Munster exposed the limited appeal of English ways on the frontier.

Elizabeth was not the only queen to find her sovereignty slighted in 1565, although the consequences of the turmoil in Scotland were more immediately momentous—for England and Ireland as well as Scotland. The Lennoxes' return to Scotland in 1564, after Elizabeth freed them from the arrest the countess's assertiveness had earned them, prompted Mary to question Elizabeth once more about claims to the succession. To Moray's dismay, Elizabeth replied that she would make no commitment until she herself was either married or had determined not to marry; Moray knew enough of her to recognize that this meant never, and that Mary would have less incentive to moderation. And indeed, as Mary ran out of marital options that might earn her a larger stage than Scotland, she seized on the return to Scotland of the Lennoxes' son, Lord Darnley, an unstable lightweight with few attractions other than a pretty face—and his mother's claims to the English throne to reinforce her own. Their marriage in July 1565 infuriated Elizabeth, appalled the Hamilton interest—the hereditary enemies of the Lennox Stewarts— and the protestants too, since while Darnley was of no known religion his mother was a strong Catholic, and Scotland now faced the loss of

Elizabeth's goodwill to boot. Moray, Argyll, and the Hamiltons promptly rebelled; defeated, Argyll retreated to the Highlands while the others fled to England.

The consequences of the ineffectual rebellion that was the Chaseabout Raid were many. Mary swung against the protestants at court, and among those to whom she gave her favour was the Italian musician David Riccio. That association was to destroy, in short order, Riccio, the murderously jealous Darnley, and then Mary herself as she clung to one of Darnley's murderers, the Earl of Bothwell. There were of course massive repercussions in both Scotland and England. Not least, Elizabeth's refusal to support godly rebels alienated Argyll. Abandoning hope of England, Argyll determined to reform and unite Gaeldom under his own auspices: not just by sponsoring evangelization in the Highlands but by reconciling all the Ulster chiefs, O'Neill, O'Donnell, McDonnell. The thousands of Gaelic swordsmen, redshanks, he dispatched across the North Channel to strengthen marriage alliances he made with them underscored how much he might have done for Elizabeth. They were to give Shane O'Neill new opportunities to make trouble.

But while Elizabeth might despair of Shane, despair too of magnates whether Anglo-Irish or Scottish, she had not despaired of a civilizing settlement in Ireland. Her decision to appoint the forceful Sir Henry Sidney as lord deputy in 1565 was at one level an expression of court politics. On his arrival in Dublin, Sidney bore Leicester's arms on his private badge: the new lord deputy's remarkable list of brothers-in-law included not only his resentful predecessor Sussex as well as Fitzwilliam, but also the Queen's favourite, now very much in the ascendant. But court politics always had a larger significance. Catholic victories in France's religious wars were leading the French crown towards a rapprochement with Spain that again threatened the encirclement of England, the more so after the Chaseabout Raid allowed Mary Queen of Scots' court to become more Catholic and French. The protestant alarm Leicester and his friends sounded grew louder, and it was fed now by Arnold's damning report on the condition of the Church, and of religion, in Dublin and the Pale, in the heartland of English Ireland. But Elizabeth was not one to move quickly. She heeded the alarm to the extent of appointing Sidney, a forward protestant, to deal with reform, with Ulster, with the Scotto-French threat, but she also knew that the world was dangerous and she must husband her resources. So Sidney, activist though he was, had to promise a 25% reduction in Sussex's expenditures, to be achieved partly by enforcing Arnold's exposure of administrative corruption. As a result, the 1,500 men committed to him scarcely outnumbered the followers of Desmond or Ormond, let alone those of Shane O'Neill.

Sidney's appointment had a governmental as well a political significance. Since 1560 he had served very effectively as president of the council in Wales and the Marches. There he had not only accommodated magnate interests (not least, Leicester's); he had also implemented and even exceeded the programme of civility the makers of the Henrician Welsh statutes had anticipated. With Wales now fully shired, the English common law courts and assize judges were able to function, while in its low-level judicial functions the Council of Wales was able to mix local custom with English law; and not only had Sidney as president sponsored the translation of protestant texts into Welsh, he had managed to patronize bards and protect Roman Catholic recusants. It was in 1563, during his tenure, that an Act was passed at Westminster for the translation into Welsh of the Bible and the Prayer Book, thus trumping with the protestant emphasis on evangelization in the vernacular the Welsh union legislation's ban on the Welsh language. That new commitment to the vernacular contrasts with the fearfulness shown in the Irish Uniformity Act of 1560. In 1567 the Welsh Prayer Book and New Testament appeared, and the entire Bible in 1588; such texts, and the steady stream of popularizations that followed, were to prove crucial to the integration of Wales in the English state, and to the fostering of Welsh national identity within that state. During Sidney's tenure too the notorious litigiousness of the Welsh became manifest in floods of suits before the Council of Wales's courts, as they found in its convenient and local jurisdiction an alternative to the feud. But contiguity again points to the advantages Wales enjoyed over Ireland: Sir James Croft's main residence was on the Welsh borders, and Sidney had an able and upward-bound vice-president in John Whitgift, future archbishop of Canterbury. The disappointed therefore had alternative points of contact available to them.

Not surprisingly, many at court believed that the incorporation of Wales so achieved constituted a model for Ireland—Sussex's belated advocacy of regional councils underscores his acceptance of the case. Some believed indeed that Gaelic and English ways might still be reconciled within an English frame. Sidney, convinced he was the man to do it, took up office not just with Welsh-style plans for accommodating to law and civility an Ireland that was being steadily divided into counties but also with a notably gradualist design in religion. Ireland would be won to a moderate protestant order that at first emphasized obedience to the royal supremacy and not doctrine. To ease the way to obedience, the largely redundant Cathedral of St Patrick in Dublin would be suppressed and its resources turned over to the deputy, who would dispose of senior clerical appointments.

Hopes that Ireland might become another Wales soon withered. Even Sidney himself was not quite convinced, for as he urged his reform plans he had to keep areas outside his main sight lines quiet, and he did not have the resources to do it in orderly fashion. Accordingly, he issued martial law commissions to local officials as Sussex had before him—at least eighty-nine in the years 1565–71. And those around him were no more of one mind than he. Neither New English nor Anglo-Irish churchmen in the Pale were eager to see the cathedral, a bastion of the Englishry, disappear. Furthermore, much of what was to derail English efforts beyond the Pale—near-universal detachment from protestantism, a landscape lying largely outside written legal record, acquisitive army officers too often equipped with judicial as well as military power, the danger of invasion—was absent from Wales.

And Elizabeth's government found it easier to concentrate on military threats than on the reforms Sidney urged. Even as Shane O'Neill protested to Elizabeth his devotion to civility—he certainly had a well-developed taste for wine—reports reached Whitehall that he had been negotiating with Argyll, with Mary Queen of Scots, and with various European powers. In Munster Elizabeth hemmed in Sidney's every move, but she quickly enhanced his budget for the pacification of Ulster. Supported by Kildare, who was eager to re-establish Fitzgerald influence even at the price of forgetting O'Neill friendships, Sidney devastated Shane's lands in 1566 and established a new garrison in Derry to the north with the aim of reducing Shane's pressure on the neighbouring O'Donnells. But he found the O'Neill chief as elusive as ever, and with Sussex now largely rehabilitated at court and magnifying every delay and setback, Sidney's stock fell fast; it did not recover when a powder accident blew up the Derry garrison in the spring of 1567.

Frustrated on every front, Sidney pleaded vainly for a recall, until Shane's over-reach redeemed him. Striving to impose regional dominance before Sidney could expand his garrisons, Shane was out-generalled in a massive raid on the O'Donnells that April. The McDonalds to whom he then rashly turned for aid—rashly, since he had butchered many of them at Leicester's invitation two years earlier—duly cut him to pieces, on the calculation that English forces were now more of a threat than Shane's. But the pickled head of the O'Neill that ended up on Dublin's gates gained Sidney only a brief political recovery. Elizabeth could not be brought to implement the rest of his ambitious programme. Like St Leger before him, he wanted to free Ulster's lesser chiefs and landholders from the dominance of the magnates, and from some of their fear of the English too, by securing their tenures. He also hoped to replace—forcibly—the Scots settlers in north-east Ulster with agricultural colonists from England. But this would cost time and money, and both were in short supply at Whitehall.

It is hard to determine whether it was in Munster or at court that Sidney was undone. As in Ulster, he sought to detach the lesser Munster lords from the magnates by converting the various arbitrary exactions—in particular coign and livery—to a regularized cess and to fixed rents, a part of which would be paid to the provincial council, whose troops would provide the protection the lords' retinues had once offered. Those broad outlines by now framed something close to an official English policy—in 1565, without a lord deputy in place, Elizabeth had responded to the challenge of Affane by ennobling Desmond's leading subject chief, the McCarthy Mor, as the Earl of Clancare. But the policy's effectiveness hinged on trust, and that would depend on an even-handed deputy and reliable provincial presidents, with force at their back. From the moment she appointed him, Elizabeth watched anxiously in case Sidney favoured Leicester's allies the Fitzgeralds against her cousin Ormond and the rest of the Butlers, who she claimed had generally been loyal to the English crown. When Sidney consulted Kildare she berated him for relying on the Irish-born, and when he tried to appoint his Kent neighbour Sir Warham St Leger—son of the Geraldine-leaning former lord deputy—as the first president of the Munster council, she heeded Ormond's fierce complaints against bias and blocked the appointment; she soon barred St Leger from the province altogether. Holding Desmond entirely to blame for the continuing friction with the Butlers, in the spring of 1567 she ordered his arrest and the forfeiture of his massive bond; she then lambasted Sidney for promoting Desmond's eminently stable younger brother, Sir John, to local office. The Lord Deputy's memoirs declare his loathing for Ormond, whom he plausibly held responsible for subverting him at court.

The consequences of the presence of a royal cousin in Munster emerged at the end of 1567, when Sidney returned to court to urge more substantial reform in Ulster. The arrest, in his absence, of Sir John of Desmond, who was imprisoned in the Tower with his brother for four years, confirmed the complaints of royal prejudice, and left the Desmond affinity open to the leadership of a much more dangerous figure, their cousin James Fitzmaurice Fitzgerald. With Sidney's nominations for appointments overridden by the Queen, with his plans for reorienting affinities in Ulster disregarded by the council, and with his policies in Munster defeated at court and disintegrating locally, by early 1568 the Lord Deputy seemed to have failed twice as fast as had Sussex.

A wider political crisis nevertheless renewed Sidney's mandate as lord deputy. Conditions in Ireland deteriorated in 1567–68, for Shane's death briefly allowed parsimony to return to the head of the Queen's agenda. Unwilling to wrestle further with the political and landed structures of Gaeldom, her council gave neither welcome nor support to the new O'Neill leader, Shane's cousin, Turlough Luineach O'Neill, against the collateral O'Neills who immediately challenged him; Turlough Luineach himself lost little time in diverting McMahons and Maguires from the English fold into his own. And in Munster, James Fitzmaurice moved quickly into revolt. By the autumn of 1568, a lord deputy's presence was needed to quell the spreading disorder.

Events in Scotland ensured it would be Sidney who would return. The great scandal of Darnley's murder and Mary Stewart's subsequent marriage to the Earl of Bothwell, one of the murderers, brought Mary's deposition in 1567. This was followed by civil war along lines of loyalty and allegiance that did not translate readily into the convenient religious labels of a few years earlier: thus, the Calvinist Argyll broke with his old Calvinist ally Moray and rallied to the Scottish queen against whom he had rebelled in 1565. Mary's flight to England in May 1568 only deepened the crisis for Elizabeth, and prompted her to appoint Sussex, possessed of reassuring dignity and a taste for simple formulae of authority, as president of the council in the north. A key anti-Sidney voice was thus removed from Whitehall.

By no means every significant response to the problems of rule in Ireland in the late 1560s crossed national boundaries. Local notables beyond the Pale spoke affectionately of the gregarious Lord Deputy as 'Henry of the Beers', and Sidney was certainly confident that he knew how to deal with Turlough Luineach. The misfortune was that as religious loyalties grew firmer and more demanding, a lord deputy's purposes no longer depended on such traditional skills.

CHAPTER 4
CAUSES OF THE LORD 1568-1585

The years after 1568 were an unnerving time for the Queen and her servants, even before she fell gravely ill of smallpox late in 1572. Troubles came fast from the north, and they had unmistakable consequences. Mary Stewart's flight to Elizabeth's unwelcoming doorstep in 1568 precipitated a spate of plotting in England, the Northern Revolt of 1569, and the destruction of the Duke of Norfolk in 1572; it also triggered civil wars in Scotland on which Elizabeth felt she could not turn her back. English forces made repeated incursions into Scotland between 1570 and 1573 to aid the protestant—or at least, anti-French—supporters of the infant James VI. Observers who noted Elizabeth's establishment of the Earl of Lennox as Scottish regent in 1570, and the apology of his successor, the Earl of Mar, for having taken office in 1571 without her permission, might have been forgiven for assuming a satellite state was forming.

The urgency of those Scottish encounters was heightened by deepening religious divisions. The Roman Catholic Church at last moved to confront the twin problems of Elizabeth and England: the papal bull *Regnans in Excelsis* of 1570 pronounced the Queen heretical and deposed, while in 1572 seminaries were established on the Continent for missionary priests who would try to win Elizabeth's dominions back to Rome. Not unconnectedly, in 1572 Elizabeth's Church establishment came under fire from another quarter, from English puritans who expressed their dissatisfaction in an *Admonition to the Parliament*. And in Scotland, crisis and civil war from the late 1560s drove the Kirk and its advocates into the militancy that was to define much of Scottish Calvinism for the next century. Beyond the archipelago, in 1572 the wider world erupted. The Dutch began what became a long revolt against Spain, the French religious wars intensified in the Massacre of St Bartholomew, and a Spanish attack on John Hawkins's ships in the Caribbean suggested that new enmities might be forming.

But despite the drama of England's engagements in Scotland and with European powers—drama that certainly consumed the attention of the Queen and her council—England's less glamorous history in Ireland proved at least as consequential. After all, Scotland did not become a satellite in this period. Ireland, on the other hand, was more forcibly opened to English attentions, and Elizabeth found herself spending as much money in Ireland as she did in Scotland and Europe combined, though the purposes of her westward spendings often eluded her. How England's Irish history acquired what seemed to be a momentum of its own is a question that involves not only international crisis and court politics but also the ways English people were taught to see themselves and those around them.

The increasing resort to the printing press makes it possible to follow some of those encounters with the world, and to follow too the formation in the mid-Elizabethan period of what seems not just a patriotic identity but an ideology of Englishness. The new polarities in religious faith provided their own powerful keys to understanding, but these were not the only ones available. Complex ways of thinking about nationhood appeared in profusion. The most famous was John Foxe's *Acts and Monuments* (1563, with revised and expanded editions in 1570 and 1576), which blended painstaking historical scholarship with religious fervour to elaborate England's appointed place in an order where God's protestant purposes were threatened by the papal Antichrist. Foxe's more advanced readers were soon able to put that apocalyptic argument together with other products of the contemporary drive to vindicate English language and culture. England's place in the world was the concern of the antiquaries who followed the Henrician John Leland into the crumbling archives to produce, most notably, the *Chronicles of England, Scotland, and Ireland* (1577) under the editorship of Raphael Holinshed. Holinshed's inclusion of subordinate Scottish and Irish narratives certainly signalled the editorial team's unusually explicit recognition that

England was not alone in its northern world. It also provided mythic justification for the old English claims on Scotland—'the sovereignty of this Isle' in the words of the *Chronicles*—and for English settlers' presence in Ireland too.

The systematic application of myth to empire originated elsewhere. After the Henrician union, the Welsh had discovered a politics of culture. The protestant need to evangelize Welsh-speakers was beginning to reinvigorate the Welsh vernacular as a vehicle for print culture. In a reciprocal process, Elizabethan churchmen followed John Foxe the martyrologist in looking to British antiquity, to the pre-papal origins of Christianity in the islands, to validate the English present and future. Welsh scholars advanced another claim to excellence as they belaboured the 'British' character of that Arthur who provided a transcendent Tudor pedigree. Holinshed endorsed the claim: 'The Welshmen are the very Britons indeed.' The printing press carried the argument of cultural unity into Wales and England both: not only was there now a Welsh Prayer Book, in 1572–73 there appeared first Latin and then English-language versions of the Welsh antiquarian Humphrey Lhuyd's *Breviary of Britain*, a defence of an Arthurian tradition in which it located 'the British Empire'.

Lhuyd's fellow countryman, the mathematician and magician John Dee, took the British project to the very centre of power. A client of the Anglo-Welsh William Cecil, Lord Burghley, Dee was from 1570 weaving economic expansion and navigation, Arthurian precedents, and claims to angelic inspiration, into a determinedly prophetic argument for a maritime 'British Empire' that was to be England (and Wales) writ large. His *General and Rare Memorials* (1577) earned him several consultations with Burghley, that 'Heroical Magistrate', and 'the British Queen Elizabeth'. The Welshman's drive to compensate for the frustration of nationhood—in demographic terms, London had become by far the largest Welsh town—took a potent form in Dee's salute: 'O Albion, O Britain, O England, and (I say) O Britain, again'.

Expansionary visions abounded. The most attractive were the works of the mapmakers, eagerly commissioned and deployed by Burghley and Secretary of State Walsingham for their consultations. Christopher Saxton's dazzling county maps of England and Wales, completed in 1579 with Elizabeth's own sustained support, are the most famous product of the period, but as English forces raided into Scotland in the 1570s Burghley followed their progress with newlymade maps. His demands are superbly caught in Lawrence Nowell's mid-1560s map of England and Ireland, with its marginal detail of Burghley sitting on an hourglass gazing impatiently at the surveyor. But it was John Goghe's 1567 map of Ireland, annotated by Burghley, that made the fears and the hopes most explicit. The waters off Ireland's south coast are labelled revealingly, 'The Spanish Sea'; on land, the empty territory of Ulster lies to one side, surmounted by the axe-wielding galloglass of the McSweenys, the main Scottish providers of these specialist warriors. Elsewhere, an array of lordships ranges outward from Dublin. On view here is not merely an anxiety about external threats; the map's unspoken message of order as well as power provided further justification for action.

The theme of order opened entrancing prospects of improvement, economic and social as well as political. Perhaps the most influential of those who sought to improve England was Thomas Tusser, whose *Good Husbandry* went through eighteen editions between 1557 and 1598, in its mundane way gratifying a broad English interest among landowners and tenants alike in raising yields for an expanding market by methods that included the enclosure of land from waste and common. As policymakers and entrepreneurs contemplated extending English power and possession outwards, to an unenclosed, under-productive, and under-exploited Ireland, they could feel confident in the public good they were doing, not least in freeing the Irish peasantry from the arbitrary exactions of their lords and clearing their way to the marketplace. Such reformers were sure they did God's work too.

Like any good ideology, 'improvement' had roots in material circumstance. Demographers have estimated that the early 1570s saw a sharp upturn in the rate of emigration from England, as a deteriorating climate put pressure on an increasing population. The net outflow continued to build until the wars of the 1590s; the Americas had yet to be settled by the English, so most migrants were heading for Ireland. The implications are momentous. While some emigrants became tenants to Anglo-Irish landowners in the Pale who previously might have leased to Gaelic farmers, and others moved to the port towns—though usually the Anglo-Irish corporations tried to exclude New English competition—still others moved to lands that had been confiscated and cleared. The initiative did not only come from below. When New English officers and officials gained estates they often looked to their native regions for tenants. Soon, as more Irish land opened by legal or extra-legal means, adventurers sensed new prospects. The dream of planting 'civility' and English ways in Ireland began to acquire a demographic meaning it had not had since the heyday of the medieval colony. Native responses changed as English pressures came to seem no longer episodic but incremental, and were overlain as well by a growing religious division.

Land hunger and the dissemination of English ways merged explosively in the Irish venture of Sir Peter Carew in 1568. A member of a Devonshire gentry family, Carew sought consolation for his indebtedness in the archive of his family's lost Irish estates. In what was to prove a lasting alliance of greed, self-righteousness, and legal learning, the Devon antiquary John Hooker sailed to Ireland to test Carew's records. Entranced by the barony of Idrone in southern Leinster, 'in all Europe not a more pleasant, sweeter, or fruitfuller land', Hooker eagerly endorsed Carew's claims on his lost inheritance. More remarkably, the lord deputy quickly upheld them, though the land had long been held by the Kavanaghs. Sidney's motives were probably partly factional, for Idrone was Butler territory, and Ormond's brother, Sir Edmund, was the Kavanaghs' overlord. But it would have been difficult for an English deputy to reject a well-turned English law case out of hand. Anyway, the southern flanks of the Pale were a headache, and Sidney hoped to use English settlers to pacify as well as to improve. Like others at Elizabeth's court and beyond, he saw the potential of Hooker's research to redraw the map of Ireland. But redrawing the map was not just a matter of taking possession like some Spanish conquistador, though many English captains fit that model. Sidney had visions of a larger reshaping.

The improving strands of English ideology came together hopefully in the Irish parliament of 1569–70. For once, a lord deputy had real plans for reform: bills to encourage manufactures and to discourage raw material exports, to secure provincial presidencies and thus prepare the way for the establishment of counties and the dissemination of law, and to establish a university for Dublin that would produce a protestant Irish clergy. Kildare's alliance with the lord deputy offered a chance of parliamentary success, for the Earl had a following among the palesmen—Kildare was even ready to condemn lordly coign and livery. But most of the programme was lost in bickering. With his eyes on detractors at court, Sidney concentrated on a long-winded and self-justifying attainder—or condemnation and expropriation—of the dead Shane O'Neill, and inexplicably missed a chance to finance reform with the lands of religious guilds and chantries. More seriously, he became caught up in a dispute with the puritan archbishop of Dublin, Adam Loftus, over St Patrick's Cathedral, whose endowment he sought to divert to a university, whereas Loftus insisted that the Church was for churchmen to reform, not any mere lord deputy. The New English community showed new signs of that old division between clergy and laity.

The New English quarrel was dwarfed, and hopes of further statutory backing for a protestant Church destroyed, by the impact of the Carew affair on relations between the New and the Old English. Carew seemed to threaten titles to land wholesale, for the Anglo-Norman colony's extent and inchoateness invited other English courtiers to conjure claims to inheritances. The parliament thus exposed new fault-lines in Irish politics. John Hooker displayed the situational ethics of the colonist, extolling royal prerogatives in Ireland that as a parliament-man at Westminster he deplored. Meanwhile, Anglo-Irish—or, increasingly, 'Old English'—anger swelled against New English carpet-baggers, and it was fed by deepening resentments at the cess that Sidney's campaigning had already necessitated and that the commutation of coign and livery would only increase. The parliament showed the difficulty of reconciling the Queen's need for economy and Ireland's need for reform. As well, it showed that though a protestant Church had not yet emerged in Ireland, the Old English dilemma of identity was taking shape.

Old English loyalties fractured in face of state-sponsored English aggression. In the nature of things, such fracturing was not straightforward: when Sir Edmund Butler, whose local position depended on coign and livery, stalked out of parliament, his revolt was as much against his brother as the Lord Deputy, for Ormond had been pushing to monetize the family's levies. But when Desmond's cousin Fitzmaurice crossed the usual magnate faction lines in 1569 to join the Butler revolt in attacking English settlements, he sought vengeance for the favourable lease of what had been the Fitzmaurice estate at Kerrycurrihy that Sir Warham St Leger had just extracted from a hard-pressed Desmond. Idrone and Kerrycurrihy together showed that court favour, written record, and commercialized tenures could undermine the Old English as well as the 'mere Irish'. For their part, Sidney's papers show his hardening and self-fulfilling conviction of Old English unreliability and ingratitude.

The troubles that broke out in Munster in 1569 underscored the inadequacy in practice of what England represented officially as it extended its hold on Ireland. Denouncing lordly arbitrariness as tyranny, Sidney hoped to diversify and commercialize Irish society, and saw in Desmond's imprisonment after Affane the chance to liberate lesser lords and trading towns in Munster: an armed provincial presidency would supply justice and protection in place of the magnate's retinue. But like other colonial administrators, Sidney was handicapped by distance, political and geographic. Elizabeth objected to St Leger, Sidney's choice for Munster's presidency, but she offered no further guidance. Distraction at the top allowed English adventurers to take the lead against Fitzmaurice locally, with predictable consequences. Struggling to secure the lesser Ulster lordships against Turlough Luineach O'Neill at the same time as he pacified the south-west, the Lord Deputy in late 1569 granted a commission of martial law in Munster to Sir Humphrey Gilbert, half-brother to the future courtier, Walter Raleigh.

What is now called social cleansing increasingly marked the violence inflicted by English commanders in Ireland. Summary hangings for those with swords whose chiefs would not or could not vouch for them by name had emerged as policy when Sussex's seneschals and captains challenged local clans in Leinster. Gilbert, a quintessential Renaissance adventurer who far out in the Atlantic was himself soon to achieve one of the classic deaths of the age, saw terror as the means to order on the frontier: in his theatre of violence, the defeated approached him down an avenue of severed heads. Munster was not the only site of English state-violence in these years. Butchery was just then being practised on many hundreds of Englishmen who had followed their lords into the 1569 Northern Rising; and Carew himself was execrated in Devon for his viciousness against the 1549 Rising there. But whereas in England state violence underwrote broader shifts, in Ireland violence in many areas stood alone; and alone it could not replace the existing power structure. So Ormond's private army of over 1,000 men had to reinforce the 700 under Sidney's Munster commander Sir John Perrot; even then, Fitzmaurice himself held out until 1573, and only submitted when Elizabeth allowed Desmond to return.

Sidney's successful request for recall in 1571 showed his recognition of the problems he faced, both in Ireland and at a court where Ormond and Sussex worked against him. He had promised the Queen speed and economy, but between 1568 and 1571 Elizabeth spent about £100,000 on Ireland, and ran up another £50,000 in debt there—a total that approached one fifth of her regular revenue in that period. He had talked—like Sussex before him—of something that looks in hindsight like state-building, the establishment of formal institutions of rule, the spread of law and law courts, the enfranchisement of subordinate landholders, with provincial presidencies as the means outside substantially anglicized Leinster. He had assured Elizabeth that the presidencies would soon be self-sustaining, but he was optimistic. The 50–100 troops Sidney projected as the permanent complement for each presidency offered little reassurance to local lords who were asked to abandon coign and livery: as Ormond had discovered before Affane, even the greatest lord, disarmed, was vulnerable. So while lord deputies regularly intervened in chieftaincy contests to secure cooperation, they were as regularly angered at the failure of the winner to deliver: under-resourced English institutions could not guarantee the winner's survival.

Bringing the magnate-dominated west into England's orbit thus proved no easier than settling the midlands, taming the lesser clans of southern Leinster, or quieting Ulster. Everywhere, material grievances dominated, though in Connacht Sir Edward Fitton, the first president, made an unusual attempt to enforce Reformation outside the Englishry by disbanding friaries and destroying images; he thus lent some plausibility to the banner of religion Fitzmaurice was trying to raise in Munster. Nevertheless, when Richard Burke, Earl of Clanricard, withdrew his support for Fitton's presidency in 1572, his complaints were secular.

Denouncing the choice of sheriff and the execution of unregistered retainers by martial law, Clanricard allowed his sons to devastate the region as they reasserted the Gaelic identities their father had forsworn. Hamstrung by internal conflicts among the O'Briens and the Burkes that surrender and regrant had intensified, isolated by the reaction against Fitton, and lacking troops, in 1573 the Connacht presidency all but collapsed.

English governmental attention soon shifted from Ireland, despite endemic unrest there. Facing renewed turmoil in Scotland (and so in Ulster too), Elizabeth could not afford further expenditure in more distant places. Amid the civil wars and assassinations (Regent Moray 1570, Regent Lennox 1571) that followed Mary Queen of Scots' fall, the Scottish Queen's party hoped for aid from France while English forces intervened five times on behalf of the protestant supporters of the infant King James VI: three times in 1570, once in 1571, and again in 1573. Elizabeth's hope was of stability and a friend across her northern border—a satellite would be welcome, but certainly and at least something other than the disorders that had allowed fugitives from the 1569 Northern Rising to find a refuge in Scotland. Elizabeth may also have seen reason for supporting the King's party in the damage that loyal Queen's man, Argyll, was doing in Ulster: 8,000 redshanks sailed to Turlough Luineach O'Neill with his Campbell bride in 1569. The captain of the English fort at Carrickfergus on the Ulster coast warned Burghley the following year that the province was 'in danger to be utterly lost for the Scots be already in such numbers and fortifying upon her majesty's land'. As a corollary to her accelerating commitments in Scotland, the lord deputy Elizabeth appointed to replace Sidney in Ireland, his other brother-in-law Sir William Fitzwilliam (lord deputy 1571–75), was a man with few plans other than containment. But while Elizabeth was far more conscious of developments in Scotland with their French ramifications, the work being done in Ireland, not always as a result of formal policy, was more consequential.

With little prospect of further support for soldiers from either her Westminster or her Dublin parliament, and not wanting to spend more herself, Elizabeth listened now to advocates of a new programme:

plantation, colonization.[1] The dream that Bellingham had first planted in the midlands of putting down settlers as islands of security, civility, and Englishness had only increased in appeal as England's own population grew. Sparsely settled Ulster had space, and Shane O'Neill's posthumous attainder allowed the claim that all his vaguely defined holding was forfeit, wide open.

Late in 1571, Sir Thomas Smith, humanist, privy councillor, soon to become secretary of state, secured a patent for a colony modelled on Roman lines, a settlement of soldier-farmers on Ulster's east coast. Behind the classicism there was organizational novelty: the enterprise would run on fashionable joint-stock principles, and Smith published a recruiting pamphlet. *A letter... wherein is conteined a large discourse of the peopling and inhabiting the cuntrie called the Ardes* (1572) aimed its sales pitch at the landless and younger sons of the gentry, and defended the removal of the Irish by stressing the better use the English would make of local resources. The fact that the lands in question were held by Sir Brian McPhelim O'Neill of Clandeboye, an opponent of Shane in the recent wars, dampened neither Smith's nor the Queen's eagerness. Nor did McPhelim's ability to protest in both Latin and English at the Queen's declarations—which he reported reading in print—ward off the charge of 'barbarity' that justified his expropriation.

Courtly enthusiasm for colonization grew. Despite warnings from Lord Deputy Fitzwilliam that plantations would broaden resistance in Ulster, and despite the abject failure of Smith's project in face of local resistance and inadequate supply from England, the Queen listened to those around her who stressed the turbulence of the Gael and the continuing danger from Scotland. In 1573—the year Elizabeth's artillery bombarded Edinburgh Castle into submission to the protestant Regent Morton to end Scotland's civil wars—she granted to Walter Devereux, 1st Earl of Essex, a patent for a larger colony covering modern county

---

[1] The development of English colonies was not quite as discontinuous as the distance between Bellingham's activity in 1549 and Smith's in 1571 might imply: in 1565, Elizabeth chartered a feudal seigneury for the then-uninhabited Channel Island of Sark. The colony of New Jersey and the troubled New England governorship of Sir Edmund Andros from Guernsey suggest that the Channel Islands had a place in later imperial history.

Antrim, facing Scotland across the North Channel. The Queen agreed to split costs with Essex; she also, and probably sincerely enough, urged a light hand against the existing population. But Essex was determined to make a profit, particularly since he had mortgaged most of his property to the Queen, and it was only through clearing the land of its occupants that his colony could hope to succeed. As Fitzwilliam had feared, colonization united O'Neills and McDonnells in resistance, and as he predicted it excited broad fears about English intentions.

In every respect, the Essex colony was a disaster, and the Lord Deputy wrung his hands at 'the shameful effusion of innocent blood'. Essex found supplies no easier to organize than had Smith, and plague and desertion reduced his party; Elizabeth sent him more troops in 1574, but would not forgive his debts. Growing desperate, Essex hardened his tactics. In the summer he harried and burned across central Ulster and then in November, under a pretext of hospitality, had McPhelim, his wife, and his brother, summarily executed, and their followers butchered. This atrocity paled in comparison with his work the following summer, 1575, in the colony's last days. Resentful of the harassment he had suffered from the McDonnells, Essex eagerly implemented the government's strictures against the Scots in Ulster. As he prepared to return home, he detailed the future English heroes John Norris and Francis Drake to take the redshanks' staging-post—and refuge for their women and children—of Rathlin Island. Hundreds were massacred. It might be uplifting to add that when the 37-year-old Essex died the following year of dysentery, the occupational disease of the English in Ireland, it was with his reputation as well as his fortunes in tatters. Instead, Elizabeth reassured him, 'You have invested yourself with immortal renown.' The only offset to the disaster was Burghley's grudging recognition that colonization was better not left to amateurs.

State-inflicted violence is always revealing, and there was plenty of it in these years, despite the narrative that celebrates England's rule of law and its privileged separateness from the world. A central chapter in that narrative is, ironically, Sir Thomas Smith's own *De Republica Anglorum*, one of the most influential and eloquent celebrations of England's legal ways, written in the 1560s and printed in 1583. At least Sir Humphrey Gilbert, returned from his campaign of horror in Munster, was consistent in his rigour as he warned his colleagues in the 1571 parliament at Westminster that princes needed revenues, and that a commitment to legal liberties could be taken too far. The parliamentary denunciations that greeted Gilbert are a reminder that coercion was reserved for others: plebeians perhaps, better yet outsiders. Fresh from brutally suppressing England's Northern Rising of 1569 and soon bound for Ireland, that frontier warrior Sir William Drury in the spring of 1570 took an army and the customary tactics of fire and sword across the border into Scotland, sacking and burning some ninety castles and 300 villages alleged to have sheltered fugitives from the English rebellion. The damage he inflicted was reported to be greater than that done in the 1540s. These were unsettled years.

A different lesson in 'civility' came from Munster, where successive provincial presidents—Sir John Perrot in 1571–73, Drury himself in eighteen months from 1576—hanged respectively 800 and 400 unregistered, or 'masterless', swordsmen by martial law. Their contemporary Sir Nicholas Malby, who earned a bad reputation as provincial president of Connacht, was a convicted felon who had worked off his death sentence in army service. Lord Deputy Fitzwilliam thought the provincial presidencies a waste of money and did not appoint an immediate successor to Perrot, and he had lamented Essex's plantation, but he too saw the sword as the essential civilizing agent for the Irish who, he judged, were sunk 'in beastly liberty and sensual immunity'. To judge by the complaints, Gaeldom found more grievous the private atrocities, which surely proliferated as the captains and settlers dug themselves in and struck out for themselves. The worst came at Mullaghmast in Kildare in 1578 when the constable of Carlow massacred several dozen O'More and O'Connor clansmen. Both before and since their removal from the midlands colonies at mid century, the O'Mores and O'Connors had committed their own killings aplenty; but, in 'mere Irish' eyes at least, levels and motivations of violence could be distinguished.

English officials did not aim at the elimination of the Gael, it should be stressed. When Sidney—*persona grata* again as Leicester rose further in the Queen's favour and Fitzwilliam's lieutenancy eroded in squalid holding operations around the Pale—returned in 1575 for a second stint as lord deputy, he did so determined to secure the collaboration of Gaelic chieftains with the old programme of translating Irish tenures and takings into English. Anyway, the Old English were for fiscal reasons his more immediate concern. He had assured Elizabeth of economy: with an army reduced to 1,100, and after an initial outlay of £60,000, he would make his government self-sufficient in three years. And since Elizabeth was at last on the point of escaping from the debts she had inherited, she was ready to listen to proposals that would entail some up-front expenditure.

Sidney's path to self-sufficiency lay in an ambitious scheme of composition for the cess. In return for a fixed annual charge on each ploughland (roughly equivalent to just over 100 acres) he would surrender the hated levy. Since settled agriculture and the cess were alike primarily features of the Old English landscape, Sidney still looked to that population, despite the rebuff in the 1569–70 parliament. But to transform an arbitrary levy into regular taxation, the holy grail of government, required tact and Sidney could ill afford emergencies: hence the importance of working with, rather than against, the Gaelic chieftains. Elizabeth tried to do her part by reassuring Desmond, whom she had freed in 1573 on the understanding that he would rein in his affinity.

Desmond's Munster was the testing-ground for Sidney. Despite the connection to Leicester they both shared, Sidney judged Desmond responsible for Affane, and worked to reduce his independence. Desmond, badly in need of royal favour to offset Ormond's family advantage, was not averse to cooperation—indeed, he agreed to convert, or 'compound', his varied 'takings' from his tenants and subordinates, nominally valued at about £13,000 sterling, into money payments. Instead of support in kind for men and horses, he received cash payments of close to £1,400 and a higher standard of living. In that sense, the English argument about the benefit of English tenures held true. The Munster president, Drury, received payments from Desmond's subordinates as a form of taxation and promised security, while the Earl retained a household guard of only twenty men. Remarkably, Sidney was able to hold Desmond in line even though Munster's president made no provision beyond hanging for those many swordsmen replaced by money-rents and dues who rejected the social and cultural calamity of farming. Indeed, Drury's own ability to establish a relationship with the Earl suggests that the latter may not have been too troubled by the fate of his kern. But Desmond's collaterals—his cousin Fitzmaurice, his capable brother Sir John—were left with little from a composition that prized primogeniture. Faction at Elizabeth's court gave them their chance. Although Sidney had thought his work was going well, in 1578 a whispering campaign by Sussex, Ormond, and Fitzwilliam, directed at the Queen's anxieties about cost, secured his recall. Fitzmaurice quickly prepared to return from exile, and in July 1579 he raised once more the banner of revolt; this time he was joined by Sir John.

The great Munster revolt was overwhelmingly secular, though Fitzmaurice's banner was provided by the pope. Indeed, the pope eventually provided 600 assorted professional soldiers and a papal emissary, and Fitzmaurice declared Elizabeth heretic and deposed. Observant Catholics did have some grounds for concern now in Fitton's recent burst of official iconoclasm and suppression in Connacht—perhaps too in the appearance in 1571 of the first Gaelic printed book in Ireland, a protestant primer and catechism. But only 200 copies of the latter were printed. Anyway, collective worship was a far more significant evangelizing tool, and flashpoint for protest, than print; few of the local elites, lay or clerical, were sympathetic to reform, so visible changes in worship had not yet appeared. What mattered were hard issues of livelihood and status. When Sir John of Desmond ambushed and killed the provost-marshal of Munster and his party—the chief executors of martial law—the rebels grew to several thousands strong. With his faith in the crown weakened by Sidney's departure, Desmond himself was in the end driven into the arms of his followers by the harsh tactics of Malby, briefly seconded to the province from his presidency of Connacht. By late 1579 the south-west was engulfed in rebellion.

If there was a single turning-point in England's troubled history in Ireland, it was surely 1580. At one level, the suppression of the Munster revolt was conventional: Desmond's lands and followers suffered scorched-earth measures at the hands of his regional rival, the loyal courtier Ormond, who took over command from Malby in one more instance of a weak central state's practice of divide-and-rule. But the threat from Europe's Counter-Reformation was changing that state's profile and capabilities, just as it was changing the character of protestantism in England and Scotland. In 1580 the first Jesuit priests arrived in England, at the end of a decade in which the pope had anathematized Elizabeth and pronounced her deposed and in which Catholics had massacred thousands of protestants in Paris. The arrival at Smerwick in south-western Ireland of papal troops and an English Jesuit declaring a crusade against the Queen could not but frighten and radicalize English and New English alike. In turn, of course, harsher English tactics radicalized those on whom they were inflicted. By the late summer of 1580, Arthur Lord Grey of Wilton, a fiercely Calvinist client of Leicester and the new lord deputy, commanded an army of 6,500 men; in November his artillery forced the foreigners at Smerwick to surrender unconditionally. His decision to put about 500 to the sword expressed the familiar calculus of deterrence applied by those sent to hold extended frontiers amid unknown dangers. The Queen immediately saw his point. As she sent troops once again to watch the Scottish border as the friendly government of Regent Morton fell, she deemed Smerwick 'next to God's divine providence...the second means whereby the whole land was preserved'.

But Smerwick was not just about deterrence. Grey denied that his victims were legitimate belligerents, to be accorded the respect due soldiers. They were in his eyes stateless agents of the pope, that 'detestable shaveling, the right Antichrist and general ambitious tyrant'. Elizabeth did not share his apocalypticism, but such polarized terms were coming into wider use.

The Counter-Reformation was indeed arriving in Ireland, in the more lasting form of committed laity and trained missionary priests. In the 1560s and 1570s, when the resource-poor government still had the field to itself, it had counted on the slow realignment of Anglo-Irish 'church papists'—traditionalists willing to make token gestures of compliance. But it failed to give them any incentive to go beyond lip-service. It could no longer buy their commitment with lands, nor could its few competent protestant clergy preach to enough of them, or preach in a language most could understand. As a result, all but a small handful of the usually loyalist urban and legal elites came to see the new Church as but one more instance of governmental arbitrariness. And there were more than enough of such instances as the Pale's 'country cause' of the cess came to a head with Sidney's composition scheme. Less and less likely to look to English universities, and with little prospect yet of an Irish alternative, they sent their sons abroad for education, where they encountered Counter-Reformation values.

The new cause of Catholicism brought the possibility of new coalitions, transcending the old division between Anglo- and 'mere' Irish. On his return from visiting Rome, James Eustace, Viscount Baltinglass, urged the papal bull deposing Elizabeth in the summer of 1580 and was joined not only by younger gentry of the pale but by O'Byrnes and O'Tooles, marginalized by surrender and regrant, and by O'Connors from Offaly, while Turlough Luineach O'Neill sent support too. The humiliating defeat that the O'Byrnes and Baltinglass inflicted on an overhasty Lord Grey at Glenmalure in the Wicklow hills in August 1580 on his way west to Smerwick presumably intensified the Lord Deputy's ferocity there. Though the crown now possessed the resources to wear down regionalized protests in wars of attrition, Elizabeth could not contain the new identifications that were arising.

New English suspicions of Old English protestations of loyalty were reinforced. To Grey, the Baltinglass revolt showed that beneath the palesmen's legalist complaints against the cess lay religious unreliability, probably treason. The odyssey of Richard Stanihurst serves as a sensitive measure of just such alienation. Stanihurst, son of Dublin's loyalist recorder, or chief legal officer, had worked on the Irish narrative in Holinshed's 1577 *Chronicles*, and claimed there that 'the English pale' had been the sole barrier against Gaelic revolt and that its inhabitants were far from the 'barbarous savageness' of their neighbours. Five years later, he published his translation of Virgil's *Aeneid* into 'English Heroical Verse'. But by then Stanihurst had left for exile in the Catholic Low Countries. When in 1584 his *De rebus in Hibernia gestis* [*Of Irish Matters*] was published, it was in Latin for a European audience, and concerned as much to argue the essential unity of Gaels and Anglo-Irish in their loyalties to Ireland and to Rome as to vindicate 'the English of Ireland'.

Grey and his New English supporters, in their growing suspicion of anybody born in Ireland, were happy to drive a wedge further into the gap. Protestantism became a loyalty test, to the growing discomfort of many who hoped to stay in the middle. Malby in 1577 had noted the divisions in government between 'we of the English' and others of 'this country birth', and Grey now insisted that only those protestants born in England could be counted on to be free of inexorably divided Irish loyalties. Kildare, who was in his enemies' eyes guilty of not having given a strong lead against Baltinglass to his own wavering affinity, was sent to the Tower; some twenty gentlemen of the Pale were executed, as was the former chief justice, Nicholas Nugent, on a trumped-up charge. At court, Lord Burghley—who did not share Leicester's Calvinist militancy—thought Grey had gone too far; nevertheless, it took reports of corruption to bring the Lord Deputy down in 1582.

Major differences in outlook on the world thus underlay the mutual frustrations of English policy-makers. To Grey certainly, and perhaps to Leicester his patron, the popish challenge was global, and must be confronted. Coercion was not merely punitive. New English opinion held that since the Irish, and above all members of the Old English establishment like Baltinglass, had absented themselves from the offerings of the protestant Church where such offerings were available, they must be driven by the sword to conform, to come to Church, so that the Word of scripture could begin to work on them. The Queen was less hopeful of the sword when the Word was not available, but in her cash-strapped condition her interest in translation of the scriptures into Gaelic and in the establishment of a university in Dublin could only be ineffectual.

Elizabeth could not afford the simplicities of Grey's vision. Ireland was far away, and countering the revolts that broke out in 1579–80 had been massively expensive. She needed to prepare against troubles elsewhere. In 1581, at the end of a long crisis, the northern Netherlands foreswore the sovereignty of Spain, a country with which England's own relations were souring fast. In 1581 too, England's friend in Scotland, chancellor Morton, was overthrown and executed, ushering in another period of intense turbulence across England's northern border—and Elizabeth had repeatedly been told that just a little money for gratuities to hungry Scots would preserve Morton. Elizabeth had little desire to ask her parliaments for enough taxation to do the job, since parliaments, whether in Dublin or at Westminster, were always readier to box her in than to bear the charges of government. Indeed, in 1581 the Westminster parliament responded characteristically to the previous year's arrival in England of the first Jesuits during an international crisis by coupling an inadequate grant of supply with draconian anti-Catholic legislation. With Smerwick retaken and Baltinglass a fugitive, the Queen felt it safe as well as necessary to reduce Grey's forces to 2,000—close to the average level for the first half of her reign. In his 1596 *Faerie Queene,* Grey's secretary, the poet Edmund Spenser, dared to chide Gloriana for cutting short her heroic *alter ego* Britomart's chastisement of the Irish rebels. His partisan temerity helped ensure his own disgrace.

As so often, Elizabeth's parsimony had consequences. Unable to deploy sufficient numbers to catch the fugitive Desmond in 1581–82, Grey resorted to a familiar anti-guerilla tactic: systematic destruction to dry up local support. This unhappily coincided with the calculation of entrepreneurial army captains seeking land: their best hope lay in clearing it. In the spring of 1582, Sir Warham St Leger reported over 30,000 famine deaths in Munster since the previous September. Spenser's retrospect in his *View of the Present State of Ireland* (completed in 1596) is famous: 'Out of every corner of the woods and glens they came creeping forth upon their hands...they looked like anatomies of death; they spake like ghosts crying out of their graves; they did eat the dead carrions...'. Sir William Bingham, president of Connacht, used some similar language as he narrated the 1586 surrender of rebels after hot pursuit there: they were 'so pined away for want of food and so ghasted with fear...that they looked rather like to ghosts than men'. Ghosts were coming into season. Grey himself reported that in his brief tenure he killed 1500 persons 'of note...not accounting those of meaner sort, nor yet executions by law and killing of churls, which were innumerable'. Ormond tallied his Munster killings at 5,650 over eighteen months. What is remarkable is the way measures to suppress an Anglo-Irish revolt had broadened into a campaign of terror. Not for nothing did the Queen instruct Grey to 'remove that false impression' among the Gaels 'that we have a determination as it were to root them out'.

The print-record as well as the body-count suggests how such an impression could form. In 1581, John Derrick's *The Image of Ireland* offered a lavishly illustrated defence of Sidney's rule that was also a vicious polemic against the Gael. With its ardent Arthurianism and pride in English arms, its contempt for those who allowed themselves to be hoodwinked by priestly acolytes of the papal Antichrist, its contempt too for an unproductive economy shaped to the needs of the thieving 'kern', the general run of Gaelic swordsmen who so heathenishly lacked civility and proper clothes, *The Image of Ireland* ran the gamut of imperialist prejudices. Its two editions suggest it also found a market for its ringing denial that the Gael was a true member of the Christian community, let alone the world of order. No wonder so many of the English in Ireland could turn to killing as well as dispossession.

Publications of these years suggest a hardening in English attitudes. Derrick's jarring claim that his account of Gaelic behaviour conveyed the very 'image of Ireland', though he published it in the midst of two Anglo-Irish revolts, typifies a growing polemical tendency to obliterate nuances. What Stanihurst argued on one side of a widening political and religious divide—that 'mere Irish' and Anglo-Irish shared a loyalty to Ireland and to Roman Catholicism—John Hooker, Stanihurst's by now apocalyptically anti-Catholic successor as the Irish chronicler for the second edition of Holinshed's *Chronicles* (1587), insisted more vehemently. It was 'a fatal and inevitable destiny incident to that nation, that they cannot brook any English governor'—and Hooker made it clear that 'that nation' covered the Pale as well as the Gael. Whatever the ancient English descent of the Anglo-Irish, they had degenerated; their true identity appeared in their popish ways and their disobedience. Amid Catholic plotting and Jesuit missioners in an England drifting towards war with Spain, the English anti-Catholic legislation of 1581 and 1584 tied patriotism to protestantism. In such a world, what were 'the Irish', when protestant clergy served almost exclusively the New English while the Anglo-Irish establishment welcomed Jesuits, and friars roamed the Gaelic countryside?

The growing English conviction of the unreliability of Anglo-Irish and 'mere Irish' alike helps explain the revival in the mid 1580s of colonization on a much larger scale than in Ulster. If no part of Irish society could be reformed, then it was not sufficient to redistribute the lands of the Munster rebel leaders to a new elite, as had been done in Kildare after 1536. English society must be superimposed. The confiscations that followed from the fall of Desmond and his followers seemed to promise a blank slate in Munster, for a re-creation of an English rural order that would allow Elizabeth to recoup some of the £200,000 she had spent suppressing the revolt. The confiscations—over half a million acres were assumed—also promised individual enrichment to the would-be English gentlemen actually in arms as servitors or as captains who yearned for land.

In this attempt at social engineering through private contracting, Burghley and his advisers intended the Munster plantation to centre on significant landholders who could rally their localities. Lords and kern were to be swept away, to be replaced by 'seigneuries' of 4,000–12,000 acres, paying rent to the crown, and each with its quota of English freeholder and farming families, villages, and mills. There was to be a scattering of market towns to foster a commercial agriculture, and a militia of English settlers organized on English county lines. 'Churls', the Irish peasantry, though pushed to the more marginal lands, would be freed of their lordly abusers and at least have a chance of civility and commerce. The symmetrical estate plans optimistically drawn up for the planters give graphic testimony to the idealizing hopes. The fallen Irish world was to be expunged in a new creation. What that new world might feel like is suggested in the famous and much-copied 'Sieve' portrait of Elizabeth of 1583: with the sun illuminating Ireland as much as England on the globe at her shoulder, and with ships sailing past on their way to and from the New World, Ireland's place in a commercial empire seemed clear. It was the vision that drove Sir Walter Raleigh and his half-brother Sir Humphrey Gilbert, and many more, to engage in projects in the Americas as much as in Ireland. But motives were mixed. To some, Munster might seem a template for an English empire in the west. The hotter protestants around Elizabeth's secretary of state, Sir Francis Walsingham—a number that included Spenser—justified new English settlements in Ireland as an anti-empire, a bulwark against the aspirations of Spain and Rome to a universal empire. For Munster's former inhabitants, the practical consequences of such differences might be minimal.

A society could not so easily be reinvented, though the fact that the state imagined it could, and that experienced land-surveyors assisted in the design, indicates that aspirations to expertise were now playing their part in England's expansion. At Burghley's invitation, gentry in western English counties and then London merchants became 'undertakers', contracting for whole or part seigneuries in Munster. But the land proved less extensive and less clear than had been imagined. In the end, only about 300,000 acres were available for plantation, and the neat designs faded. The most important complication was the informality of Irish tenures, an informality that made ownership, and therefore forfeitability, hard to determine for an administration that despite its impatience with all things Irish intermittently protested its respect for the rule of law. There were other impediments: confiscated estates were scattered, making surveying difficult; undertakers who could travel staked pre-emptive claims, while special treatment for the well-connected disrupted the proportions of estates. Soon the objectives were compromised. Raleigh, the most favoured—who had risen far since serving as the leading English butcher at Smerwick—sublet his massive 42,000-acre estate instead of residing in person; all the undertakers accepted Irish tenants instead of fostering a new England in the west; and by the mid 1590s there were only 4,000 English families in the plantation (yielding a total English population of near 22,000) instead of close to 12,000. But when Sir John Perrot, who became lord deputy in 1584, tried to question Raleigh's special treatment, Burghley warned him that policy must give place to politics: Raleigh 'is able to do you more harm in one hour than we [on the council] are all able to do you good in a year'.

Elizabeth's unpredictability and unreliability are legendary, but her personal interest only shaped policy up to a point. Nor was lack of money the only other constraint, even once the war with Spain began in 1585. When the issues of religion and the succession crystallized at the end of the 1560s, two sets of policy options had taken shape. Each found advocates among distinct groups of courtiers with their own analyses of, and links to, the contending groups on the European continent, in Scotland, and in Ireland too. The Queen tended to lean towards the more conservative grouping that included Ormond, Sussex until his death in 1583, and—depending on circumstances—middle-of-the-road figures like Burghley and Lord Chancellor Hatton. But in the early 1580s, the growing Catholic and Spanish threat gave the firmer protestants around Leicester and Secretary Walsingham the upper hand at court. The resurgence of partisan turbulence in Scotland exemplifies the world with which Elizabeth had to deal as she increased the watchfulness of her soldiers on the northern borders. In 1579 James became fascinated with Esmé Stuart, Lord Aubigny, created Duke of Lennox, who had just been seen off from Paris by the hard-line Catholic Duc de Guise; that dependency allowed another *politique* soldier from France, Captain James Stewart, the new Earl of Arran, to focus noble jealousies and destroy Morton in 1580–81. To break that politique hold the group of Calvinist militants known as the Ruthven Raiders seized the King in August 1582. When James escaped in the summer of 1583 they fled to London before returning with the support of Walsingham's friends to seize power in Edinburgh in 1585. It was in this environment that pressure grew on Elizabeth to intervene in the Netherlands.

The tensions this mood could set up in Ireland are evident in the career and indeed the personality of the new lord deputy appointed in 1584, Sir John Perrot. A soldier who had grown up in a bilingual household in south Wales and seems to have gained there some sympathy for Celts, Perrot was also Walsingham's friend and a hotter sort of protestant. His first move on taking office was to go campaigning into Ulster, but in the intensifying European crisis the Queen would not give him the resources to establish better defensive lines there. Instead, the council in 1585 denizenized—granted resident alien status to—the encroaching McDonald chieftains. This remarkable shift in the Queen's attitude to Scots in Ulster may have stemmed from her growing confidence in the Anglo-Scottish amity as James took power. But though Perrot was dismayed, he too showed considerable flexibility in his dealings with the remaining centres of Gaeldom.

Perrot's strategy for civility was Sidneian. He aimed to establish legal tenures in land and to focus on the prime lineages. His first significant composition agreement, in East Breifne on Ulster's border with the Pale, carefully established freeholds for the leading collaterals of the O'Reilly lord, but gave the current chief about half of the lordship and significant quasi-feudal rights over much of the rest. Perrot's hope was that a secured lordly presence could ensure stability. And while a full division of Ulster itself was too large a problem to take on, he sought to establish three

clear zones of influence in the centre and east of the province: one for
Turlough Luineach O'Neill; one for Sir Nicholas Bagenal, now marshal
of the Irish army, with his garrison at Newry; and one for the carefully
cooperative figure of Hugh O'Neill, Conn's grandson and son of
Matthew, Baron Dungannon. To crown the achievement, and usher the
Gaelic leaders back into the English fold, Perrot had the parliament he
called in 1585 nominate Hugh to his grandfather's earldom of Tyrone
under the acquiescent gaze of Turlough Luineach, now Sir Turlough and
garbed English-style. It was testimony, Perrot declared, that the Queen
sought to govern 'with equal care and without distinction of nation,
English or Irish'.

Even-handedness was to be on English terms. Recognizing that the
sept leaders could only fight as long as they could billet their kern arbitrarily on the farmers, he determined to end 'the name of churl and the
crushing of a churl'. Emancipation of social relations and of the market,
and the extension of the English legal system into the localities, would
make Irish society more peaceful and more productive. Perrot busily set
about extending the framework of English local government. In 1585 a
swathe of northern Ireland was at least formally 'shired', or given county
status, as the precursor to the dissemination of English law and civility:
Leitrim, Fermanagh, Monaghan, Armagh, Tyrone, Coleraine, Donegal.
Though the chiefs might run the new sheriffs out of town (as some of
them did), they were put on notice.

Perrot's major restructuring work was in Connacht, which like Ulster
had lain outside the late-medieval English orbit. He aimed at revenue as
well as civility when he propounded composition for the cess and lordly
takings in 1585. The province's president, Malby, had until his death in
1584 been persuading the great lords of southern Connacht, Clanricard
and Thomond, to follow Desmond and shed the burden of lordly military preparedness in return for a greater rental income. Unlike Desmond,
these lords were strong enough to impose the scheme on their collaterals. Perrot's key enticement was the exclusion of a portion of their lands
from liability for composition payment: the 'freedoms' from payments
the lords gained for their estates proved unexpectedly attractive to prospective tenants—and, in thinly populated Connacht, prospective tenants were a valuable commodity. That rarity of English Ireland, a success,

was taking shape, at least in the south where there were magnates. Not only did composition establish English authority, such that by 1586 the Connacht presidency was operating financially at a 20% surplus and able to field an effective and mobile army. It also introduced the kind of social reform that officials had talked about for decades. 'Civility' was on the march.

But civility and godliness proved incompatible. Although Perrot's soldierly bluffness and Welsh ways might fare well enough in Gaelic quarters, he was Walsingham's client and accordingly ill-equipped to deal with the more ardently Catholic Old English who made up the bulk of the Dublin parliament. The Lord Deputy went to parliament in 1585 not only to integrate the O'Neills but also hoping to secure the national composition for the cess that had eluded Sidney—and determined to enact the fierce anti-Catholic measures that had passed at Westminster in 1581 and 1584. These declared Catholic priests traitors, and thus required their execution and the ruin of their supporters' estates. The all-too-predictable failure of Perrot's anti-Catholic designs might not have wrecked the 1585 parliament: the Queen herself criticized him for broaching religion 'in these dangerous days'. But the chief governor's initiative certainly raised Old English suspicions about government intentions. Perrot was treated to a harangue by the Commons' Speaker, Nicholas Walsh, on the evils of overweening power: the Irish body politic was a community under constitutional safeguards akin to those in England. Walsh, the protestant chief justice of Munster and a government nominee, declared the Old English conviction that they were the inheritors of a frame of law that was threatened by the government's agents.

The English government needed an army to impose its will on the swordsmen and their lords in the provinces, and the Irish parliament had repeatedly shown its unwillingness to fund an army. It is no wonder that parliament did not meet again for nearly thirty years, that the vision, whether Perrot's or Walsh's, of a national community faded fast, and that the English increasingly came to see the Old English as bigger problems than the native Irish.

CHAPTER 5
ENDGAMES 1585–1603

England's entry into a major European war in 1585 quickly made explicit what had long been apparent: neighbours to the north and west were not Elizabeth's highest priority. Her reluctance to spend money now gained the certainty of national emergency. Provided Scotland and Ireland were quiet, all was good enough. Accordingly, Elizabeth barred successive lord deputies in Ireland, Sir John Perrot and then (for a second term) Sir William Fitzwilliam, from military adventures, and stressed the importance of economy. More urgently, she worked to secure the goodwill of James King of Scots, who came of ruling age as her war began. The fact that England's foe was now Spain rather than France obviously lessened the danger that an adventurous young Scottish king with French relatives would otherwise have presented, but James certainly showed his independence by occasional gestures of friendship to Spain and approaches to the pope. Elizabeth saw the point, and she knew that she had something James wanted: recognition as her heir. But she could not give him this—it would embolden trouble-makers, she told him; as well, she refused to look mortality in the face.

The agreement the two monarchs reached in 1586 nevertheless worked surprisingly well. Elizabeth did not grant James the English ducal title and lands he demanded to ease his succession, but she agreed not to impede his claim without cause, nor to intrigue with discontented Scots as she had done ever since her accession. And she intermittently sent him small subsidy payments and letters full of unsolicited advice. In return, James did not open his ports to the Armada or even to the Armada's survivors. Perhaps if the Queen had given him a dukedom he would have done more for her, but the agreement did manage to weather the trial and execution in 1587 of James's mother, Mary Queen of Scots. Elizabeth then did her gnomic best to sound reassuring and James did his best to confine his statements of outrage to a domestic audience. Meanwhile, Elizabeth censored or isolated English authors—such as John Hooker and Edmund Spenser—inclined to tactless vaunting over Mary. If one was needed, the history of English incursions between 1559 and 1573 and the very recent memory of the Ruthven Raid must have served as unspoken reminders to James of the value of cooperation. And he did want to be England's king. In 1594 he even delayed for six months the christening of his first-born son, Henry, until Elizabeth's representative arrived to stand as sole godparent.

To an extent, the non-Spanish world was turning in Elizabeth's favour. The death in 1584 of the 5th Earl of Argyll helped dry up the flows of mercenaries into Ulster that had given such clout to his evangelist's vision. The very success of his efforts to spread protestantism in the Highlands was anyway beginning to divide Gaeldom along national lines; James's own efforts to 'civilize' the Western Isles were to work to the same effect. And France was soon neutralized by the assassination of Henri III in 1589 and the contested succession of the protestant Henri of Navarre. Although in 1593 Henri IV converted to a politique Catholicism in order to end the civil wars, France's concern for some years thereafter remained survival in face of an intransigent and encircling Spain rather than making trouble for Spain's other enemy England in Scotland or Ireland.

But in the end, James's goodwill was invaluable. Despite minimalist goals and Scottish and French neutrality, the Queen spent almost as much on Ireland in her final decade as she did on wars in the Netherlands and at sea combined. Ideology—the honour of monarchy—as much as national security helped ensure this. There is real despair in Elizabeth's reported comment in 1598, as her forces faced defeat, that Ireland doomed her: 'My sister [Mary] lost her life for displeasure at the loss of a town [Calais], I can not tell what I may do at the loss of a kingdom.'[1]

---

[1] Jane E.A. Dawson, *The Politics of Religion in the Age of Mary, Queen of Scots* (Cambridge, 2002), 218n.

Had James been otherwise inclined, he could have made her last years even more uncomfortable.

Elizabeth's motives for holding so tightly to what cost so much were mixed. The weight of honour and history made English policy in Ireland unnervingly reflexive: Ireland must be held because Ireland was there. Nevertheless, the calculus of national security is unmistakable. Ireland's long eastern coastline left nearby lowland areas of England and Wales dangerously exposed, and the arguments of English councillors in favour of involvement in the French wars in the 1590s, that to see the Spanish take nearby Brittany from France would be almost as bad as to see them take Ireland, suggest the stakes. For many of Elizabeth's subjects (though not the Queen herself), what was at stake was much larger: the Spanish enemy was the right hand of the papal Antichrist. It had been natural enough for hard-pressed Irish leaders, from the Geraldine league to Fitzmaurice, to look to England's enemies. But the times were out of joint, and the 1584 assassination of the Dutch leader William of Orange only reinforced the alarm among protestants sparked by the 1572 St Bartholomew massacre in France and the upheavals in Scotland. The confessional polarization of Europe in the 1580s increased the risks that when Irish Catholics appealed to Spain and Rome for aid, English protestants would draw apocalyptic conclusions.

But the harsh unpredictabilities of English policy in Ireland, which made Irish elites so distrustful, stemmed from causes mundane as well as apocalyptic. Successive innovations by governments with neither the will nor the capacity for supervision had created a series of local political centres—not only the provincial presidencies, but also constables like Sir Nicholas Bagenal and his son Sir Henry at Newry in Ulster along with their lesser equivalents in Leinster, and the planters in the midlands and Munster. Royal parsimony and indiscriminate grants of powers of martial law encouraged a dangerous independence among these. The consequences became clear in Elizabeth's later years as war expanded the range of governmental activity and demography increased the numbers of the ambitious and of the hungry who might hope to take advantage. In England, where political and legal constraints were stronger, an impoverished Queen's resort to grants of commercial privileges to reward servants led in her last years to parliamentary protests and legal challenges. In Ireland, checks on officials were ultimately extra-legal. Common law courts were only slowly being established outside the traditional Anglo-Irish areas; those that functioned were under the control of interested parties, both New English and Old English, and the Irish parliament ceased to meet for a generation after Perrot's 1585 venture. As a result, officials generally had a free hand at a time when the Munster plantation declared confiscation state policy. However much the crown tried to create a respectably hierarchical colony, the conclusion others all too easily drew was piratical. Fair estates could be carved out of Irish soil, and the indigent and those on the edge of gentility might claw their way to them. Such calculations gained extra force in regions like northern Connacht where instability, occasional violence, and limited information-flows allowed the energetic and well-armed to justify themselves with the prevailing rhetorics of popery and the wild. The eyes and ears blazoned on the Queen's Irish mantle in the 1601 Rainbow portrait constituted one of the most hopeful of all the period's many declarations of royal competence. A more realistic assessment comes in Lord Deputy Perrot's advice to an underling: 'Stick not so much upon Her Majesty's letter, she may command what she will, but we will do what we list.'

Perrot's composition of Connacht did not therefore check the further alienation of Gaeldom. Sir Richard Bingham, the soldier appointed to succeed Malby as president there in 1584, made no secret of his self-interest when he immediately challenged the landholdings of other English officials in the region on the grounds that they limited his own possibilities. The power of the two earls in southern Connacht ensured that English intrusions there were limited. In the north, Bingham forcefully intervened in the succession disputes of both the Sligo O'Connors and the McWilliam Burkes to carve out holdings for his brother and several cousins, and to reward a handful of cooperative Old English lawyers from the Pale.

English self-seeking became painfully evident everywhere. Sir William Herbert, a leading undertaker in the Munster plantation, wrote to Burghley in 1588 deploring the conduct of the New English, and warning that lesser army officers, thwarted by the hierarchical concerns of the plantation, were so harsh in their efforts to compensate themselves that they were likely to spark a new rebellion. But the most proficient self-server of them all had only just begun. Richard Boyle, later the great Earl of Cork, arrived in Munster from England in 1588 as a lawyer's clerk from a minor gentry background. Securing a deputy-escheator's post that gave him responsibility for the identification and leasing of confiscated estates and of lands to which the crown had claim, Boyle had by the end of Elizabeth's reign acquired an estate worth close to £4,000 p.a. He scarcely needed the example of the Lord Deputy, but if he did it was probably there, for Fitzwilliam on his return to office in 1588 quickly incurred multiple allegations of corruption. Hugely indebted to the Queen after failing to balance the books in his long service in the Irish treasury, Fitzwilliam had ample incentive to restore his finances. He denied the allegations and was not convicted. Nevertheless, in order to protect his own position he fabricated charges of treason against Perrot, who left Dublin in 1588 for appointment to the privy council and who was soon endorsing the reports of Fitzwilliam's corruption. Such vicious in-fighting for self-ends was hardly the mark of administrative coherence.

Perrot's deputyship and his fall cast a harsh light on the contradictions of the English effort in Ireland. In many respects he was one of the abler English administrators there—and despite the disasters, there were some able ones. He had learned the inadequacy of a merely punitive response to the swordsmen. In Connacht he made serious efforts to stabilize a Gaelic presence within an English order, and in Ulster in 1584 he aimed not just to establish forts but also to recognize contending spheres of influence; in pursuit of the latter enterprise he persuaded Gaelic leaders to participate in the parliamentary parade of 1585. The zeal of his protestantism was hardly Perrot's best bargaining chip in Ireland, but it was English, not Irish, obstruction that brought him down, as it had other deputies before him. Faction at court as well as in Ireland was a perennial obstacle, but from St Leger to the end of the century deputies faced an insoluble structural problem as they attempted what amounted to social engineering and nation-building with trifling resources at considerable physical distances and with poor communications. Much therefore hinged on personality, and Perrot's temper and body were increasingly impaired. His confrontations with colleagues (especially

Bingham and Bagenal) multiplied. Burghley was deluged with their complaints, and those as well of the Yorkshire-born and puritanical Archbishop of Dublin, Adam Loftus, who—revealingly—accused Perrot of favouring the Irish. It was these that led to his recall, though it was Fitzwilliam's outrageous accusation of treachery with Spain and with Rome that led to his arrest. Beyond these, it was the strains of reconciling an active military policy with rule by a notoriously inconstant and parsimonious queen that led to his conviction. Sidney, and later Mountjoy, managed to contain their frustrations in the language of chivalry; Perrot, like the younger Essex after him, failed and fell. Perrot's tirade against the Queen—'God's wounds, this it is to serve a base bastard pissing kitchen woman, if I had served any prince in Christendom I [would] have not been so dealt withal'—gives some flavour of the predicament of Elizabeth and the soldiers alike as they tried to deal with each other.

The venality, the bigotry, and the confusion are apparent, but there was some logic to English policy. This did not stem from any sustained protestant evangelism in Ireland. The arrival of the first Jesuits in England—they did not reach Ireland until 1596—at last convinced Elizabeth's government of the need for outreach, but the Queen had no money and the output of the English universities was woefully small even for England's needs. Loftus's refusal to shift ecclesiastical resources away from the beneficed clergy, and as well from himself, delayed the establishment of Trinity College Dublin until 1592; by then, an anxious New English establishment that had little trust or concern for those who did not already share its values confronted hardening Counter-Reformation loyalties. There were diminishing possibilities there.

The secular vision of civility had more to offer. The promotion of tillage and the substitution of the market for the sword in landed relationships imagined a more productive and peaceful world. As the Connacht composition had shown, these values could win the support of the chiefs, at least some of the subordinate landholders, and the farmers. But they threatened an ancient way of life that was celebrated by a confident bardic culture and that centred on the lordship of men. The bards, the collaterals, and the swordsmen could all put pressure on the chiefs, particularly since the Englishmen urging the new values were far from peaceful, were indeed exactive rather than productive as they moved across Ireland. There was an instructive contrast between Perrot's composition of Connacht and the settlement he attempted the following year in the province's north, an area without lords as powerful as Clanricard and Thomond; here, he took further the approach pioneered in East Breifne. A succession dispute among the McWilliam Burkes seemed to offer the Deputy the possibility of social redistribution, of breaking up the lordship among the six claimants' septs and making the portions of each freehold. The composition in the south had showed that local interests might accept demilitarization, but dismantling a lordship was another matter. For the last time a major contingent of McDonald redshanks rallied to the aid of a chiefly contender; it was cut to pieces by Bingham's troops, but the region's instability continued for years. The neighbouring Ulster chiefs found the bearing of reformers' logic on their own unreconstructed lordships easy to calculate.

And English governors were rarely subtle in their attentions to Ulster. Lord deputies had for decades played off O'Donnells against O'Neills, but crisis encouraged heavy-handedness. When in 1587 the O'Donnell heir, Hugh Roe, was set to marry Tyrone's daughter, paralleling Tyrone's own marriage to Sir Hugh O'Donnell's daughter and giving promise of a major new alliance, Perrot kidnapped the young bridegroom-to-be and took him prisoner to Dublin. In 1589–90 Fitzwilliam intervened in a succession dispute in Monaghan, and then hanged Hugh Roe McMahon, the contender he had promoted. The new chief had continued to take coign and livery and thus broken a promise of reform, and likely enough had added insult to injury by withholding a promised pay-off to Fitzwilliam himself. But the outcome was as provocative as the hanging, for the Deputy not only divided the lordship but also established 287 lesser men as freeholders, who paid dues to the crown as well as to their superiors. The dismantling of the McMahon lordship became a by-word among the other Ulster lords.

In what really mattered to Elizabeth and her council—combating the Spanish threat—Gaelic powers were willing to cooperate with English purposes. When the scattered Armada of 1588 straggled to destruction on rocky Irish coasts, the hapless survivors were robbed and butchered by those who found them, whether English, 'mere Irish', or Anglo-Irish.

But Bingham's remorseless pressure for performance drove the McWilliam Burkes again to take up arms, while one of the few Gaelic lords who protected the castaways, Sir Brian O'Rourke of West Breifne— long a thorn in Bingham's flesh—was himself hunted into exile for his pains. James King of Scots then showed his support for the Queen's purposes (and his anticipation of a larger crown) by handing him over for a traitor's death in her capital. That undignified but metropolitan end suggests that the 'mere Irish' were not victims of empire in quite the same way Amerindians were to become, and that their identities within the English world were more complicated. Had they known it, of course, the Ulster Irish would have found scant consolation in this.

Left to herself, Elizabeth might not have pressed so hard on the northern province. English governments were able to live with such anomalies as the semi-autonomous Lordship of the Isle of Man and papal warranty of the Channel Islands far into the seventeenth century when it felt no pressure from them. Elizabeth was desperately preoccupied with Spain and the Netherlands, and beset with cries for aid from the new king, Henri IV, of France against the Catholic coalition challenging him. She did not seek to obliterate Gaelic lordship in Ulster. She opposed Fitzwilliam's execution of McMahon for breach of his commitment to English ways, and observed realistically though ineffectually that his crimes were only 'such march [i.e. frontier] offences as are ever ordinarily committed in that realm'. But as that execution showed, Elizabeth's servants did not leave her to herself.

English ambivalence is clearest in the saga of the leading Ulster magnate, Hugh O'Neill, now Earl of Tyrone. With his anglicized upbringing and periodic service to English interests—with Essex in Ulster in 1573–74, with Grey against Desmond in Munster—Tyrone sometimes seemed to the Queen 'a creature of our own'. He was after all Dungannon's son. And he chose a good moment to visit court and make his pitch, for in 1587 the Dublin government was torn by Fitzwilliam's campaign against Perrot, and Whitehall and Edinburgh were distracted by the fallout from Mary Queen of Scots' execution as well as by the Spanish threat. Backed by Ormond, who himself resented the English military officials, Tyrone came away with an enhancement of the deal his grandfather Conn had achieved in his visit forty-five years earlier: tacit agreement that Ulster would not become a presidency and that he would remain dominant, and explicit recognition of the subordination of the lesser lords of central and eastern Ulster to himself. The outcome seemed likely to be a larger version of the kind of regional autonomy under the crown that Thomond and Clanricard had gained. And Tyrone quickly did the crown's business as he executed hundreds of Armada survivors and protected the Pale by martial law.

But English officialdom would not treat Ulster as southern Connacht. Not only did the north remain strategically sensitive because of its proximity to Scotland; it was patently the last bastion of the Gaelic order, and an affront to any standardizing dreams officials like Fitzwilliam and Bingham, and indeed Perrot too, might entertain. More importantly, the most entrenched of all the captains, the Bagenals of Newry, had their own aspirations in and for Ulster: not least, they hoped for the presidency. They therefore urged Tyrone's unreliability, his ambition, his covert sympathy for Spain, and they amplified the complaints of Shane O'Neill's sons against their rival's excesses. When Sir Henry Bagenal succeeded his ageing father in 1590 as marshal of the Irish army and member of the Irish council, he and Fitzwilliam persuaded Elizabeth's council to summon Tyrone for questioning. As so often in Ireland, public policy—never clearly defined, always wavering—was open to exploitation by private ambition deploying the uncontestable slogans of loyalty, civility, English law, and the protestant religion.

The 1590 hearing left Tyrone's position reduced. He was constrained to agree to something more like composition, the establishment of lesser families as freeholders paying rent to the crown as well as to himself—a prelude presumably to the funding of a governmental military force in the province. He agreed too to the institution of a sheriff, though he insisted this should be his brother Cormac MacBaron and the lordship should not be fully shired—English sheriffs, usually soldiers to free them from local faction, were all too often rapacious and had been sources of disruption elsewhere; local writs would therefore still run at his behest if in the Queen's name. And he took a more traditional route to accommodation by proposing a marriage with Sir Henry Bagenal's sister Mabel. Since an earl of Tyrone significantly outranked a Bagenal, the marshal's outrage at this as an affront to family honour may manifest

New English ethnic prejudice. It certainly manifests his distaste for Gaelic serial marriage practices, since at least one of Tyrone's previous wives was still alive. Bagenal's outrage intensified when Tyrone and Mabel eloped for a protestant church wedding; the personal quarrel deepened when Bagenal refused to hand over his sister's substantial dowry. Tyrone now had ample reason for concern about his security.

But did Gaelic intransigence have a larger politics? By the 1590s some Gaelic verse, particularly that composed in the long-contested uplands of Wicklow, seems to show traces of what might almost be called Gaelic nationalism: not just the usual identification with the land of Ireland but with a specifically Irish Gaeldom threatened everywhere by the English. If so, this parallels—and not entirely coincidentally—the emergence of a more assertive national element in late-Elizabethan English culture. But on the whole, the highly formal praise poems of the Gaelic bards focused still on the virtues and achievements of the patron: not just traditional princes like O'Donnell but even doughty English invaders like Malby. On the other hand, the cause of religion was beginning to generate a more inflamed resistance to English encroachments. A few new, and Counter-Reformation, Catholic bishops had begun to appear piecemeal in Gaelic as well as Old English dioceses across Ireland in the late 1580s, paralleling and challenging the English Church structure. The Old English of the Pale—many of whom had advanced further in Counter-Reformation purity than their less cosmopolitan Gaelic co-religionists—successfully urged Rome to soften its call to rebellion against their Queen. But some northern bishops who had trained in Spain and were responsive to the anxieties of northern lords sought Spanish military support against the heretic.

In the surviving political centres of Gaeldom, opposition to English encroachments was becoming radicalized. Hugh Maguire's lordship in Fermanagh had suffered from Bingham's campaign of enforcement against the Armada survivors and again when Fitzwilliam moved against the McMahons; Maguire later insisted plausibly that such excesses drove him into rebellion. But though local grievances also pressed on Hugh Roe O'Donnell, when he escaped from his arbitrary imprisonment in Dublin Castle and headed back to Tyrconnell in the winter of 1591–92, he made contact not just with Maguire but also with Spain through the northern Catholic bishops. When Bingham intercepted the churchmen's pleas for Spanish support for a Catholic rising, English protestants were only confirmed in what they had long thought they knew—the more so when in 1593 Maguire attacked the Binghams in Connacht after the president installed a particularly aggressive English sheriff in Fermanagh. At the same time, Maguire added another link to the Ulster chain of dynastic alliances, and another element of uncertainty for the government, by marrying one of Tyrone's daughters. The Queen, with thousands of troops committed in the Netherlands and also now in France in support of Henri IV, had little choice but still to hope that Tyrone would hold steady.

Hugh O'Neill, after all, was no intransigent, religious or otherwise. He had had a protestant wedding ceremony, and though the Earl of Essex exaggerated when he later alleged that his nemesis had as much religion as his horse, Tyrone was surely torn ideologically. His objectives will always be debated, but he does seem to have tried to continue Elizabeth's subject, and at Dublin's prompting even cooperated with Bagenal in a 1593 campaign against Maguire, protesting angrily when Bagenal received the credit for the capture of Maguire's base of Enniskillen. But Tyrone was surely now playing a double game, encouraging his relatives to attack the English on Ulster's peripheries while he kept his own hands clean, in order to extract concessions from a government desperate to avoid one further conflagration. And his strategy seemed to work. His complaints of English ingratitude and the biased dealings of Fitzwilliam and Bagenal—complaints supported by Ormond, and by a growing English literature of complaint about corruption in Ireland—secured Fitzwilliam's recall, and an order excluding Bagenal from Tyrone's territory. So when in 1594 his brother Cormac MacBaron joined Maguire in a dramatic raid on the English at Enniskillen, Tyrone ostentatiously displayed his own loyalty by appearing unbidden before the new deputy, Sir William Russell. But the desire of both parties to avoid confrontation was diminishing. With the ageing Ormond, who had acted as a mediator at court, now permanently returned to Ireland, Elizabeth berated Russell for allowing Tyrone to ride away from the meeting unhindered. Greater stability in the Netherlands and peace in Brittany in 1595 soon enabled her to divert 2,000 troops from France to

Ireland, to give substance to that impatience. That spring, Cormac MacBaron helped Maguire and O'Donnell recapture Enniskillen; by midsummer, Tyrone himself had attacked Bagenal's marauding forces, and had been proclaimed traitor. Three months later, in September 1595, he reasserted his Gaelic autonomy by having himself installed as the O'Neill at the ceremonial site of Tullahoge.

'The Nine Years War'—the term is not that of the English crown, since the crown called its Irish enemies rebels or worse, not belligerents—did not open with a herald's declaration. Its putative beginning, if such a decentred and sporadic conflict had a single beginning, lay in Maguire's 1594 raid on Enniskillen. But the war owes its character and duration to Tyrone, who had been as single-minded in building a position of regional strength as Elizabeth was distracted. Indeed, it seems likely that Tyrone had thought his position in Ulster, with its natural defences of mountain, forest, and bog, so strong that Elizabeth would negotiate a settlement. There were certainly English commentators who advised as much. But the Queen rarely brooked resistance from those she deemed her creatures, still less one she could deride as a 'bush kern'. On the other hand, Tyrone was correct in assuming she did not have the resources to impose her will efficiently. By the summer of 1595 he was credibly reported to have 1,000 horsemen, 1,000 pikemen, and about 4,000 musketeers; the Lord Deputy, whose reinforcements from Brittany had not yet arrived, then deployed less than 1,500, many of them poorly trained cast-offs from the English countryside, and many of the others just as 'Irish'—mercenary kern of the kind who always filled out Tudor forces in Ireland—as those they fought against. In his ability to support his forces and to train them with foreign captains in the arms he imported from Scotland and Europe, Tyrone was a modern commander, and not the savage enemy of the 'civil' that his royal foe sometimes alleged.

And Elizabeth had repeatedly to temporize with him. Although in February 1595 the crown issued a proclamation calling for the expulsion from England of all Irishmen, 'who cannot have any good meaning towards her majesty', unless they were identifiable householders or others of good standing, Elizabeth was not convinced the Irish were all lost. Anyway, her court was riven by the Essex–Cecil feud, her commanders in Ireland—Lord Deputy Russell and Sir John Norris—were seriously at odds, and her energies and resources consumed by the 1596–97 raids on Cadiz and the Azores. These predictably enough sparked Spanish attempts to counter with new Armadas—from which England was spared by the weather—and sparked Spanish interest too in striking at Elizabeth through Ireland. Tyrone joined the other Ulster chiefs in encouraging such interest with proposals for a war to restore Catholicism, but the failure of the Spanish to do more than send him a little money left him content in 1596 to accept a truce. The crown's position continued to worsen on the expiry of that truce. Russell's preoccupation with his quarrel with Norris and with securing the Pale against resurgent O'Byrnes in Wicklow allowed Tyrone to press against Bagenal's position in Newry while O'Donnell reasserted his dominance over much of northern Connacht. This damaging period of drift forms the context for the notorious assessment of English policy and options, the *View of the Present State of Ireland*, that Edmund Spenser wrote, apparently in the summer of 1596.

The *View* was not published until 1633: presumably its sardonic references to factions around a Queen given—too given?—to listening to 'pitiful complaints' gave sufficient warrant to a council nervous of disaffection in that blighted time to suppress it. The amount of interpretive weight the text can bear is a question, since Spenser's authorship has been disputed and anyway the author crafted a dialogue, thus giving any particular argument deniability. But there can be no doubt of the fissures the *View* reveals in English thinking. Spenser begins with criticism of unnamed 'counsellors' for wishing that 'all that land were a sea-pool', while the question whether Ireland had a 'fatal destiny' reverberates throughout, surely reflecting some desperation in official circles. Spenser's overt argument is that Ireland had neared catastrophe in 1596 only as a result of repeated English mistakes and half-measures, and that it—or at least England's grasp on it—could be rescued only by a sufficiently tough policy against the swordsmen and the structures that sustained them; these must be destroyed before new could be built. Accordingly, the *View* proceeds remorselessly from its horrific account of conditions in Munster after the Desmond revolt—the work of a properly determined Lord Grey, Spenser's hero—to a no less startling advocacy of starvation tactics against Tyrone's forces in Ulster and

O'Byrne's in Wicklow. It urges too an equally breathtaking programme of garrisons, martial law, confiscations, and forced population movements. But Spenser's angry insistence that the disloyal Old English were in their 'degeneracy' more guilty, worse traitors, than the rebellious mere Irish suggests an uneasy suspicion that the country that could corrupt them may indeed have been 'accursed'—ironically, Spenser's own descendants were to be dispossessed in the seventeenth century for their opposition to English protestant regimes in Ireland. His sophisticated ethnographic analysis further declared the faintness of his hopes for reform. True, he pointed out that the English at the time of the twelfth-century conquest of Ireland had not been very civil; but like many others he argued the Scythian origins of the Gael, and so brought the 'mere Irish' elite within the apocalyptic compass of the curse Shakespeare's King Lear threw at his daughter Cordelia when he accused her of emulating the legendary cannibalism of the Scythian.

But if the Irish could not, the English would not change their ways. Russell's replacement in late 1597 by a more dynamic deputy, Lord Burgh, brought only temporary improvement, since Burgh and Norris quickly died, leaving the less than competent Bagenal with the task of relieving and resupplying a dangerously exposed English garrison on the Blackwater River in central Ulster. Tyrone's victory at the Yellow Ford in August 1598—Bagenal was killed along with over 1,000 of his troops, and much of the munitions lost—transformed the war. By the end of the year the Munster plantation had collapsed as the displaced local elites reclaimed their own. Only Ormond saved Leinster.

The prospect of its loss made Ireland for once the priority of the English government. In March 1599, after some delay in the factional morass at court, Elizabeth's last favourite, Robert Devereux, 2nd Earl of Essex, accepted the enhanced title of lord lieutenant of Ireland that signalled the Queen's commitment to the cause as well as the man. Popular approval may be read in the chorus's unusual endorsement of 'the general of our gracious Empress' in Shakespeare's *Henry V*, a work of 1599; Francis Bacon, one of Essex's advisors, rejoiced that now was the time to return the Irish 'to humanity' from a 'more than Indian barbarism'. Furious at the damage inflicted by 'bush kerns' and with her commitments in Europe reduced by peace in France, the Queen also and at last dispatched a huge force, whose paper strength of over 17,000 exceeded any sent to the Netherlands. But though this army cost her £300,000 in seven months, it was one of a long series of forcible levies for war since 1585, and it had to be raised amid the atrocious harvests and acute dislocation of the later 1590s. The men chosen, or passed off, by the English counties were all too often ailing and inadequate, and the rainy weather and harsh conditions in Ireland killed them almost as fast as they landed—certainly faster than the enemy did. Nor were they, or Essex, helped by the planners. As the chequered record of English raids on Spain showed, combined operations were hard to coordinate, and Essex's promise that he would proceed promptly with a joint naval and land assault on Ulster evaporated when ships, horses, and carts failed to arrive. Instead, he turned aside for a show-the-flag expedition to Munster, a not entirely irrational move when Spanish invasion was feared and Old English loyalties were wobbly, but by the time he headed north in September his troop-strength had dwindled below 4,000, while Tyrone's force that confronted him was twice the size.

However justifiable it may have been militarily, Essex's decision to negotiate a truce—Tyrone still hoped that Elizabeth might compromise—finished him politically. Already in the summer he had sent the Queen a memorandum arguing that though the war could be won it might not be worth the winning, whether materially or—in terms of what such a war might do to Old English loyalties—politically. The risks inherent in a high-visibility commander now became clear. Essex was earl marshal of England as well as lord lieutenant of Ireland, and for him to walk away from confrontation was to raise his own judgement and honour against the impatient Queen's, and to encourage speculation about what Tyrone and he said to each other alone in the river's shallows near Dundalk. All parties were in some sense playing for time now, and the kinder readers of lips hinted, plausibly enough, that preparations were being made for the event of her death; others conjectured something even more outrageous. Within days, Essex abandoned his command and rushed to court to try to undo the damage, but it was too late. He was only to escape by rebellion and death the disgrace that now engulfed him.

Tyrone's objectives seem to have been as fluid as his generalship. He favoured ambushes and raiding rather than set-piece engagements, and in his politics he similarly avoided formal confrontations. So while in 1595–96 he and O'Donnell made overtures to Philip II about transferring sovereignty over Ireland to Spain—just as the Dutch rebels had a decade earlier tried to transfer their sovereignty from Spain to either France or England—he remained reluctant to push the struggle with Elizabeth to the utmost. There was prudence in this, for he recognized the complex loyalties of the Old English who were increasingly estranged in religion and politics and yet committed to their inherited identity. It was surely to them he spoke as well as to Elizabeth when in 1599 he published his terms for the government of what would have been a largely autonomous Ireland. These show a significant effort to preserve the royal honour and the fundamental royal prerogative of control over foreign policy: the formal head of government, to be termed the viceroy, would be a senior English nobleman serving under the crown, with perhaps half the army fully English, though the rest of the government and the judiciary would be the preserve of those born in Ireland, and the established church would once more be that of Rome, not Canterbury. The Queen's Secretary, Sir Robert Cecil, famously scrawled 'Utopia' in the margin of his copy, and while the comment is dismissive we may hear a note of wistfulness too. Almost as unrealistic were Tyrone's hopes that his sophisticated appeals not just to a Catholic cause but to an undifferentiated Irish nation—'we Irishmen'—and to the soil of a suffering Irish fatherland, the Roman *patria* as opposed to the female 'Erin' of the bards, would rouse the Old English in revolt against English heresy and tyranny. But no shared nationhood could yet be found among those born in Ireland. In Munster, the McCarthys, with unhappy memories of Desmond as neighbour and aspiring overlord, remained divided as the plantation fell; conversely, the gentry of the Pale, the coastal towns, and the Dublin oligarchs clung determinedly to their ancestral English identities. As a result, the map of Ireland in 1599 looked much as it had done a century earlier, with the English hold reduced to a Pale that seemed impervious to the assaults of Gaeldom.

But the level of outside interest had grown over the century. Although both Philip II and Lord Burghley had died the year before, their sons

Philip III and Sir Robert Cecil recognized the same strategic realities: Spain could strike at the Dutch and at England through Ireland, and indeed one more defeat for England there might prove fatal. Accordingly, while Spain prepared yet another fleet, the Queen in February 1600 dispatched a new lord deputy in Charles Blount, Lord Mountjoy, whose remarkable personal appeal—he managed to be friends with both Cecil and Essex, and his looks had caught Elizabeth's eye—was matched with an impressive military record. The court rivalries might still have derailed the new command: Mountjoy listened to Essex's frantic urgings—seconded as these were by his mistress, Essex's sister—that he bring his army to England against the Cecilians and to secure the succession unilaterally for James of Scotland and the Essex interest. Thinking himself fatally compromised when Essex so disastrously rebelled in 1601, he almost fled to France. But Elizabeth chose to ignore the evidence against him, and Mountjoy played it safe politically and also militarily. There were to be no grand gestures, since any mistake now would be catastrophic. He would proceed against Ulster gradually and on a number of fronts, allowing regional commanders—especially Sir George Carew in Munster—the discretion to offer terms and vary tactics in a way the jealous Essex had not. By proceeding methodically and ruthlessly with scorched-earth tactics against Tyrone's resources, human as well as material, by careful use of the navy to support English garrisons around the Ulster coast, and by brutal marauding through the winter of 1600–01, Mountjoy within a year of his arrival reduced Tyrone to desperation. Crucially, the Scottish monarchy's consolidation of western Scotland in the 1590s meant that the usual flow of galleys bearing redshanks from the Hebrides dwindled to a trickle—had it not, Elizabeth would surely have lost. Spain remained now the rebels' only hope.

Advances in state formation, in logistics and supply, were fundamental to the war Mountjoy waged, and to its success. The English army was at last able to operate year-round, able to prevent Tyrone hiding his cattle and supplies in the winter woods, and Mountjoy was determined to deprive his foe of that or any other capacity. The violence of his campaigns resulted in part from the years of frustration—a frustration that is palpable in Spenser's yearning for Talus, the iron man of *The Faerie Queene*, whose flail would sweep away the corrupt along with their corruptions. It resulted too from the familiar cultural division: those from the European heartland had long been uneasy about Gaels, and Lord Deputy Sidney had been far from alone when he dismissed Shane O'Neill as 'that cannibal'. The overlay of religious war, the creation of what has been justly called an ethno-religious conflict, hardened the lines mercilessly, making violence-as-cleansing as easy to perpetrate as it was to imagine. So, while soldiers played football with the severed heads of their enemies, English commanders like Sir Arthur Chichester, a future lord deputy, could report without remorse or shame indiscriminate—or rather, systematically indiscriminate—killings and burnings of entire villages. The laws of war were increasingly familiar in the European theatre—Fluellen in *Henry V* denounces the French massacre of serving-boys as 'expressly against the law of arms'. But in Ireland few voiced any qualms as they devastated Ulster and parts of Munster at the end of Elizabeth's reign. Not for nothing did Elizabeth in the proclamation sent with Essex in 1599 feel obliged to defend her government against allegations 'that we intended an utter extirpation and rooting out of that Nation'.

Spenser's *deus ex machina* did not appear, and the Spanish came too late to help Tyrone, exposing him instead to catastrophe. As Mountjoy penned him into an Ulster increasingly emptied of crops and people, Tyrone urged Madrid to send to a south-western port a force large enough to distract much of the English army, but to choose a port more accessible to Ulster for anything smaller. To his dismay, Spain's distractions in France meant that its troops only arrived in early October 1601, after Carew had divided and stabilized Munster and after the English strength in Ireland had been brought up to the remarkable level of 19,000. Worse, the Spanish numbers—under 4,000—were few enough and their landing-point at Kinsale in the far south-west distant enough for Mountjoy to get there first and bottle them up. The endurance of all sides must be credited. Tyrone and O'Donnell broke out of Ulster in atrocious winter weather to relieve the Spaniards, while Mountjoy maintained a siege in appalling conditions, with thousands of dying men scattered among the tents. When the northern lords arrived in front of Kinsale at the end of the year their greater numbers might have pinned Mountjoy's wasted besiegers against the city's walls, as the cautious Tyrone wanted to do though his own men were starving; but the clerical advisers and the Spanish urged battle. Communications and the terrain worked against them. The Spaniards never left the city, and the heavier English cavalry proved decisive in the open country. The Christmas Eve battle of Kinsale left well over 1,000 Irish, but few English, dead. Mountjoy soon took the Spanish surrender and allowed them, as regular belligerents—which the papal irregulars at Smerwick had not been—to evacuate in good order. In default of catching Tyrone, he then turned to the slow task of obliterating the base for resistance—Ulster's economy.

Tyrone made his peace as Elizabeth lay dying in March 1603, though in military terms Kinsale fifteen months earlier had been decisive. The delay was socially and economically ruinous: the English resorted to systematic debasement of the currency to fund the war, and intensified the famine and the killing in Ulster. Until late in 1602 the Queen refused to contemplate a pardon for the 'Archtraitor'. Furthermore, her government could see practical advantages in harshness, since a plantation of Ulster emptied of its leaders and many of its people could settle a province that had preoccupied every governor since Sussex, and would allow some recouping of the ruinous sum of nearly £4 million that the Queen had spent in Ireland since 1588. Munster had, by contrast, been planted after a war costing one-sixteenth of that. But though in September 1602 Mountjoy symbolically terminated O'Neill political culture by destroying the ancient stone inauguration chair at Tullahoge near Armagh, Tyrone's remarkable hold on Ulster loyalties despite Ulster's suffering enabled him to evade capture. Only when Mountjoy was himself desperate, as an aspiring courtier, to get to London to make contact with an unknown king and Cecil was desperate to end a war that had consumed almost all the crown's financial reserves did Tyrone come in.

As Elizabeth's grip loosened, Mountjoy persuaded Cecil to approve a remarkably generous settlement. The surrender terms signed at Mellifont on 30 March 1603, after Elizabeth was already dead, resembled the agreement Tyrone had made at court in 1587, and they would probably have satisfied him even in 1594. Though he was now required to abandon the title of 'the O'Neill', his earldom was confirmed to him and the earldom of Tyrconnell granted to Rory O'Donnell, brother of the dead Hugh

Roe. Surely more important, the treaty confirmed their dominance over the lesser lords of Ulster, even those who had fought for the crown, and it did not impose composition on Tyrone's lordship. As he made the deal, Mountjoy may have been acknowledging the Scottish king's, his king's, generally more relaxed relations with Gaeldom.

Had Essex been wrong, then, to ask whether the war would be worth winning? With an outcome as compromised as that of 1603, second-guessing is almost unavoidable. The magnitude of the stakes involved by the end of the 1590s, especially after Tyrone called for the restoration of the Catholic Church, meant that it was a war Elizabeth could not afford to lose—she may have been melodramatic in her invocation of her sister Mary's fate, but she had a point. Did she need, though, to fight the war to the point of exhaustion? An early settlement could have been gained on terms like those of 1603, and would surely have avoided the devastation of Ulster, the impoverishment of the crown, and perhaps the full playing of the religious card. The role of material pressures—Bingham's rigour, Fitzwilliam's abuses—in Maguire's rebellion, and Tyrone's evident lack until very late in the day of the religious devotion that might have driven an intransigent to war, push the questions further back, and prompt questions about the responsibility of English policy-makers for the war itself. True, the Ulster lords' determined resistance to a settlement along Monaghan lines—the dismantling of overweening lordship and the allocation of resources to lesser lineages—suggests an underlying conflict between English policy as it had developed in the sixteenth century and Tyrone's aspirations, suggests indeed that Bagenal, Bingham, and Fitzwilliam were superficial problems. On the other hand, Tyrone at the end, and in 1587 too, proved ready to settle for a position not unlike those of Thomond and Clanricard—'civil' because demilitarized but a magnate's dominant position nonetheless. Elizabeth's own ability to recognize Hugh Roe McMahon's misdeeds in Monaghan as but 'march offences' suggest that—had the Bagenals' calumnies not disrupted the 1587 agreement—she might have been able to live with the adjustments that would have been needed. To put it another way: was the principle of social levelling worth the cost?

Map 3 Jacobean Plantations

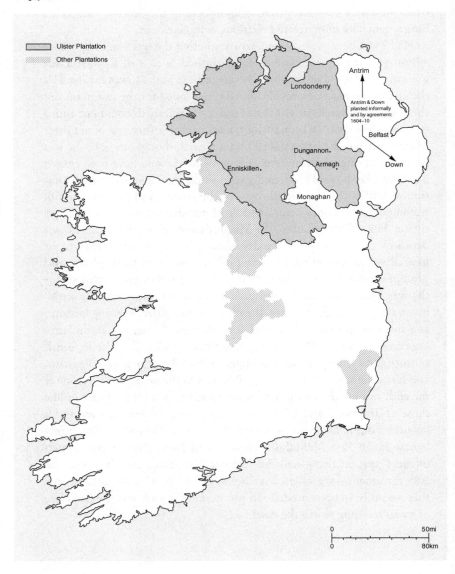

CHAPTER 6
TOWARDS A GREATER BRITAIN?
1603–1618

The panegyrists' customary salute to a new reign as a new beginning for once made sense. Few could have known of Secretary Cecil's own growing desire for peace with Spain, fewer still of James VI of Scotland's occasional contacts in the 1590s with Madrid and even Rome. But none could ignore Edinburgh's distance from the narrow world of Elizabeth's court in her last years. With a new king who had been no party to the court's wartime mood since the 1580s, peace and lower taxes ought to be possible. Accordingly, the poets celebrated the prospect of patronage flowing more freely, of corruption banished, of moods lightened. Not only had an aged and cramped regime gone; the new king had three children, whose lives dispelled the dynastic uncertainties that had for so long clouded England's political culture.

James was to take as his motto '*Rex Pacificus*', the royal peace-maker, though his active responsibility for the cease of arms might be questioned. After all, Cecil needed little encouragement to begin the Anglo-Spanish negotiations that resulted in the 1604 Treaty of London, with its general and uncomplicated return to the *status quo ante*; peace had already been signed in Ireland, the conquest ruinously made; and it was the mere succession of James Stewart to Elizabeth's throne, not any canniness, that smoothly closed that 'postern gate' to the north which had for nearly three centuries opened England to fears of France. But the succession so accomplished did inaugurate a new geopolitical order, even as the dynastic vulnerability vanished. Furthermore, the multiplication of kingdoms ensured international respect, or so James—now gracing himself with the more cosmopolitan surname of 'Stuart' (the

French had always had trouble with the 'w' in 'Stewart')—assured his first English parliament. That claim to dignity might be genuinely British, and so those Scots assumed who continued to look to a protestant union for security and for continuance of those British support networks so many Scottish protestants had enjoyed in Elizabeth's reign. The King's English subjects took an English focus for granted. For them, the moment marked a welcome step away from the old awareness that the reduced England of the Tudors, shorn of its French possessions, was in European terms rather peripheral. A trace of relief can be heard in the boast of the English antiquarian Sir Henry Spelman, 'We...are now invincible.'

Yet new anxieties appeared, unavoidably perhaps with a foreign king on a new throne. The anxieties were less urgent than those of survival in the grim days of 1598–99, but they did occupy the mind. What would the political arrangements be, and how would they work? If some gained, some must surely lose, and Europe's post-medieval history abounded in formerly proud states curtailed in their autonomies by dynastic unions. The force of Henry VII's prediction that the greater would draw the less was clear: Scots assumed they would lose their king to the attractions of the south, and the English expected nothing less. But what would that mean in practice? In England and Scotland alike, most could see that the accession of a king of Scots to the English throne would be a transition of significance, but for the moment they had to rely for its meaning on the assurances that James—who went south not only exuberant in his new-found prosperity but confident in his king-craft—gave on every hand. Anyway, the most immediate concerns of courtiers and would-be courtiers were the windfalls of favour that attended any new regime.

As the first king of both England and Scotland, and king of Ireland too (like others, he was not inclined to give equal weight to a title dependent on the English crown), James meant to redraw the map. An imperial and protestant British monarchy would offer the kings of Europe a model to set against blasphemous papal claims to hegemony. More prosaically, a dual king could in his person put an end to the mutual bellicosities of England and Scotland, even remove their causes as he united the kingdoms. By 1617, on his first and last return to Scotland, he was perhaps only singing an old song to his attendants when he dismounted from his horse and lay athwart the border to dramatize his royal body politic, but at the start of his British reign he had had high hopes. As he set up a bi-national commission in 1604 to work towards union, he insisted to Sir Robert Cecil, his English secretary of state, that he intended 'the uniting of both laws and parliaments of both the nations.' He softened this only a little when he told his first English parliament soon afterwards that he sought to effect that impressive formula, *unus rex, unus grex, una lex*—one king, one people, one law. And there were reasons for the west to hope for more extensive reconciliation: Irish bards delighted in the Gaelic origins of the ancient Scottish kings, finding in James 'a monarch of their own race and blood,' and consolation for their sufferings under the bastard Elizabeth Tudor. 'Mere Irish' were later to show a striking commitment to the Stuarts, even amid catastrophe.

There was much that James could do on his own to effect his vision of British union. The 1604 Anglo-Spanish peace that followed and capped the Irish peace at Mellifont gave him more freedom than Elizabeth had ever enjoyed. Although his opening proclamation that he was king of Great Britain failed to persuade either British kingdom of the title's merits, contemporary Europe was more familiar with composite polities. He managed to secure appropriate recognition from northern states used to dealing with Scotland, though French and Spanish diplomats thought they were still dealing with England and its king; perhaps a few of their countrymen along the coasts were gradually won over by the common flag (the 'Union Jack' named after him) that James enjoined for British shipping. But undoubtedly of greater practical significance were his efforts to create an Anglo-Scottish court, and to rely on English and Scottish nobles equally for his intimate attendants. Their dangerous rivalries quickly turned him towards an entirely Scottish bedchamber to offset the English institutions of formal rule that surrounded him. The decision occasioned considerable English heart-burning, but the success of the bedchambermen—crucial intermediaries for suits and petitions—at integrating distant Scots into the new polity testifies to James's political good sense.

In many matters beyond the court too, a king could achieve much without waiting for a parliament. James aimed for an average seven-day delivery time for royal mail between London and Edinburgh—crucial for a king who intended to govern Scotland from afar—and he quickly (though a little prematurely) pronounced the irrelevance of the Anglo-Scottish Borders, the ancient reiving and raiding zone: they were now the 'middle shires' of his British kingdom. On the English side of the border, the militarized tenure of tenant right soon gave way to more pacific and commercialized forms of holding, and some of the Grahams, the most troublesome of the Border 'names', or clans, were resettled in an Ulster depopulated by war. Spreading civility by such means smacks of approaches to Gaeldom taken by both the English and the Scottish crowns over the years. Indeed, there were signs that in Ireland James hoped to use the still-ambiguous figure of Tyrone—with whom he had long been in contact—as his lever with the 'mere Irish', just as he and his predecessors had used Argyll to control Gaelic western Scotland. This was a king who, whatever his grand scheme of union, intended to bring his Scottish style of personal, problem-solving kingship to bear across his dominions.

The long Anglo-Scottish peace that had followed Mary Queen of Scots' abdication in 1567 had certainly allowed the ancient resentments to subside. But could watchfulness be transformed into warmth? Some clearly doubted this. One high episcopal churchman, Richard Bancroft, bishop of London and future archbishop of Canterbury, had aimed his *Dangerous Positions* (1593) at puritans in 'this Island of Britain', and clearly saw Scottish presbyterians as a significant threat to English happiness. On the other confessional side, the Catholic Gunpowder Plotters of 1605 hoped to exploit broader anti-Scottish feeling in their 'blow' against the new monarch and his followers. The mood in London at the accession at best suggested only introversion. *The Magnificent Entertainment* put on by the City for the King's March 1604 entry (delayed by the devastating London plague of 1603) spoke ringingly of the ancient grandeur of Britain and its promise under its new monarch, but the text by Thomas Dekker and Ben Jonson generally imagined these in terms of the City's place in the brave new world. Anthony Munday's pageant for the following year's Lord Mayor's show, *The Triumphs of a Re-united Britannia*, was still more preoccupied with London's antiquity and claims.

The idea of Britain certainly had imaginative purchase. The poets' evocation of an island Eden, separate from the world—England as 'this sceptr'd isle' in Shakespeare's *Richard II*—gained greater geographic precision with Scotland's addition in and after 1603. King James exploited the figure eagerly (and in so doing and not insignificantly omitted Ireland from his vision) when addressing his first English parliament. The dream of an island fortress combined nature with destiny for that minority of militant protestants in both kingdoms who wanted to drive the papal Antichrist from Europe and the world—an objective that seemed to grow more urgent in the wake of the 1605 Gunpowder Plot. More pacifically, Welsh panegyrists celebrated James's unification of the British kingdoms as the fulfillment of Merlin's ancient prophecies. Legends of early British Christianity were central to England's protestant genealogy, but Welsh claims to founding-Britons status did not go unchallenged: London audiences delighted in the increasingly frequent theatrical appearance of the proverbial stage Welshman, and resident Welshmen—perhaps 7% of the Jacobean City's population—brave enough to flourish a leek on St David's day risked a beating. More learnedly, Sir Henry Spelman warned his colleagues in the Society of Antiquaries against those nameless ones who sought to sacrifice the name of England, and with it 'the glory of a nation triumphant through all the world to restore the memory of an obscure and barbarous people', the British, or Welsh.

The matter of Britain was, for the English if not for the Welsh or for zealous Scots, easier to talk about than to warm to. William Camden, the greatest of the scholars and Elizabeth's favourite antiquarian, had sought in his Latin *Britannia* (1586, final expanded version 1607) to authenticate pre-Roman Britain and to connect it lineally to its descendant, a greater English present. But he tried to be tactful: not only did he puncture English Arthurian fantasies, but in the English translation that appeared in 1610 he welcomed non-British Scots to the royal and English sunshine with the assurance 'We are all one nation at this day'. There were other lavish surveys of the King's collected dominions. Around the time of *Britannia*'s appearance in the vernacular there were published John Speed's wildly successful *Theatre of the Empire of Great Britaine* (1611) and Michael Drayton's verse chorography *Poly-Olbion* (1612). But these signalled enthusiasm less than they did curiosity, and of course an authorial pitch for patronage. Speed's atlas is, at the conceptual level, remarkable for its rare attention to all three kingdoms within the covers of one book, and its attempt to fix a label onto them ('the empire of Great Britain'—though was 'Great Britain', with Ireland somehow included, an empire, or did Great Britain have an empire in Ireland?). Its impressive cartography is more notable for its domesticity, its plans of English towns, its attention to gentlemen's parks, its flourishing of noble coats of arms; though it maps in some detail the three southern Irish provinces, its map of Ulster is (and remained in later editions) oddly out of date. And the atlas gives short shrift to Scotland—indeed, the vignette of Edinburgh in the main-page spread of 'The Kingdom of Great Britain and Ireland' actually shows the city in 1544 under English siege, shortly before it was burned. Empire may have been the announced theme, but this was an unsteady rallying-cry for Britain.

Other imagined ventures into British territory were no more enthusiastic. Shakespeare turned his energies away from the English history that had preoccupied him in the 1590s to works on British (but not Irish) themes: *Macbeth*, *King Lear*, *Cymbeline*; lesser authors followed similar trajectories. Nevertheless, Shakespeare's tone had shifted across the dynastic watershed. The notes of English patriotism heard in *Richard II* and *Henry V* leave little doubt of the author's sympathies in the 1590s; but while he was ready enough after 1603 to explore the British histories, his plays suggest he may not have found much in Britishness to cheer him. In the wasteland of *King Lear*, Edgar, with his impeccably English name, is the one good man left standing; in the grand catastrophe of *Macbeth*, England provides safe haven for Scotland's heirs; and in *Cymbeline*, Rome's empire and its civilities may seem compromised, but the Queen and Cloten her son are no less beastly than they are British. Still more remarkably, there may be in Caliban's lament for his receding island in *The Tempest*, with its verbal echoes of Shane O'Neill's lament for his island home reported in Holinshed's *Chronicles*, a rare recognition of what others lost as 'civility' advanced.

When James made British union his objective he therefore encountered not quite the reaction he had anticipated. Neither his Westminster nor his Edinburgh parliament objected to the repeal of mutually hostile laws, but the Scots were nervous that freer trade would open their markets, and particularly their trading privileges in France, to English competition. They surely derived some satisfaction when they learned of royal anger at the English MPs who worried that mutual naturalization might open them to a flood of 'beggarly' Scots eager to use royal favour as a stepping-stone to English jobs, estates, and wives. Sir John Holles, an aspiring courtier, was making a significant point when he protested that in a monarchy royal favour mattered: 'The Scottish monopolize his princely person, standing like mountains betwixt the beams of his grace and us.' But the English were not just jealous. They had their own fears about lower-cost, and therefore lower-priced, Scottish competition in textiles, coal, and salt. The disproportion between the two economies—a generation later, the value of Scottish external trade hovered around 5% of the English total, though Scotland's population was about 25% of England's—gives some colour to the English jibes at Scottish beggarliness. Chauvinism and carping were to disrupt the 1604 and 1607 sessions of James's English parliament, leaving the King with a bitter aftertaste and leaving parliament-men sorely distrustful of royal intentions.

James's dream of rebranding his two ancestral kingdoms as 'Great Britain' provoked much deeper suspicion than his distribution of favours, whether political or commercial. It is not clear that James ever recognized the complexity of the task he had set himself. English common law was the most centralized legal system of its day, and alone in Europe in its determinedly uniform application to a whole nation. Since 'England' was written across the statutory record, would English laws vanish with the name? The judges in conference in 1604 declared they would, and that was worrying enough. Worse, the peculiarly national character of English law had been the watchword of Henry VIII's Reformation statutes against Rome, and of his incorporation of Wales. English law made England an empire of itself, and the patriotic meaning of that claim had been heightened by the long Elizabethan conflict with Rome and Spain. The King tried to woo his English parliament-men: Britain, united, encircled by the ocean, was 'become like a little world within itself'; he was 'the husband and all the whole isle [his] lawful wife'. In that domesticating vision, unity, singularity, was essential. By the time of the 1607 session, James had been schooled both by the 1604 outcry and the sophisticated civil-law theories articulated by Sir Thomas Craig, one of the Scottish union commissioners, and tempered his rhetoric with a dash of realism. He protested his determination to leave the 'municipal' laws of his kingdoms untouched in their particulars and unite only their shared principles. And he acknowledged too that Scotland would be the junior partner—even hinting, to Scottish dismay, that its status might resemble Ireland's. But who could be certain when the stakes were so high?

The strength of English fears that the nation's distinctiveness, its essence, would be lost is palpable: 'We cannot be other than we are, being English we cannot be Britains [sic],' one member declared in 1604. Sir Maurice Berkeley appealed emotionally in the 1607 debates to 'laws written in the blood of our ancestors'; Sir Edwin Sandys—who was soon to prove something of a shaper of empire as treasurer to the Virginia Company—exploited the fears, and the manifest contempt for the Scots shown by noblemen and MPs alike, with the brilliant wrecking proposal that Scotland would benefit most from a 'perfect union': a full incorporation of the nation and its laws into England, on the Welsh model. This appealed hugely to English MPs and offended a king proud of his Scottishness. Far from the new beginning of which James and the panegyrists had dreamt in 1603, stasis remained the order of the day, since so few had anything to gain from change. Frustrated, James had to content himself with a lawyers' containment of the big issue. In *Calvin's Case*, a collusive action brought to the English courts in 1608, the judges resolved unanimously that the *post-nati*—that is, those born after James's accession to the English throne—were *ipso facto* naturalized in either kingdom. The doctrinal underpinning for the decision—allegiance was personal, to the king and not to the office of king, and therefore not tied to any place—was to prove crucial in the long term to British nationality law. In the shorter term, English antipathy to the King's Scottish compatriots and to his dreams of Britain was to colour his sense of the value of parliament.

The *Calvin's Case* ruling had a further significance. Sir Edward Coke, who reported the case, may, as the greatest lawyer of his age, have been unusual but he was surely not unique in his ability to grasp and even to try to impose some rules upon what he emphatically understood as a multiple kingdom, rather than the composite and even coherent state James had dreamed of. He certainly said he was not alone in that effort: all the judges were of one accord, he reported, and more spectators crammed into Westminster Hall for the hearing of this cause than had ever been known. Such turnout reflected the sensitivity of the Scottish matter; it may also have reflected curiosity about the implications for the remote and struggling English settlement in Virginia, founded the year before, and perhaps some broader interest in the meaning of England's expanding sphere of influence. High-profile plans for Ulster were now beginning to take shape, and Coke as reporter went out of his way to reflect on the status of Ireland. The Old English may have found some comfort in his dictum that, though conquered, Ireland was a Christian kingdom whose laws must be respected. Surviving privy councillors from the 1590s perhaps also found some satisfaction in Coke's insistence that since medieval kings had subordinated Ireland to English laws and writs, Sir Brian O'Rourke and Sir John Perrot had been properly tried in London for treasons committed in Ireland. Surely more important, though, was his conclusion that 'in the case of a conquest of [a] Christian kingdom, as well those that served in wars at the conquest as those that remained at home...are capable of lands in the kingdom or country conquered,...and have the like privileges and benefits there, as they may have in England'. Prospective planters and absentee investors could expect legal security in their investments.

As James's Whitehall years passed, his rule came to exemplify two very different meanings of empire. On the one hand, there was the story told in *Calvin's Case*, of a king who ruled over multiple kingdoms, that characteristic early-modern consequence of dynastic accident and military adventurism. Like some Habsburg lacking (as yet) his American lands, James kinged it over several polities, each with its own institutions and frames of governance, all joined in and through his own person—the very bigamy he objected to in his speech to his Westminster parliament in 1604. The three-cornered relationship of the King and his two British kingdoms conformed to this pattern throughout his reign, despite his brief attempt to transform it; aspects of the King's relationship with Ireland were no different, since as Coke pointed out, and as the Old

English frequently complained, Ireland had its laws, and they should be respected. But as Ireland became more stable it increasingly resembled that familiar modern pattern of empire, the extractive. The woodlands that had given refuge to Irish fighters soon fuelled New English iron-works and provided barrel staves for the salt beef—increasingly of Irish origin—bound for the multiplying settlers in the New World. The economic recovery that came with peace gave an unexpected incentive even to English property-owners to join their hungry younger brothers in looking for profit across the Irish Sea. Indeed, some of those in favoured positions made out like proverbial bandits.

In the first years after Tyrone's surrender at Mellifont the leading extractors were local. Tyrone had fared well in the treaty, and proceeded to rebuild his lordship and take revenge on those who had deserted him. But his position, and still more that of Tyrconnell, was vulnerable, for the usual difficulty in translating the imprecise dues and entitlements of Gaelic lordship into English legal tenures generated disputes between the earls and such sub-lords as Sir Donnell O'Cahan (Tyrone's) and Sir Cahir O'Doherty (Tyrconnell's). Royal officials exploited these skilfully. O'Cahan, for example, was urged on by a well-connected Scottish prot-estant cleric, George Montgomery, newly appointed to an Ulster bishopric and eager to regain Church lands given to the chiefs at the Dissolution. The arrival in November 1603 of an ambitious and creative lawyer, Sir John Davies, as solicitor-general for Ireland changed the game. Davies had a lawyer's distaste for overmighty lordship, and secured a 1605 proclamation that made formal doctrine out of Tudor policy: no Irishman's relation to the king could be mediated through a lord, for all were 'free, natural and immediate' subjects. The line from this position to that of Coke in *Calvin's Case* is clear.

Like John Hooker before him, Davies articulated a settler's double standard: in the Westminster parliaments of Elizabeth he had opposed abuses of the royal prerogative in England, but in Ireland he discovered a deep concern for royal rights. His favourite device was the commission to investigate defective titles to land. This inquisition caused anxieties enough in England but in the confused and sparsely documented ter-rain of Ireland it was explosive—as the King's chief minister, Cecil, now Earl of Salisbury, observed sagely in 1607, 'There is nothing more sure than that [land] titles are obscure in Ireland.' Davies' favourite argument was the dictum that land once forfeited to the crown remained the crown's: because of the posthumous attainder and forfeiture of Shane O'Neill, this doctrine threatened both Tyrone and O'Cahan. The local beneficiaries of such lawyerly enterprise included Davies himself, the new lord deputy Sir Arthur Chichester, and Scottish informants of the King like Bishop Montgomery and James Hamilton, who rose from a schoolmastership in Dublin to become Viscount Clandeboye.

Remnants of the old Gaelic leadership might nevertheless have survived in Ulster. Bards and even exiled theologians had rejoiced at James's accession; James had a Catholic mother who had died at Elizabeth's hands, and Irish mantles became briefly fashionable at his court. More important, he remained well disposed towards Tyrone. They had gone hunting together, and in the summer of 1607 the King gave a friendly ear to the Earl's claims against O'Cahan; Tyrone seized the moment to negotiate his son's marriage at court. And whatever Davies' dreams may have been, Lord Deputy Chichester seems not to have intended a total reconstruction of northern Ireland. But the Mellifont framework crumbled faster than most had expected, though certainly no faster than some desired. Tyrconnell and Cuconnacht Maguire, the chief of what remained of the Maguire lordship in neighbouring Fermanagh, despaired as lands and livelihoods were whittled away, and increasingly came to think exile preferable to humiliation at home.

Religion was no less entwined with land in Ulster than it had been in Munster. Despite James's own instincts, the beginning of his reign brought a burst of persecution in Ireland, for Chichester was a hard-liner in religion, if not in his attitude to land-claims. He responded fiercely to the so-called 'recusancy revolt' of 1603, when the Old English enthusiastically reclaimed the Munster towns for Catholic worship in hope that James Stewart would prove tolerant, and in protest too at the military burdens imposed on them in the war. Dissatisfied with the crown's retreat into occasional fines for recusancy—non-attendance at church—Chichester and Archbishop Loftus of Dublin seized on the opportunity presented by England's Gunpowder Plot of November 1605 to target the Catholic elite of Dublin. These were presented with individual 'mandates' requiring them to attend English Church services as law required, and requiring their removal from office for any non-compliance. Although the victims of the mandates were overwhelmingly Old English, Tyrconnell and Maguire read their own sorry futures in the recent arrival in Ulster of a few protestant clergymen like Montgomery. Tyrone was taken by surprise at news of their plans to leave, but he quickly concluded that he must join them. The 'flight of the Earls' with their families and a few followers into obscurity on the European continent is one of the most poignant moments in Irish history, and Tyrone's reasons for going will always be debated. He clearly felt that his neighbours' flight would hopelessly compromise him, since he had been told that the crown knew of his own desultory contacts with Spain. Since the bride the Earl had chosen for his son was the daughter of Argyll, that greatest of all the Gaelic magnates, perhaps Davies had been right to believe he would never reform.

The consequences were fully as dramatic as the 'flight of the Earls' itself, for new prospects suddenly appeared in Ulster. The land settlement Chichester had intended before 1607 had been a partial plantation, intermixing English and Scottish colonists with sitting Irish tenants. James himself had followed such a moderated approach when in the 1590s he had vainly attempted to 'civilize' the Hebridean island of Lewis with plantations of Scottish Lowlanders. But most of Ulster was now opened up by the lords' flight—and still more opened in the spring of 1608 when O'Doherty was provoked into rebellion by the aggressions of the new governor of Derry. If even O'Doherty, after fighting with the English against Tyrone and Tyrconnell and presiding over the grand jury that declared them traitors after their flight, could rebel, could any Gaelic chief be trusted? Chichester provided his answer when he sent O'Cahan off to die in the Tower, along with Sir Niall Garbh O'Donnell, the loyalist rival to Tyrconnell; meanwhile, the crown determined to maximize its opportunities, and to civilize at a stroke. It did so by reversing, and surely cynically, what had been its underlying policy towards Gaeldom throughout the sixteenth century. Its vision of a properly landed society in Ireland had assumed that the lords did not *own* all the territories from which they drew their exactions: collaterals and subordinates also had claims, and were accordingly allocated land in the composition schemes. But if chiefs who were adjudged traitors could be declared to have owned everything, then all their lands would be forfeit: the attainder of Shane O'Neill had pointed the way, though then the power had been lacking to follow through. So in 1608 six entire counties of Ulster escheated to the crown. This was not to be the piecemeal confiscation of individual rebels' estates that had preceded the doomed Munster plantation, and nor would Sir John Davies's legalisms be needed. With the lords gone and title vacant, expropriation could become simple government process across most of Ulster.

The territories of the O'Neills, the O'Donnells, the O'Cahans, the McSweenys, and the rest, were in the course of 1609–10 pared away. Close to four million statute acres were confiscated and redistributed to British undertakers, to Trinity College Dublin, to protestant clergy, and to around 300 'deserving natives'. The internal rivalries of the O'Neills ensured that a few loyalist branches with claims on government gratitude survived, but the O'Donnells almost disappeared from the newly redrawn map of an Ulster they had so long dominated; the O'Reillys, whose Cavan lordship Davies had already dismembered after Perrot's initial composition, were caught up again and more thoroughly expropriated under the new application of the treason law. It should be stressed that it was the elite that was displaced and not the Gaelic population as a whole. A broad population redistribution was certainly intended in pursuit of 'civility' and profit, but this proved beyond the undertakers' capacity or indeed their interests, since they needed tenants and labourers and too few were yet willing to leave Britain for a devastated Ulster. It remains an open question whether the peasants, the 'churls', fared worse in simply material terms under new market-oriented proprietors than they had under the takings of the swordsmen. But there can be no mistaking the transformation. Over the next generation, Ulster—which had been the Gaelic heartland of Tudor Ireland—assumed something of its modern character. That character has famously been presbyterian as well as commercial, but King James, with his own painful memories of turbulent Scots presbyterians, scarcely intended that coupling. He gave 20% of the redistributed lands to the Church (of England in Ireland), and worked to strengthen episcopal structures. Scottish clergy were welcome, provided they conformed within the king of England's Irish kingdom.

Only in the next generation did the new society in Ulster begin to assume its hybrid institutional form.

To the remodelling of Ulster James's government devoted considerable attention—indeed, perhaps too much for the tastes of a huntsman-king. When a few years later he was given a tour of his own state paper office, he remembered feelingly, 'There was more ado with Ireland than all the world beside.' And at least some of the work was of high quality. In just two months in 1609 the office of Sir Josias Bodley—the chief military surveyor in Ireland and brother of the founder of Oxford's university library—drew up a superb set of detailed maps of the escheated Ulster counties to facilitate the planning. The crown had learned from the 1598 Munster collapse to put security at a premium in the new colony. Not only was Ulster's land not confiscated piecemeal, leaving planters scattered and vulnerable; the crown insisted that on certain strategic estates all the native inhabitants be removed, and insisted too that the leading settlers provide themselves with a fortified dwelling and enclosure, a bawn. The English objective had of course long been anglicization as well as security. The shift in plantation design here points to changing English realities, for the social vision tilted now towards commerce rather than great estates. In place of the massive seigneuries of Munster, the largest Ulster undertaker's portion was to be 3,000 acres, and all the settlers were to be within a day's journey of one of the hundreds of new markets projected for this new landscape.

Sir John Davies elaborated on that vision in his self-righteous defence of conquest as improvement, *A Discoverie of the True Causes why Ireland was never entirely subdued* (1612). The crown, 'always...tender and careful of the good of this people', aimed only to make them 'a Civil, Rich, and Happy Nation'. Forcible pacification—which King James had provided after four centuries of lamentable English inconsistency and failure—was, he explained, essential so the law courts could function properly; and the enforcement of English law, with its protections for property and inheritance, was the prerequisite for agriculture and improvement. But nowhere in Ireland did enforcement of law have quite the same consensual meaning that it did in England. 'The English empire in Ireland'—the phrase of Sir William Parsons, Bodley's colleague in surveying work—found substance in the new gun platforms at Limerick and Waterford that Bodley installed in the aftermath of the 1603 recusancy revolt, platforms that faced onto the city as well as across the water. With its garrison remaining steady at a peacetime level of over 2,000, and provosts-marshal and martial law retained, albeit generally for use against the poor, Jacobean Ireland scarcely conformed to the English vision of liberty under law that Coke held dear. But, Davies insisted, disorder in Ulster had been so systemic that plantation offered the only means to reform, and particularly to make possible the foundation of towns and markets 'to increase their trade of Merchandise... to cherish Mechanical Arts and Sciences'. The result of such English labours was, he reported proudly if a little prematurely, 'the clock of the civil Government, is now well set, and all the wheels thereof do move in Order'. The suffering, the breaking, entailed upon the inhabitants was all warranted by the onset of civility.

The law brought to the new Ulster was to be English common law, but the order Davies saluted was in key respects British. An English army had defeated Tyrone, but the colony began and grew in a newly British context. The stabilization of Ulster was part of a much larger consolidation of the Stuart monarchy's authority in its outlying territories. In 1611 Norse law was eliminated in the formerly Danish Shetland and Orkney islands; in Scotland's Western Isles, the English navy blocked the ancient two-way flows of swordsmen that had disrupted previous English efforts in Ulster and might have threatened not just the new settlement but also James's continuing efforts to reform the Highlands. So in 1609 agents of the Scottish crown (assisted by English warships and artillery) were able to impose on the Highland chiefs the so-called Statutes of Iona. Now bound to an annual sojourn in Edinburgh while they accounted for their clans, the chiefs were drawn into expensive consumption habits that inexorably spread 'civility' piecemeal by forcing them to treat their lands as an economic rather than a clan resource, even as they renounced 'Irish' ways by sending their sons to the Lowlands to learn English. Fully aware of the geographic reach of a Gaeldom he despised—'These unhallowed people, with that unchristian language,' he was to protest—the King had been sufficiently worried by the 1607 crisis to consider moving his court north to York, and soon appointed one of the architects of the Statutes of Iona, Bishop Andrew Knox of the Isles, to the Ulster diocese of Raphoe.

Many others crossed the North Channel too, and not just from England. The undertakers' grants for settlement in the new plantation went according to James's design, almost equally to Lowland Scots and to English. Among the actual settlers, the proximity of the plantation to Scotland meant that the ratio by the 1620s was about three to two. The Scottish complement was much thicker in the two strategically crucial counties of Antrim and Down, outside the six-county plantation proper but closest to western Scotland: these had already become the preserve of the acquisitive Hamilton and Montgomery interests which busily imported settlers from the Scottish Lowlands. It was Ulster therefore that witnessed the birth of a new 'British' race, one that was to be distinguished from the ancient British, the Welsh, of the bards and the antiquarians.

The progeny did not match its royal father's aspirations. The lesser members of the landed elites, largely from nearby south-west Scotland and north-west England, who could be drawn into the venture lacked the resources to sponsor and equip enough farmer and craftsman settlers; anyway, they preferred to find tenants among the existing Irish occupants who were willing to pay exorbitant rents to stay on the land. Some settlers seemed unperturbed by the security implications: one English projector, Thomas Blenerhasset, in 1610 urged regular headhunts for Gaelic trouble-makers, 'and no doubt it will be a pleasant hunt...the charge, none, the pleasure, much, the profit, more'. But though the privy council had neither the resources nor the energy to restrain trouble-makers, whether Gaelic or British—it showed little sense of how to use systematically the maps Bodley had drawn up, for example—it did want more stable improvements. Accordingly, between 1610 and 1613 the crown forced an unenthusiastic corporation of London to fund the new county and city of Londonderry in northern Ulster. When Bodley surveyed the whole plantation in 1613–14 he found 'British' numbers 25% below target, and native Irish still everywhere preponderant. Nevertheless, by the end of the decade the British total had tripled, with over 6,000 male British settlers in the plantation; economic calamity in Scotland in the following two decades dramatically increased the pace of immigration, and by 1640 Ulster's British population may have reached 40,000, around 20% of the province's probable total. The Scottish influx was certainly protestant, but whether it otherwise met the hopes of Davies and the King—that plantation would spread English ways in church and state as well as in farming and commerce—proved a question.

Questions must also be asked of the centrality of that civilizing agenda. Somewhere between 1615 and 1630, a member of the Gaelic elite apparently in south-western Munster wrote *Pairlement Clann Tomais*, a tract that lamented the willingness of the local 'churls' to learn English and enter the money economy in their lust for tobacco. There seems therefore to have been a potential for patient and law-abiding reform. But the voluminous correspondence of James's chief minister, Salisbury, lord treasurer until his death in 1612, indicates the limits of the government's reformism and its patience. Facing the herculean task of reducing James's burgeoning deficit and debt, Salisbury noted that, despite the onset of peace, Ireland remained the largest recurring charge in a budget whose deficit was running close to £160,000. To cover its Irish costs, the crown shipped an average of £47,000 sterling p.a. in silver coinage from 1604 to 1619. Salisbury noted too the importance and the difficulty of cutting costs while leaving sufficient force 'to enable the State to speak in the imperative mood'.

Although the Lord Treasurer knew that 'oppression will force a rebellion', he could no more withstand those who sought to profiteer in Ireland than he could the speculators closer to home. The servitors—the officers and administrators in Elizabeth's wars—had watched enviously as others profited in Ulster; from 1610 they initiated a new wave of legal challenges to Irish landholders, first in Wexford in the south-east, then spreading into the midlands and through to the south-western edge of Ulster. Utilizing the proven and potent argument that land once formally claimed by the crown was always the crown's until it was properly granted away with written charters, they forced Kavanaghs, O'Farrells, and others to surrender a quarter or a third of their holdings. The process intensified towards the end of the decade when James's hungry new favourite, George Villiers, soon to be Duke of Buckingham, saw the potential for Irish revenues. The rhetoric of plantation and civility gave a veneer of legitimacy to the extortionist's version of composition that was fast becoming English policy, as favoured English and New English took their portions and did little to encourage improvement or settlement. Seeing the writing on the wall, between 1616 and 1618 the landowners of distant Connacht agreed to pay the considerable sum of £10,000 for ratification of their titles. In one of the period's more egregious pieces of brigandage, the money disappeared—probably split between the pockets of the New English official Sir Charles Coote and Buckingham—and no deeds were drawn.

Something might still be achieved and the Stuart kingdoms could yet be more than sum of their parts. Perhaps James's greatest successes came in Church matters, though these were in the next reign to pull the kingdoms apart. James famously stumbled at the Hampton Court conference he summoned in 1604 when he mistakenly believed he had found militant Scottish-style presbyterians masquerading as moderate English puritan clerics, but otherwise his churchmanship in the greater part of his British rule was remarkably sensitive. He came to the second and third of his thrones sure of the merits of Scottish preaching and the Scottish Kirk's Calvinist theology, but sure too that the presbyterian church structure that had emerged during Scotland's Reformation troubles dangerously challenged royal authority. He had spent years in his native kingdom trying to temper presbytery with some episcopal forms. Despite the contempt of some of Elizabeth's bishops for Scottish ways, the full-grown and self-confident episcopacy he encountered in England proved a taste he could enjoy. Perhaps the most lasting fruits of James's episcopalianism appeared in Wales, for it was in his reign that a high-Church axis formed linking Oxford and south Wales. Like Elizabeth before him, James appointed a succession of Welshmen to Welsh bishoprics, and the Anglican culture he fostered there was to shape the region's politics and identity for over a century.

But James had no wish to try to impose the full-grown English Church style on his countrymen: he was too much a political realist, and too proud of Scotland's dignity, for that. Furthermore, his great hope for a divided Christendom was to confront the universalist claims of the papacy with a union of mutually respectful national churches at peace under beneficent kings. Imposition of uniformity across his kingdoms would undercut that vision. Instead, James sought to harmonize his Churches' difference. He spiced up English preaching by judicious appointment of Scots to southern pulpits, and he dignified the Scottish episcopate in 1610 by a few properly ceremonial consecrations in which the participation of English bishops—but not archbishops, lest English claims to primacy were reinforced—allowed him to reclaim a continuity of episcopal succession for Scotland. In 1611 and in response to Scottish promptings he appointed the Calvinist George Abbot as archbishop of Canterbury. Only in his last years, when he determined to import more ceremonial into Scottish worship, did he run into trouble.

Much less successful, on every front, were James's aspirations for his Irish Church. The sizeable endowments for protestant churches and churchmen that he wrote into the new Ulster settlement went disproportionately to Scots clergy, whose relative poverty at home provided them some incentive to move the short distance across the North Channel. Sixty-four Scots ministers had moved to Ulster by 1625. The Church that took shape there was British not just in origin but in ministration too, since its clergy overwhelmingly tailored their services to the recent immigrants whose language and sense of isolation and embattlement they shared. What was true of Ulster was increasingly true of the protestant Church that was emerging beyond, as the new graduates of Trinity College Dublin slowly dispersed into the few parishes endowed enough to support a married, graduate clergy. Overwhelmingly of New English descent or British immigrants themselves, at Trinity they had been taught by a faculty whose own Calvinist intransigence had exiled them from the British universities. As they contemplated the alien and alienated population around them, their sense of election, of separateness, indeed of superiority, grew stronger. This was not a clergy convinced of its broad missionary role in Ireland: perhaps the Irish-born were Roman Catholic and suppressed because that was God's purpose? Such thinking was elaborated in the Irish articles of religion of 1615, whose Calvinist certainties and exclusiveness went some way beyond that found in the Church of England in this its most Calvinist phase. But at least James could find reassurance in the fact that his Irish Church now had the formality of defining articles.

The King's Irish Church was shaped as much by the competition it faced as by its creed. If peace allowed protestants to organize, it also provided opportunity to Ireland's Roman Catholics, and they used it to greater effect. The recusancy revolt in the Old English southern towns in 1603, and a resurgence of observance at St Patrick's Purgatory and other centres of Gaelic piety, had provided dramatic evidence of the vitality of lay Catholicism. Soon this found reinforcement in a stream of priests and friars arriving from the new Irish colleges in the Low Countries and Iberia, and as well in the trickle of Gaelic devotional literature that began to appear in the 1610s. If Catholic identity in the middle of the Elizabethan wars had been largely inchoate, an anti-government reflex, by the middle of James's reign Counter-Reformation practices and loyalties had formed. The readiness of some seminary priests to refer to their labours in Ireland as 'this new plantation' underscores both their consciousness of their departure from old and unreformed ways and their conscious challenge to the crown's efforts.

Churchmen and government ministers alike were far from sure how to confront the problem of Ireland's Catholic resurgence. The Elizabethan debate between those like Sidney or Spenser who wanted first to secure Ireland and those like Archbishop Loftus of Dublin who insisted on reinforcing protestants' commitment had never been resolved, though war had inexorably privileged security. The Jacobean peace opened the door to inconsistency, and the ineffectiveness that came with it. Insofar as the government had a general prescription, it seems to have been the assumption that slow attrition—the work of penalties and disabilities—reinforced by the civility and anglicization born of prosperity would eventually prevail; for one thing, greater resources would mean more could be committed to evangelization. But however tolerant James's instincts—and Old English declarations of loyalty certainly appealed to these—the recusancy revolt and then England's Gunpowder Plot of 1605 rattled his nerves. The fiercely anti-Catholic Chichester quickly gained the King's approval for further coercion in the campaign to weed out Catholic office-holders through the mandates and widespread fines for recusancy. For a moment, the flight of the earls and the beginning of the Ulster plantation bred some optimism, but the assassination of Henri IV of France in 1610 brought a new sense of crisis. With English stereotypes of the popish enemy confirmed, James and his advisers in London determined to expel the clergy who were so busily strengthening the Catholic backbone in Ireland, and to bar Irish youths from travelling to the seminaries. To their dismay, they found that the failure of Sir John Perrot's parliament had left the Irish statutory framework inadequate in this key respect. A parliament to pass penal laws was imperative.

Such a descent into partisanship outraged the surviving Old English establishment. To pass protestant penal legislation in a Catholic kingdom, the government needed to transfer dominance to the New English minority. Accordingly, a handful of new protestant peers joined the protestant bishops to secure the Irish House of Lords; meanwhile, forty new parliamentary boroughs, largely in Ulster and many of them little better than villages, gave promise of New English control over the lower House. Perhaps Chichester hoped that the public execution in 1612 of two senior Catholic clergy would cow any disquiet, yet when Mountjoy's former secretary, Fynes Moryson, revisited Ireland the following year he noted 'our degenerate [Old] English Irish' firm in their contempt for the 'poor and beggarly' Englishmen, the new servitors, who came to compete in Ireland for whatever was to be had. Chichester therefore found his control challenged when parliament opened in 1613. The vast bulk of Sir John Davies's corpulent body was needed to hold the Speaker's chair against an Old English caucus which then sent a delegation to Whitehall to protest. Ben Jonson's *Irish Masque* (1613) held the Old English visitors up to courtly ridicule, and the King was perplexed as he faced men protesting their loyalty but emboldened in their religion by the two recent martyrs, and fearful that the new plantations would be extended to their lands. Although a Calvinist himself, he still dreamed of reigning over a willing people. So he followed the usual royal practice and tried to fudge: on the one hand he imprisoned several of the Old English spokesmen and issued a stern proclamation against their presumptuousness, and on the other quietly abandoned the attempt at penal legislation. But the Old English were clearly growing more estranged: Butlers were prominent in the protests as they had been in 1569, and the heir to the Ormond earldom was himself a devout Catholic. Renewed Gaelic restiveness—in 1615 the McDonalds retaliated once more against Argyll's pressure in western Scotland—eventually reminded the Old English in the Irish parliament of their English roots and secured the grant of supply the King badly needed. But he showed his distrust of Old English Catholics as he moved quickly to break up the Ormond holdings.

By the middle of James's British reign, the prospects for mutual respect among the parts of the Stuart multiple kingdom looked faint. Anglo-Scottish frustrations simmered, and the King grew impatient. In 1613, Patrick Gordon composed an 8,000-line epic on the Scots' anti-English hero Robert Bruce, while English resentment of Scots courtiers who consumed so much royal largesse resounded in James's disastrous 'addled parliament' of 1614 as it had in the 1610 session. Sir Edward Coke, now lord chief justice, challenged the King's 'British' and imperial claims more fundamentally as he laboured over the *Reports* and *Institutes* that so shaped the common law, and systematized his treasured thesis that England's law defined the community of the land. Other legal antiquarians—Spelman and the greatest of them, John Selden—similarly were working to counter the King's arguments by insisting on the immemorially Gothic origins of English law. Sir John Davies, then Ireland's leading common lawyer, certainly agreed with the thesis, though for him English law had its own imperial cast, for the common law being imposed in Ireland was a partisan English tool. Under it, the political culture of Gaeldom lay broken while the Old English were discovering the extent of their marginalization. True, a more commercialized economy was developing, but extraction was its defining note as new landowners cut timber and occasionally, in the midlands and south, began to work iron. Meanwhile, English courtiers and hangers-on exploited Irish land-titles. There was some evidence of English interest that was not merely predatory, not least in the publishing industry that was Barnabe Rich, ageing servitor and author of *A Short Survey of Ireland* (1609), *A New Description of Ireland* (1610), *The Irish Hubbub* (1617), and much else besides. Rich's hyperbolic accounts of the fragile progress of cultural transformation presumably appealed to English readers who had served in the wars, or who had trading or family ties to Ireland. There was little such common ground with Scotland. It took the royal visit of 1617—a visit that drew along such inveterate self-publicists as the elevated poet Ben Jonson and the humble versifier and waterman John Taylor—to elicit English curiosity. And yet there were signs of connectedness. The Scottish tales that the 1617 travellers brought back to England told of an uncouth gastronomy but reassuringly courtly ways. For the King, the visit occasioned nostalgia and some lamenting for the closer union that might have been. For his Scottish subjects, it brought a brief return to the old sociabilities of a personal monarchy, and a welcome reaffirmation of nationhood. It was also a time for work. Scots found James still hoped to 'conform' his kingdoms a little more closely. Even before 1603 he had worked to replace Scottish hereditary feudal jurisdictions with justices of the peace on something like the English model; those efforts continued, and continued to inspire noble foot-dragging even as they elicited approval in other quarters. The traffic of borrowing may not have been all one-way. There is something suggestive in the proximity of the act of prescription James issued in Scotland in 1617, giving immunity from crown questioning of title to those who had held land for forty years, to the 1624 English statute conferring security after sixty years' prescription. Might the powerful enunciation in Ulster of the doctrine that royal claims could not lapse have inspired some nervousness in both the other Stuart kingdoms?

In Church matters, to Scots' dismay, English practices were held out as a model. The King had shown considerable tact as well as determination in his long-standing efforts, which came to a head in his reforms of 1606–10, to reintroduce a measure of episcopal hierarchy to Scotland's Kirk, and protests had come from only a handful of die-hard presbyterians. But quite another matter were the effects of James's discovery on his 1617 visit of how much he preferred the dignity of his English Church to bare-bones Scottish ways. Sustained royal pressure to heighten the ritual element in worship secured the passage of five articles—the most provocative required kneeling, English-style, in the communion service—through a general assembly of the Kirk at Perth in 1618; further pressure gained their ratification in an unusually stormy Scottish parliament in 1621. The Scots were now finding new meaning in this British kingship. Not only did it deprive them of James and turn his Scottish courtiers into anglicized absentees. His old countrymen found something worryingly new in a king eager to impose an alien ecclesiastical vision from distant London.

In Ireland, meanwhile, there were unmistakable signs of what we now call state formation—and with equally unmistakable partisan applications. Even with the peacetime army now reduced to 1,500 men, military costs in James's later years averaged about £40,000 sterling p.a., while the increased expenditures on a civil administration that now covered the whole country ran close to £13,000 p.a. The English government under Salisbury and his successors worked steadily, if not altogether single-mindedly, to offset those costs by increasing Irish revenues. The Dublin parliament of 1613–15 showed what Elizabeth had learned so often at Westminster, that direct taxation carried political risks; like most early-modern states, the English-Irish regime therefore looked elsewhere. It did so fairly successfully, and by the 1630s revenue from the customs made the largest single contribution to the Irish state, though in 1600 that input had been close to nil. The recusancy revolt of 1603 had given the crown the incentive to move against the Old English port towns' control over customs collections, and as a result the government's receipts rose more than seven-fold (from around £200 sterling) between 1606 and 1612. And in 1613, the now-streamlined Irish customs were farmed, to an (English) merchant syndicate, for a rent of £6,000 p.a. Another measure of the crown's growing fiscal reach is provided by wardship fines, paid by heirs to feudal tenancies who inherited as minors. Irish wardship revenues, averaging around £300 p.a. early in James's reign, had risen more than ten-fold by 1617, and doubled again in the following decade. The Irish state was becoming more efficient fiscally, usually at the expense of the Old English elite, whether as landowners paying higher feudal dues or as merchants paying and no longer collecting higher customs dues. At the same time, it was being reshaped along confessional lines, as feudal wards seeking to enter their inheritance and lawyers practising in the Dublin courts had to swear the oath of supremacy, to the king as head of the protestant Church, as well as the oath of allegiance. This was anglicization with a vengeance.

Although he had backed away from the sweeping vision of unity he announced at the beginning of his reign, by the time of his return from Scotland James could surely pride himself on the progress made in 'conforming' his kingdoms. In their public face at least, both Scotland and Ireland were recognizably civil kingdoms. In the aftermath of the McDonald troubles of 1615, Scottish statutes in 1616 codified Lowlands prejudice as they instructed the Isles clans to send their children away to learn 'the vulgar English tongue'; Gaelic, which was to be 'abolished', was declared a main cause of 'the continuance of barbarity and incivility'. But no provision was made for erecting schools, and of course government was nowhere in Scotland (or in England for that matter) as easy, as fully 'by the Pen', as the King had in 1607 boldly claimed— 'I write and it is done.' Government everywhere was in the hands of the landed elites but particularly in Scotland, where much of the administration of justice lay with the nobles; in the western Highlands, an extreme case, James made his will felt only through cooperation with the Earl of Argyll. Much was still to be done if civility was to be more than mere prescription, and if there was to be more to a common monarchy than the crown itself.

But if bringing congruence to government in the three kingdoms proved more tiresome than their king had anticipated, he could still congratulate himself on his pastoral care. The 1615 articles laid down the platform for a reformed Irish Church, and the Five Articles of Perth aligned the Scottish a little more closely to the ways of its English neighbour. In 1618 James seized on the opportunity presented by some Dutch ecclesiastical disputes to promote an agreed public face for international Calvinism. The British—in fact, almost entirely English—delegation he dispatched to a synod at Dort in the Netherlands joined the majority in asserting Calvinist orthodoxy; no less dear to James's own heart was the way the rigour of the Dort resolutions was softened by an emphasis on careful pulpit-work. Most of the serious protestants of his three kingdoms could find satisfaction within such a framework. They might yet grow together.

CHAPTER 7
CONFORMING MULTIPLE KINGDOMS
1618–1637

James's post-1607 retreat from his hopes of a fuller British union left him to rule a not unusual early-modern phenomenon: a multiple kingdom whose common monarch permanently resided in a major metropolis that was geographically decentred. The minimal nature of the early-modern state and the prevalence of habits of local self-government meant that the maintenance of an unwieldy structure ought not to have been difficult, though communication networks were thin and slow. Rulers normally had little enough they wanted to do that could not be done by the judicious exercise of patronage, and while competition and resentments were inevitable—as the history of James's bedchamber showed—these were manageable.

Wars presented a problem, however, since they not only had to be fought but paid for. The ability of the Elizabethan regime to weather the long, expensive, and inglorious wars in Ireland suggests that the crown could draw on considerable reserves of obedience and convictions of common interest, at least within a single kingdom. But in the Stuarts' larger world? One solution, widely attempted in an early-modern Europe eager for ideological cohesion, was the elevation of the royal person and the royal will. It is no accident that key early writings of Thomas Hobbes date to these years, nor that James's son Charles should have so much made an issue of his will as king. An alternative means to a conviction of common interest was the cultivation of ideological solidarity, as the intermittent collaboration of English parliamentarians and Scottish Covenanters between 1640 and 1646 was to demonstrate. The Stuarts' misfortune was that their multiple kingdom straddled a major ideological fault-line that sharply divided the protestant ground England and Scotland shared from a largely Catholic Ireland. The establishment of even partial religious consensus would take time. But perhaps it was under way. Although in Ireland the crown's struggle with the Roman Catholic Church was about to be lost, elsewhere in the English-speaking world the 1611 publication of the Bible translation King James had authorized, and that is still associated with his name, was to do its mellifluous work, even overlaying Scots vernacular usages in James's native kingdom. And in the Welsh corner of the world, the appearance in 1620 of another Welsh translation of the Bible and of the English Prayer Book, to supplement that of 1588, furthered the remarkable Welsh achievement of cultural nationhood within a state and economy firmly centred on London.

A common civility might also arise from commerce and cultivation. Here, the auguries seemed good, and not just in England. Fair harvests in the late 1610s and a quickening of trade from the Mediterranean as well as other seas invited townsmen and farmers, incomers and natives to respond to the market economy to the best of their abilities; thus, tobacco could be had in Scotland's Western Isles in the 1610s. Indeed, even in the harsher conditions of the 1620s and 1630s, all the Stuart kingdoms witnessed the patchy spread of new goods and tastes: most obviously tobacco and its paraphernalia, but also new textiles, glassware, wines, and spices. Sir John Davies had argued that prosperity would prove transformative: would a commercial—and thus perhaps metropolitan and thus surely anglicized—culture spread through all the Stuart lands? Already at the end of James's reign, over 20% of Scottish customs revenues came from English imports.

But conflicts in Europe ensured that the Stuart dominions were not to enjoy peaceful progress towards civility. Ironically, James's efforts helped bring about the crisis he tried to avoid. He had inherited with his disparate kingdoms two discordant alignments: one, Scotland's 'auld alliance' with France, and Scotland's regional ties to the now-protestant states of northern Europe; the other, England's old though interrupted friendship with Spain. As his motto 'rex pacificus' declared, a British king—and particularly one with the resources of all his kingdoms to draw on—might play a decisive role as bridge-builder in a divided

Europe. James's pursuit of that vision gained urgency in 1618 as his heir apparent, Prince Charles, reached marriageable age. James then looked to Spain for a Catholic bride for Charles, to balance Charles's sister Elizabeth's marriage in 1613 to the German Calvinist prince, Frederick of the Rhineland Palatinate. His hopes of bridging Europe's religious chasms grew more pressing, indeed desperate, when in 1619 Frederick accepted the invitation of the Bohemian nobles to become their protestant king, and so plunged the continent into what became the Thirty Years War. The outbreak of what looked like a war for religion inflamed passions everywhere, and dark apocalyptic fears grew in Britain when the war went badly for the protestant camp. As Frederick lost first Bohemia and then his Palatine inheritance to Catholic forces that rapidly dominated central as well as much of western Europe, volunteers and mercenaries flocked into the belligerents' ranks, especially from Scotland, where the Stuart princess, 'the Winter Queen' Elizabeth of Bohemia, had a large following: over 25,000 joined the various protestant armies between 1620 and 1625. But recruits flocked too from Ireland, into the Imperial forces and also into the Spanish armies that confronted the protestant Dutch from 1621. The alignments born of the German wars were to shape the history of the Stuart kingdoms for decades, disrupting and almost overthrowing the slow work of commerce. And since taxation and war are inseparable, the identifications shaped by conflict merged in all the Stuart kingdoms, and sometimes to dramatic effect, with dawning apprehensions about the nature of rule.

The delicacy of the task of pursuing diplomatic alliances predicated on religious difference in a time of internal religious division quickly became clear. English policy-makers had reacted abruptly to the assassination of Henri IV of France in 1610 by tightening enforcement of anti-Catholic measures, and now James's marital diplomacy prompted a lurch in the other direction. Unable to secure a Spanish Catholic bride for Charles while persecuting Catholics, James eased enforcement of the penal laws. This new swing of the policy pendulum had a dramatic and lasting effect in Ireland, where Roman Catholics constituted perhaps three-quarters of the population. Priests had remained active in the years of persecution, but attempts to organize formally had been set back—the Dominican order, for example, had closed all its Irish houses by 1608, and by 1618 there were no Roman Catholic bishops left in the country. Persecution could be remarkably effective if a competitor church had yet to organize and put down roots. But the relaxation of 1618 proved a crucial turning-point in Ireland's history, allowing the re-establishment of an illegal but increasingly effective Catholic episcopate; soon the outlines of a Counter-Reformation Church that was structured in parishes, disciplined by bishops, and focused on the sacraments became clearer. By 1623 there were at least 1,100 Catholic priests and friars in Ireland, and the possibility was lost that the populace would drift into protestant Churches because they had nowhere else to go. Through the 1610s, close to a quarter of the students at Trinity College Dublin had been of Gaelic or Old English stock, but by 1640 the proportion was closer to 5%, as the established Church of Ireland became ever more clearly the Church of the New English.

In his British kingdoms, James's pursuit of religious peace caused more immediate political disquiet. Europe's growing instability and a royal debt in England of close to £1 million pointed to the need for taxes, particularly since there was little enthusiasm for the King's attempt in 1620 to raise money for the Palatinate by the non-parliamentary means of a benevolence. But when the following year he finally summoned a parliament to Westminster he soon regretted it: the relaxation of fines for recusancy—for not attending the established Church—had intensified the perplexity caused by the quest for a Spanish bride when the King's daughter languished stateless. An unhappy dissolution ensued. The Scottish parliament that year was almost as fractious, since James's determination to gain approval for the ceremonies enjoined in the Five Articles of Perth, and to secure a tax grant of the equivalent of £100,000 sterling over four years without committing to the religious war many of his subjects wanted, provoked unusual parliamentary opposition. The sum he gained was unprecedented in Scottish terms, but since Scotland contributed only about 3% of James's regular revenues, his English subjects might—had they known the figures—have renewed their old complaints about his beggarly countrymen. But in this respect at least the changing face of Europe refocused anxieties away from the animosities against the Scots that had disturbed James's earlier English parliaments.

At the English court, clarity of purpose was hard to find since the first decade of the European conflict was also the decade of George Villiers, Duke of Buckingham, and the King's over-reaching intimate. Buckingham's political impact is apparent in the turbulent parliamentary record of the 1620s, but his dominance had governmental consequences too. The rise of a hungry favourite with many kinsfolk at a time of massive royal indebtedness intensified normal pre-bureaucratic habits of private enterprise. Pay-offs for new appointments and skimming from revenue-streams multiplied, and helped stir the parliamentary protests of 1625–28. Scotland, a separate (and poor) kingdom escaped more or less unscathed from Buckingham's attentions, and even benefited indirectly since the domestic taint diverted English complaints away from Scots recipients of royal bounty. But Ireland was now to learn some further disadvantages of its status as an increasingly civil kingdom within the Stuart fold as spreading war intensified the crown's sense of need.

Indeed, Ireland in James's reign became open country for a civil sort of predator as war increased the stress on the crown's finances. Buckingham, the most illustrious and successful of these predators, gained massively from a series of Irish pay-offs and rake-offs. The Ulster plantation had shown courtiers the scale of potential pickings, and it had left many servitors unrewarded and jealous. In the second half of James's reign these groups made common cause, the servitors pointing the courtiers to properties and arguments, the courtiers urging the claims of the servitors in return for a percentage. The new plantations in Wexford and the midlands saw some particularly sharp practice; nevertheless, amid growing fears of religious war at the end of the 1610s, alarmist English eyes found complacency—the undertakers' focus on 'civility', on houses and cultivation rather than settling protestants—perhaps more troubling than corruption.

Issues of Irish land therefore played out in a complex environment—Irish, English, Scottish, as well as European. Complaints reached the English parliament of 1621 from New English planters in Ulster who hoped to pick up delinquents' properties through complaints that rivals—Scots, London companies—were defaulting on their plantation agreements; the following year, the English privy council, not averse to a reformist mantle, established a commission of inquiry into all the plantations. This faulted planters' performance of their obligations generally. The new lord treasurer, Middlesex, who saw peace and retrenchment as the only way to preserve the crown's finances, seized on the evidence of abuse to try to plug the Irish drain on the budget, instituting an oversight committee in London and moving to cut pensions and the size of the army. This was a direct challenge to a New English establishment that had long ago learned to cultivate contacts at court, and in the 1624 parliament at Westminster Middlesex fell victim to Buckingham, who was eager now for war with Spain and eager too to protect his already-extensive and remunerative Irish interests. Unapologetically, the Duke then deployed the familiar argument of defective legal title to carve the 11,000-acre 'Villiers' manor from the lands of the loyalist McGillapatricks in Upper Ossory. When the crown, once more with Buckingham's involvement, managed between 1618 and 1629 to divert much of the Ormond inheritance, it became clear that the Old English were as vulnerable as the Gael. The probably deliberate failure of earlier English officials to process formal confirmation of the Elizabethan composition of Connacht then allowed the lord deputy—Buckingham's client Viscount Falkland—and his New English allies to move towards plantation of that province. Nor were the New English themselves safe, for the 1622 commission had found flaws in all the plantations. By the end of the decade Falkland was even contemplating a legal assault on Ulster, and the rhetoric of improvement and civility that had buttressed the plantation would have amply justified such a raid.

The royal pursuit of money was not felt only in a local or regional context. The king of each of the early-Stuart kingdoms needed money, and the exportability of some fiscal expedients provides a measure of the crown's ability to think systematically across its territories. Much early-modern ink flowed into assertions of the crown's role as 'the fountain of honour' against those who thought titles originated in immemorial usages or ancient deeds of valour: kings alone made nobles. If the crown had something that people wanted, it surely could be marketed. So, with varying regard for what might seem policy considerations or for nuances of hierarchy, between 1618 and 1629 James and then Charles put titles of honour out to sale; and in the four years from 1618, Buckingham raked off nearly £25,000 from the proceeds. The sales reflect both market conditions—that is, the money available—and the strength of any local objections to the devaluation of honour. Sales in England were far livelier than in Scotland, but they were liveliest of all in Ireland, for there few conventions existed to restrain the crown. By 1629, the early Stuarts had created some sixty-eight new Irish peerages, even selling titles to Catholic 'mere' Irishmen with money who otherwise might have expected to be excluded from public life: thus, Tyrone's son-in-law Arthur Magennis became Viscount Iveagh, while Randall McDonnell, the chief of the southern branch of clan McDonald, became Earl of Antrim. But most titles went to Englishmen, since England was the richest kingdom and demand was involved as well as supply. Thirty of the Irish sales went to men with little or no connection with Ireland; Englishmen bought a handful of Scottish titles too, though—suggesting the priority the crown assigned to England—no Scot or Irishman was sold an English title. When, in the financial and political crisis of 1627, Charles sold a Scottish viscountcy to Sir Thomas Fairfax, grandfather of the future parliamentarian general, another Sir Thomas Fairfax, also from Yorkshire and not to be outdone, bought an Irish viscountcy—and all to the great favourite's benefit. Such sales across different kingdoms' ladders of honour bore fruit in convoluted precedence disputes, including one that disrupted the 1625 naval expedition to Cadiz, and in protests from holders of older titles at the promotion of 'foreign' upstarts: one such dispute was still disrupting Cheshire politics as civil war loomed. The web of marital ties the Earl of Cork spun on both sides of the Irish Sea for his many offspring may seem a more elegant way to pursue supranational goals. Nevertheless, the sales point to the crown's growing confidence in its ability to impose new forms of unity on its territories.

The pickings and pre-eminence of the Duke of Buckingham through most of the 1620s provided of course their own form of geopolitical unity; nevertheless, 1625 marked an important watershed. The accession of Charles I brought the changed tempo of a new king, and a king who went immediately to war: with Spain first of all and then in 1627 with France too as Charles's predicament grew more complicated. Young kings are often opinionated and wilful, and wars require taxes, with consequences that are all too often disruptive. The effects of this new beginning are clear in all three kingdoms.

The turbulence of England's parliamentary history of the middle and later 1620s, culminating in the Petition of Right in 1628 and the Three Resolutions of 1629, is famous, even celebrated. A more revealing measure of the work of a young king—worse, a young and distanced king—is the Act of Revocation that Charles issued in Scotland at his accession. The 'Act' was a royal decree rather than a parliamentary statute, and a quintessential product of non-consultative processes. In what Charles declared were the interests of both crown and Church, he aimed by his Revocation to restructure relations with a significant group of Scottish landowners—perhaps 40% of the whole small group in that feudal society—who had obtained from successive kings grants of lands and rights confiscated from the Church. Much of the local justice on the lands in question, as elsewhere in Scotland, was hereditary, and in nobles' hands. Following practices of composition developed elsewhere in his kingdoms, Charles sought to compound with nobles for their claims where he could: revoking the grants altogether was as good a way of spurring landowners to compound as were the activities of those who investigated defective titles in Connacht. Charles also sought to extract better provision for local clergy—who were often woefully paid—by redirecting tithes from the lands in question, while retaining a percentage for the crown.

Revocation was a familiar Scottish device by which new kings responded to the frequent plundering of the crown's estates during royal minorities, and Charles's overall goal of endowing the Church and reducing the powers of landowners was quite consistent with James's practices. Nevertheless, the scale of the measure—its assault on grants extending back variously to 1560 or even 1455—the lack of consultation or even explanation, the requirement that nobles submit to royal authority before it was clear what in practice they were submitting to, and the fiscal implications not only in payments to the Church but in payments to the crown, made it easy to see it as a piece of high-handed fiscal adventurism. More obviously, it was the work of an absentee whose obliviousness to Scottish concerns ensured its practical failure, but not before it had generated a storm of unease among the nobility. The workload and disillusionment of those drafted onto the local subcommissions to evaluate tithes were, furthermore, to thwart Charles's efforts in the 1630s to enhance the work of the English-style, and non-feudal, justices of the peace that his father had begun to establish.

If the royal will was firmly engaged in Scotland's turmoils with the Revocation, it was the work of war that disturbed Ireland in Charles's first years. The Old English elite had not yet accepted King James's judgement that they were but 'half-subjects'; in Charles's wartime needs—by 1627, the army in Ireland had swelled to 5,500 men, largely unpaid and forcibly billeted on householders—they saw an opportunity to return to full participation in the political community. For them, the central Irish dynamic was still the advance of civility against the untutored Gael, not the struggle for religion. It was entirely possible, they insisted, for individual Catholics to be loyal to the king. Accordingly, they offered to replace the floundering and unpaid army with a trained and funded militia, on the English county model, that would keep the 'malcontent mere Irish' down and the Spanish out. The price-tag would be their own reinstatement: they would become officers in the new militia, and the oath of supremacy—which conscientious Catholics could not swear—would be withdrawn. A near-bankrupt crown found the offer appealing, but the New English were appalled by the challenge to their privileged position, a challenge they claimed threatened their very existence. With Lord Deputy Falkland encouraging the opposition—doubtless spurred on by his wife's very public conversion to Catholicism in 1626—the crown changed the terms.

Across two years of negotiations, the 'Graces' of 1628 took shape. The crown conceded on the oath of supremacy, thus allowing Catholic lawyers to practise and Catholic heirs to inherit feudal tenancies; as well, it agreed to relax the recusancy laws. Such was Charles's desperation that in return for an Old English offer of £120,000 over three years he agreed to two further demands that transcended Old English sectional interests. These sought to block the onslaught on defective titles and the regime of plantation by confirming the composition of Connacht and applying to Ireland the English statute of 1624 which secured against the king titles to land that had been held for over sixty years. The prominence of these demands suggests how broadly in Ireland the crown was now seen as predatory.

The crown was soon seen as untrustworthy as well, for the Graces had originated in the pressures of war on a divided monarchy, and as war receded Charles found the bargain less compelling. As he hedged his diplomatic bets in Europe between a pro- and anti-Habsburg alliance, the stormy English parliament of 1628–29 and the political divisions in his own court gave him reason not to appear too soft on Catholicism. Ireland thus seemed a low-risk arena for a reassertion of protestant zeal. As Archbishop Ussher of Armagh and his New English allies fulminated against those who put religion to sale, a procedural error in Falkland's summons for a parliament in Dublin in November 1628 to confirm the Graces gave the King the opportunity to distance himself from the two key concessions, though he had taken the payment offered for them. Falkland himself, recalled in semi-disgrace after the assassination of his patron Buckingham, was replaced by two New English lords justices, Lord Chancellor Loftus and Richard Boyle, Earl of Cork. With the invasion threat gone, these two personal enemies could find common ground in a hard line against Catholics. Recusancy fines were revived, the major pilgrimage centre of St Patrick's Purgatory was destroyed in 1632, and Cork urged the plantation of Connacht, 'the only neglected part of this kingdom in which no English...are yet planted'. The Old English had gained little for their money.

The political strains on all the Stuart kingdoms arising from involvement in Europe's spreading war are central to any account of the upheavals of the seventeenth century. That involvement offers a number of perspectives on the relations of the Stuarts to their various subject groups, and the relations of their kingdoms to each other. One important caveat is that involvement was a matter of opportunity as well as cost. In the 1620s and 1630s, the worsening climate made itself felt as viciously as it had in the 1590s. Scattered starvation in England's upland north-west and a rise in vagrancy paled in comparison with the experiences of those in rainier and more marginal regions of Scotland and Ireland; there, starvation deaths soared in the late 1620s and again in the mid 1630s. Local authorities in England readily consigned surplus males to recruiting sergeants raising forces for desperate and doomed ventures to Germany in 1624, to Cadiz in 1625, to the Ile de Rhé in 1627; local notables in Scotland and Ireland did much the same, although often in the guise of private contractors to whom the crown sometimes gave licence. The need for such employment ran strong, since the Elizabethan conquest of Ireland had put an end not just to open warfare but to the contracting of clan mercenaries across the North Channel. The pressures to demobilize clans' human resources were reinforced by the Scottish statutes of Iona of 1609 and their reiteration after the abortive McDonald rising on Kintyre in 1615, for clan chiefs compelled to sojourn in Edinburgh needed cash—needed, in other words, to commercialize their lands. Fighting-men made redundant accordingly needed employment.

The role of Scottish and Irish regiments in the later British Empire is legendary. The tens of thousands of Scots—some 10% of Scotland's adult males followed the Palatine cause in Danish and Swedish armies between 1625 and 1632—and the similar numbers of Irish who found employment abroad in the early seventeenth century suggest the pressures of demand and supply in the development of that history. Some contingents might seem mercenary or merely conscripted, but others served under more partisan leaders like the exiled Owen Roe O'Neill with the Spanish forces in Flanders; on the English and protestant side, the renowned Vere brothers led troops in the Netherlands and Germany. If central and local authorities were pleased to see men removed, the intersection of ideology and arms signalled domestic dangers. Charles was anxious to avoid these, as well as the costs of deeper involvement. However elevated his sense of the respect due from the other belligerents to himself, to his hard-pressed sister, and to his kingdoms, he tried to keep on the periphery of the continental war even as he encouraged proxies to regain the Palatinate for his sister's family. The potential of what cannot quite at this juncture be called the British state is apparent in the fact that Scottish and English, and indeed a few Irish, recruits constituted the largest quasi-national element in the forces fighting for the Palatine cause. The complex reality appears in the fact that the 6,000-strong Anglo-Scottish contingent that the King's cousin, James Marquess of Hamilton, led in 1631–32 into Swedish service for that cause went under a private contract.

There were without doubt those who thought about the nature of power and rule in a multiple kingdom. When wartime pressures were at their height, Sir John Coke, one of the English secretaries of state, urged Charles in 1627 to draw proportionately on the resources of all his kingdoms for common defence, but the King's retreat from active belligerency allowed a retreat too to less demanding options. The most notorious English levy of the 1630s is revealing here. The warrants for ship money that Charles first issued in 1625 and then systematized from 1634 laid the material base for the long-term expansion of a fleet. The rhetoric justifying the levies and the resulting naval build-up talked grandly of the shared interest of the King's subjects in the security of the 'British seas' from pirates and other dangers. The lawyer John Selden's *Mare Clausum* (1635, though written in 1619) pitched the claim to control over shipping and fishing in British waters at the highest intellectual level; royal entertainments like the masque *Britannia Triumphans* (1638), which presented the King as true British hero in his maritime enterprise, made it rather more accessible to Charles himself. But ship money fell only on the English counties, and the navy it funded was an English navy, if occasionally put to use in Scottish or Irish waters. A still more striking contraction into a single national interest and indeed private interest appears in the King's proposal in 1630 for a British fishing company that would monopolize fishing in British waters. The project was touted as an anti-Dutch measure, and of common concern. Nevertheless, the roll-call of courtiers heading the under-capitalized company suggested an English take-over bid for herring that swam thickest off the Scottish coasts. Charles's Scottish privy council made clear what it thought of his attempt to make (objectionable) practical politics out of the royal transnational dignity when it protested at use of the British label, 'there be[ing] no union as yet with England'.

But there was one area where Charles was acutely conscious that he was more than a king of parts, and that was the Church. At the very beginning of his reign, the struggles in England between a Calvinist establishment and anti-Calvinist hopefuls alerted him to the distance between the doctrinal ambiguities of the defining Thirty-Nine Articles of the English Church and the more rigorous Calvinism of the 1615 Articles in Ireland. When the future parliamentarian leader John Pym observed yearningly in 1628, 'These islands are sisters,' he invited the King—doubtless encouraged by his ecclesiastical guide, William Laud, future archbishop of Canterbury—to draw his own conclusions. Argumentative loopholes must be closed, and unity among the kingdoms secured in a world where religious passions ran high. And Charles certainly believed in unity as a value; he had a profound sense as well of his duty to God to establish the Church order in which he believed. It was an order replete with ritual, and fundamentally episcopal in its structures. It departed from prevailing patterns in all his kingdoms—patterns in which many of his subjects believed at least as deeply as he scorned them. Charles was undaunted, and for reasons that we may suspect owed as much to temperament as to ideology, above all since his ideology was in an important sense also his dominant character trait. He had an unquenchable conviction of his own authority or, to put it more broadly, of a royal authority that transcended local traditions, rights ('privileges', and therefore revocable, he thought them), and institutions; and he had a divinely enjoined obligation to put that authority to work.

That divine mandate did not commit Charles either to 'British'—that is, programmatically transnational—or to English-oriented schemes. English-derived attitudes and tastes inflected how he appeared and expressed himself and the friends he chose, but he certainly thought there was much to reform in the English polity: for example, in its lamentable particularism and its taste for 'popularity', for courting the unruly people. Charles deplored a lack of ceremoniousness and decorum wherever he found it, in London churches whose altars were not railed off quite as much as in Scottish kirks that lacked organ music. But he did not insist on Anglican modes of altar-railing for Scottish churches, nor did he seek a free hand in Scotland for Laud, or imply that Scotland was subordinate to the archbishop of Canterbury as primate of all his dominions. Laud certainly wanted to institute episcopal order in England's toe-holds off-shore, whether the Channel Islands, Massachusetts, or the trading concessions abroad of English merchant companies, and he hoped to 'conform Scotland to the Church of England', as he revealingly put it; but Charles was never so merely English in outlook. The work towards a mandatory prayer book for Scotland that James had set desultorily in motion late in his reign and which Laud thought could best be achieved by the imposition of the English book was, Charles insisted, to be left to Scottish bishops, albeit under Laud's guidance and correction. Few of his Scottish subjects would have found reassurance in the distinction.

The channels of communication that might have offset Scottish mis-givings over religious difference were left to dry up. Learning little from the storm over Revocation, Charles neglected the personal contacts that had compensated for his father's absence and that had allowed the mul-tiple-kingdom relationships to work fairly smoothly. Immediately on his accession Charles rather pointedly turned away from James's old noble friends, and though after the Revocation he leaned for a while on the scholarly Earl of Menteith, the latter's near-treasonous genealogical speculations about his own blood royal—always a sensitive area for hereditary kings—brought his downfall early in 1633. Thereafter, Charles lacked a Scottish conduit and, insofar as he sought advice, turned towards a handful of anglicized Scottish courtiers, several with past links to Buckingham. Scots' ability to get business done at court suffered; it suffered still more from the economic depression which brought a near one-third decline from the informal exchange-rate for Scottish coins against English that had prevailed in the 1620s. Suitors contemplating a visit were discouraged, while their ability to do business in Edinburgh dwindled as the King increasingly staffed the Scottish council with bish-ops, who could be relied upon not to question his wishes.

When at last Charles himself headed north in 1633 for his Scottish coronation, he did little to encourage acquaintance or a sense of mutual respect. The coronation ceremony declared his taste for episco-pacy and for ritual vestments, both of them abhorred locally as dregs of popery; when he opened the Scottish parliament that followed by using the crown's procedural advantage to push through affirmations of Kirk ritual as well as the more predictable taxes, he alarmed those who believed that Scotland's identity centred not just on its ancient monarchy but on the pure Kirk outlined in scripture and tested in the Reformation struggles. One alarmist in the parliament was Lord Balmerino, who was shortly afterwards convicted of treason for pos-sessing a copy of a petition for Church reform that the King had rejected. Charles thus contrived to identify royal authoritarianism indelibly with what the Scots took to be religious innovation. Although Balmerino's sentence was commuted, Charles had created a martyr, and given dangerous point to a host of more mundane aggravations. Even the least apocalyptically inclined could see an affront to Scotland's honour in an absentee king's disdain for Scottish institutions as he insisted on his prerogative power.

Although they had gained some benefits—peace with England had stimulated livestock raising in the southern counties—Scots could be forgiven for suspecting that they were being drawn in England's wake. The continuation of the high taxes granted in the 1621 parliament presumed a wartime need, though little was done to aid the Palatine cause and Elizabeth Stuart. Instead, Charles's war-effort of 1627–29 called on Scottish contingents to fight against their old French ally, and as a result jeopardized Scotland's lucrative favoured-nation status in the Bordeaux wine trade; worse, the King's 1634 attempt to refurbish Scotland's defences through duties on coal exports, rather than through new taxes which would have required consent, threatened Scotland's competitive advantage against England in the important Dutch market. The British fishing company affair of 1630 gave further evidence of royal unconcern for an economy already in crisis. But that crisis—the long climatic down-turn in the 1620s and 1630s that disrupted Scottish cereal and livestock production alike—seemed to speak of more than mere royal neglect. The departure of so many of the hard-pressed to settle in Ulster—which by the 1630s had a settler population of more than 34,000—or to fight in Europe was of course not just Scotland's story, for England (and much of Europe) experienced similar adversity. That did not lessen the suspicion of the Scottish godly that God's judgement was upon the land.

Ireland too experienced catastrophic harvest failure in the later 1620s, though the 50% increase in population between 1600 and the troubles of the 1640s indicates considerable recovery from the Elizabethan devastations. Perhaps half of that demographic recovery was the result of natural increase, and the rest the consequence of choices made by Britons hard-pressed in their island and drawn to Ireland as a land of relative opportunity. And opportunity took a variety of forms, political as well as economic, since government itself was growing. The population of Dublin—capital city as well as commercial centre—doubled over these years, to over 20,000, making it one of the three or four largest cities in the three kingdoms. Sir William Brereton, visiting from Cheshire in 1635, thought it already a finer city than Edinburgh, and capable of catering to reasonably cosmopolitan tastes.

The English conquest and consolidation were reshaping the Irish economy in various ways—indeed, reshaping Ireland itself, since it was the systematic devastation of the woodlands for fuel that allowed the Earl of Cork to build lucrative iron works in the south-west and Sir Charles Coote in the midlands in the 1620s. The effect of such clearances is evident too in the ability of Ulster, until recently almost wholly pastoral, to supply 18% of Ireland's grain exports in the 1620s: but here, the heavier ploughs and more sophisticated mills brought by immigrants with access to capital also played their part. Change was certainly partial and patchy: pastoralism remained dominant in Ulster, the planters' goals both demographic and economic were never met, and most of the new market towns they optimistically projected in the first decades withered. Nevertheless, consumer goods were imported into Carrickfergus and Belfast, and in larger quantities than the immigrant British population could warrant, suggesting that new tastes were spreading. Indeed, they were spreading at both ends of the island, since the re-established Munster plantation, with perhaps 20,000 newly arrived English residents in the 1630s, was exerting commercial pressures in the south-west and stimulating urban growth regionally. Above all, a dramatic expansion in livestock exports to England up to 1640—perhaps seven-fold since the 1610s, if we are to believe the customs figures—points to the advance of commerce.

Watchers in England could therefore find much that looked promising in Ireland once the Graces affair was past. Eager to ensure that some of the gains should be his, Charles appointed the one strong-man of his reign as lord deputy to replace the New English lords justices who had succeeded Falkland. Thomas Viscount Wentworth—like Elizabeth's Sir Henry Sidney, a provincial administrator in England before appointment to Ireland—had learned from the fates of Sidney and other deputies the importance of protecting his back at court. Wentworth took office in 1633 having extracted guarantees of non-interference from Charles; perhaps more importantly, he had mortgaged Church policy in Ireland to Laud in order to secure the Archbishop's support at Whitehall. It proved a decisive combination.

Wentworth saw himself, and certainly advertised himself at court, as giving effect to the King's overriding objectives: to make Ireland a model and sustaining part of the royal dominions, and to reduce its ecclesiastical disarray to order on Charles's, and Laud's, preferred model. And, of course, he sought to make his own fortune as well as the King's, and to advance in the King's service accordingly. The Irish administration had been running at a 30% peacetime deficit in the 1620s and, by doubling the customs revenues and laying what would have been the basis for a major expansion in the revenue from feudal tenures, Wentworth came close to eliminating that. More signally, he cleared the accumulated debt (the equivalent of two years' of pre-1632 revenue) by brilliant manipulation of the 1634–35 Irish parliament—in the first session allying with the Old English members against an exploitative New English establishment he sought to curb, and in the second and third reversing the alliance in order to block Old English progress towards the key Graces outstanding from 1628 that at the outset he had seemed to promise. These cynical reversals secured subsidies of over £200,000 sterling with a new and more effective method of levy, setting fixed sums due from each county, that was soon to provide a model for others of the King's dominions. More immediately, Wentworth trumpeted the political achievement to Whitehall as an example of obedience for the King's other parliaments.

The management of the 1634–35 Irish parliament also gave notice of the malleability and arbitrariness of Wentworth's attitude to law and consent. Although surely no more than his king, he saw law as a tool of state. Fresh from his Dublin triumph, Wentworth justified the Irish fears of the 1620s by then proceeding to Connacht to demonstrate his contempt for the 'darling articles'—confirmation of land titles in Connacht, and security against the crown for tenures of more than sixty years' standing—the Old English had sought in the Graces of 1628. By pressuring and imprisoning sheriffs and juries alike, Wentworth established the crown's title to most of the province. He then set about perfecting the model of composition that Chichester had intended for Ulster before the flight of the earls and had pioneered later in Wexford: existing landholders, secured now with English title to three-quarters of their old holdings, would be liable to feudal dues and loyalty oaths, while the King and his deputy could bestow the remainder on themselves and favoured protestant undertakers. The Elizabethan dream of civility in Ireland was within reach, even as the King's revenue soared. John Milton's *Lycidas* (1637), with its lament for a godly stalwart drowned crossing the Irish Sea, suggests that it was not only courtiers and businessmen who wanted to export English ways westwards.

Wentworth did not limit his attentions to the Irish-born, whether Gaelic or Old English. With his watchword of 'Thorough'—the establishment of royal authority 'thorough' or through all vested obstacles—only reinforced by what he found on the ground in Ireland, Wentworth believed the New English as great a threat to government in Ireland as the other interest groups. Their pursuit of recusancy fines seemed to him mere vindictiveness when the Church of Ireland was unable as yet to evangelize among, or even to accommodate physically, the Catholic populace in the protestants' churches, and fines were anyway likely to provoke resistance; New English plunder of Church lands explained why the parish ministry was so deficient; and their rapaciousness in office explained why the crown's income was so much less than it should be. His alliance with the Old English in the first session of the 1634–35 parliament on the apparent promise of the Graces had in this context seemed plausible enough. After all, he had very publicly befriended the new and protestant Earl of Ormond; he was already breaking the corrupt New English deputy-treasurer, Lord Mountnorris, while hounding the former lord justice, the great Earl of Cork, to force him to disgorge the Church wealth which he had ploughed into his vast Munster estate—hounding him too to dismantle the massive family tomb he had erected behind the high altar in Dublin cathedral. Moreover, Wentworth's successful fiscal reforms very much aimed at New English evasions. Yet, as the Connacht plantation project showed, Wentworth shared the prime New English objective of an Ireland made safe for protestants. The question remained, protestantism on whose terms?

The Calvinist redoubt that was the Church of Ireland held almost as little appeal for the King and Archbishop Laud as it did for the Irish population at large. And the ambiguity of Ireland's constitutional status—unlike Scotland, a kingdom subject to English law and dependent on the imperial crown of England—was such that the Archbishop had few qualms about intervening, and with Wentworth's full support. Whatever the Deputy's own views of Laud's vision of the 'beauty of holiness', he recognized that the King shared that vision. As important, he believed that the effectiveness of the Irish Church, and thus the creation of a protestant Ireland, hinged on the recovery of the Church's material assets. A materially independent Church was central to Laud's programme in England, and Wentworth determinedly extended that campaign to Ireland: indeed, his energetic chaplain and Laud's chief instrument, John Bramhall, soon promoted bishop of Derry, made it his central task. But the independence of the Irish Church was to be measured only against the laity, not against England. That Church's articles of 1615 had enshrined a Calvinist orthodoxy which Charles and Laud abhorred. When Wentworth coerced the Church convocation of 1634—as successfully as he manipulated the Irish parliament of that year—to adopt England's Thirty-Nine Articles, he effectively wrote an end to the short history of an independent Church of Ireland.

The question remains whether Wentworth's campaign for the Irish Church might have been successful if it had not been brought down by the political crisis that broke in Scotland in 1637. To the outrage of Irish landowners of all persuasions, the reclamation efforts of Wentworth and Bramhall his tireless enforcer had considerable effect in the short term: the revenues of several Irish bishoprics increased three- or four-fold over the decade. But the Laudian model of bishop as administrator and dues-collector, exemplified in Bramhall, was scarcely suited to the work of evangelization and arousal Ireland's condition surely demanded. Wentworth probably knew this, and certainly saw Bramhall's labours as a means to an end of eventual liturgical and pastoral improvement. Not coincidentally, he also drew considerable satisfaction from the penalties and humiliation exacted from landowners of all stripes, and above all from the greatest, the Earl of Cork, as Bramhall and his henchmen forced them to disgorge their takings from the Church. But when the Catholic clergy were working energetically and Catholic bishops were already building an organizational structure across the country, we must wonder at what point the Church of Ireland would have been in a position to compete. Strikingly, another style of protestant churchmanship was available in William Bedell, bishop of Kilmore in the north midlands. Bedell, a brilliant linguist and former provost of Trinity College Dublin, in 1631 published *The A.B.C. or The Institution of a Christian*, a protestant primer in parallel English and Gaelic texts, and by the time of his death in 1642 he had nearly completed a collaborative translation of the Old Testament into Gaelic. He sought out Gaelic-speaking clergy, he was moderate in his polemical manners after spending years in Italy, and he despised the officiousness of contemporary ecclesiasticism. For his pains, he earned the respect of his Catholic neighbours, the distrust of Wentworth and Laud, and still more that of New English neighbours, who thought him soft on popery. Nor is it clear that he won many converts.

There was yet another model of protestant churchmanship, a creation at first of Wentworth's and Laud's fantasies, and far more alarming to them than Bedell's eirenicism. Scottish emigrants had taken ministers with them to Ulster, and the numbers of the latter had grown with the migrations of the 1620s and 1630s. The new arrivals brought a Calvinist fervour with them born of their discomfiting experience in a Scotland unnerved by the Five Articles of Perth and the Thirty Years War crisis more broadly. Wentworth and Bramhall quickly read outdoor prayer-meetings and liturgical nonconformity as presbyterian challenge. Though they harried a few ejected ministers back to Scotland—Robert Blair and John Livingstone by way of a storm-tossed and (they claimed) providentially aborted voyage towards New England—such successes proved two-edged, as the events of 1637–40 were to show. They provided data for Scots alarmed at the meaning of English policies, and data too for Wentworth's unceasing efforts to educate Laud, and through him the King, in the obstacles to an English style of civility in Ulster, and to a common and obedient churchmanship across Ireland and all the Stuart kingdoms. Those lessons soon became self-fulfilling prophecies.

The objectives of Charles and his advisers in the 1630s were order, ceremony, the financial recovery of the crown, and an increasing congruence of religious and governmental practice among the kingdoms—by no means a simple anglicization, when England too needed reform. Despite the challenge of ecclesiastical competitors, by 1637 these goals seemed in most respects on their way to attainment. Royal revenues in all three kingdoms had increased, in the cases of England and Ireland substantially. Despite the worsening climate, there were across the map encouraging signs of commercial diversification and growth, yielding higher customs dues and changing consumption habits. Backed by courts of ecclesiastical high commission in Scotland and Ireland which were newly established and modelled on English forms, episcopacy and ceremony seemed everywhere ascendant. Wentworth was creating in Dublin something of a vice-regal court in a nascent empire, with a vibrant theatre in the city and a governor's palace a-building just outside Dublin, at Jigginstown. Meanwhile, malcontents sailed in numbers for the New World. The triumphal notes of the royal court's masques of the later 1630s must have seemed to the select audience not altogether fanciful. And while most of those in England outside the court resented the burden of ship money and the 'pomposities' of the clergy, they had as yet infinitely less reason than their king to think in terms of three kingdoms. If they thought in other than local or national terms, it was likely to be of the popish foe in Europe and not—unless they or someone they knew was contemplating emigration westwards—of their fellow subjects in Scotland or Ireland. But horizons were soon to intersect, with disastrous consequences for all.

Map 4 Conflicted Kingdoms, Summer 1643

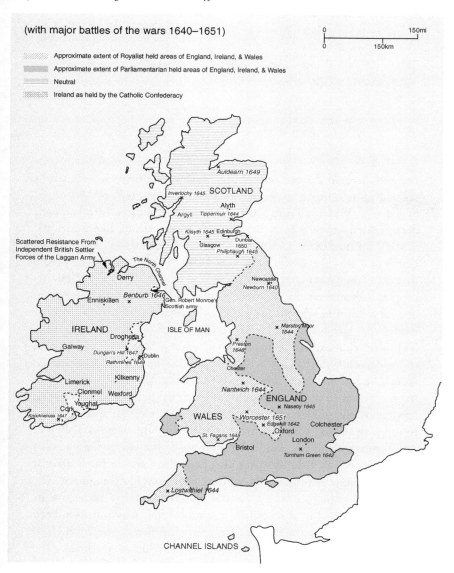

(with major battles of the wars 1640–1651)

0   150mi
0   150km

/////   Approximate extent of Royalist held areas of England, Ireland, & Wales

▓▓▓   Approximate extent of Parliamentarian held areas of England, Ireland, & Wales

≡≡≡   Neutral

░░░   Ireland as held by the Catholic Confederacy

SCOTLAND

Auldearn 1649

Inverlochy 1645

Alyth

Argyll   Tippermuir 1644

Kilsyth 1645   Edinburgh
      ×   Dunbar
Glasgow   1650
       Philiphaugh 1645
           ×

Scattered Resistance From
Independent British Settler
Forces of the Laggan Army

The North Channel

Derry

Benburb 1646

Enniskillen   ×   Gen. Robert Monroe's
              Scottish army

Newcastle
Newburn 1640

IRELAND   ISLE OF MAN

Galway

Drogheda

Marston Moor
    1644 ×

Dungan's Hill 1647
Rathmines 1649   Dublin

Preston
1648

Limerick   Kilkenny

Chester

Clonmel   Wexford

Nantwich 1644

ENGLAND

Youghal

Cork

Knocknanuss 1647

Naseby 1645 ×

WALES   × Worcester 1651
           × Edgehill 1642   Colchester
          Oxford
St Fagans 1648   London
       Bristol   ×
          Turnham Green 1642

× Lostwithiel 1644

CHANNEL ISLANDS

CHAPTER 8
CONFLICTED KINGDOMS 1637–1646

For a moment at the end of the 1630s, each of the three Stuart nations seemed united, though scarcely as Charles had anticipated. Affronted by a distant Whitehall, the Scots and even the fractured Irish had each been welded—if only for a moment—into something like a national cause. And if only for a moment, many in England—with their own conviction that the crown's fiscal activities of the 1630s represented a threat to law, their own certainty that Laud's and Charles's ecclesiastical practices subverted a cherished Church—were ready to cheer them on. John Milton, who in 1645 was to lament the barbarous Scottish names that war forced before the eyes of the English reading public, had once rejoiced, like so many others among the godly minority, in those 'dearest brothers', the Scots. Waxing prophetic in *Of Reformation* (1641), he imagined the two nations marching forward 'both hand in hand... never to be dis-united'; he also offered pointed analysis when he praised 'the nobles and people of Scotland, striving against manifold provocations', who had first stirred against the bishops' Babylon. The Scottish nobility's role in the protests of the late 1630s signalled the extent to which the absentee king had affronted not just Calvinist zeal but national sentiment, as Milton's tribute tacitly recognized. The Covenanting army's startling funeral march through Flodden on its way into England in 1640 points to a mood that may not have been entirely anglophilic, but there is no denying the cooperation. It is harder to find English celebrants of Irish virtue; nevertheless, the English parliament found Irish complaints of misrule sufficiently credible to base its own 1641 impeachment of Ireland's governor on the

Remonstrance that passed the Irish parliament unanimously in November 1640.

The achievement of such united nations had taken hard work. The King's hand is clearest in Scotland, since he had insulated himself against advice as he pushed for ecclesiastical conformity. Charles it was who had alarmed the nobility by victimizing Lord Balmerino for voicing his conscience in 1633, Charles who had insisted on new canons, or rules, for the Scottish Church in 1636, including ones asserting royal supremacy over and episcopal government of that Church, although his actions were fast persuading many of his Scottish subjects it could never be episcopal, had to be presbyterian; Charles it was too who promulgated the new Prayer Book—with its rash requirement that the communion table be removed from the body of the church to the secluded east end—the following year by prerogative alone, without consultation of any Scots beyond a few bishops. Even for the ambitious young Earl of Montrose, who was not much given to apocalyptic excitement, there were provocations enough in such conduct and in the lessening of political opportunity that the King's absence in England entailed. For more godly nobles, like the chancellor, Lord Loudoun, or Balmerino himself, the road to leadership of what was already a national cause was direct. Robert Baillie, a leading cleric and future Scottish commissioner in London, was not alone in fearing in 1637 that 'our poor country [would be] made an English province'.

Unity in Ireland, more fleeting but certainly more remarkable, owed everything to the determination and skill with which Wentworth had implemented the policies of Charles and Laud while pursuing his own considerable enrichment. In the plantation of Connacht, Wentworth himself had attacked the status quo, and while the plan for a legal onslaught in 1634–35 on the City of London's Londonderry plantation in Ulster originated at court, Wentworth helped carry it through. In so doing, he added London and its protestant tenants in Ulster to his extensive list of enemies; he also earned dangerous new foes by rejecting sweetheart deals in the plantation lands for two leading courtiers, Hamilton and Antrim. The complications of human interest hardly escaped Wentworth's notice: John Pym's brother-in-law Sir John Clotworthy was one of the Londonderry tenants and also a zealous presbyterian with good Scottish connections; Antrim—a (Catholic) grandson of Tyrone married to Buckingham's widow and, as the head of clan McDonnell, ever hopeful of reviving the Lordship of the Isles—was a bitter enemy of the leader of clan Campbell, the Earl of Argyll, who was soon to emerge as the greatest presbyterian opponent of royal policy in Scotland. To drive together, in the name of 'Thorough' and the royal prerogative, court adventurers, Irish Catholics stung by the betrayal over the 'Graces' and outraged by the Connacht plantation, New English magnates like Cork, and Ulster protestants of all stripes, was a major achievement.

It was an achievement that transcended borders as well. When in February 1638 Charles's Scottish critics channelled the outcry against the 'creeping popery' of the new Prayer Book into a National Covenant, or collective oath, binding a Calvinist Scotland to God, they found a way to take and to justify action independent of an uncovenanted king. Their assertion of a contract that was political as well as religious had major implications, not least in that the Covenanters had found a counter—an apocalyptic trajectory that would bring a self-consciously Presbyterian Reformation to the wider world—to the medieval English archbishops' claims to primacy over all Britain. The cause was not quite as unanimous as the Covenanters claimed, and coercion was needed in the north-east, those parts of the Highlands that were not the Campbells', and among the more conservative nobles too. But the Covenanters were right to assume that in a time of religious war, few causes could be limited to one kingdom. Spain had been recruiting volunteers in Ireland for its Flanders regiments; Wentworth quickly held these back for likely royal service in Scotland, and then imposed on the Ulster Scots a 'black oath' forswearing the Covenant. He also furiously resisted Antrim's proposal, which he thought both provocative and half-baked, to lead his clansmen against western Scotland. Fearing assault from Ireland, and outraged by Wentworth's challenge to Scottish consciences, the Covenanters began to bring Scottish soldiers and supplies for them home from the northern European theatre. Meanwhile, as the black oath worked to convince Ulster Scots that their way was indeed not the Church of England way, Clotworthy journeyed from Ulster to Edinburgh before heading on to London.

Neither for King nor Covenanters was this merely a Scottish crisis. Presbyterians recognized that their Kirk would always be vulnerable to a hostile king who could deploy English resources against them; they believed too that their God-given truths would spread once English eyes were opened to them. So they sent propaganda and agents south, to excite British fellow-feeling. They were confident that, faced by a united Scotland and disaffection in England, the King would have to concede. But Charles, divinely appointed king of many kingdoms, was determined to resist. His English treasury was too empty in 1638 for a quick strike, but he had grounds for hope. In Scotland, Hamilton's regional strength around Glasgow would dominate the General Assembly of the Kirk that Charles allowed to meet there in late 1638; in England, aristocratic retinues, backed by the trained bands of the English county militias, would suffice when a show of strength was required; and Wentworth was rendering Ireland usable. But, as so often, the King ignored wider opinion. Hamilton's local standing suffered from Charles's drive to equalize Scottish and English customs tariffs, which had damaged Glasgow's trade, and he promptly lost control of the Assembly and of the politics of Kirk. As the Covenanting nobles and their clerical and lawyer allies consolidated the autonomy of the Kirk through 1638–39, they built through the General Assembly a sophisticated committee-based executive as a way to circumvent both the Scottish privy council and the majority of the Scottish nobles who were at best luke-warm. And in England too, hierarchy was crumbling, while Wentworth was finding, like Tudor deputies before him, that submissiveness in Ireland might be more apparent than real.

The significance of the 'Bishops' Wars' of 1639–40 was almost masked by the bluster that attended them. Custom barred the English militias from deployment outside their counties, but around 20,000 troops mustered at York in the summer of 1639. Some were trained bandsmen, but many more were paid substitutes or resentful conscripts, and the nobles were uneasy and fractious; one English observer judged that there had never been 'so raw, so unskilful, and so unwilling an army brought to fight'. Nevertheless, they did turn out. Though Scottish morale was better, anti-Scottish feeling might have persuaded the English to fight: they outnumbered the Scots, and the Scots were no better equipped than they. But Charles lacked funds and knew that returning Scottish veterans from the European wars had been training the army of the Covenant; his nerve failed. The inconclusive Pacification of Berwick that the King signed in June 1639 to put an end to the First Bishops' War was one of his greatest mistakes. He was never again to be in such a promising position, and the retreat proved politically disastrous.

A royal strategy of divide-and-rule emerged after the fiasco on the border. Wentworth's recall to power in England, and to the earldom of Strafford, signalled the new approach. Aspects of the old remained: Ireland would still be a model for Britain and an instrument, and early in 1640 Strafford pressured a new Irish parliament into granting £180,000 for the creation of a 9,000-strong army to be sent against Scotland. Confident of his management skills, he persuaded the King to call the first English parliament in eleven years to Westminster that spring. Confident too that Englishmen shared his distaste for the Scots—particularly since Charles now claimed evidence of treasonable ties between Covenanter leaders and France—Strafford aimed to counter the history of the Stuarts' British kingship since 1603 by reviving the old enmity. But however plausible his plan to magnify the Scots' threat to England's borders and to its king, he was delayed by illness; by the time he arrived, the 'Short Parliament' had demanded major policy concessions in return for supply. These Charles refused, and in this Strafford of course supported him. In council following the dissolution, Strafford was uncompromising: 'You have an army in Ireland you may employ here to reduce this kingdom.' By 'this kingdom' he probably meant Scotland, but—while Scots thought that inflammatory enough—Wentworth's English enemies saw in his words a threat to themselves.

The British solidarities revealed by the 'Bishops' Wars' dashed Strafford's hopes. The Covenanters put some 2.5% of the Scottish population in arms, a virtually unprecedented achievement in early-modern Europe. The English war-effort, by contrast, disintegrated both materially and politically in the summer of 1640. In the summer of 1639, Lords Saye and Brooke famously refused to swear to fight for the King; in 1640, along with the Earl of Warwick and other peers and gentlemen, they were intriguing with the Covenanters. Unlike their medieval forbears, these had no thought of using noble retinues against a failed king;

instead, their hopes lay in parliament, and especially in a Scottish invasion that might force the King to call and retain one. That August, the Covenanters duly routed Charles's disorderly army at Newburn and went on to occupy England's two north-eastern counties and take an ominous control of London's coal supply. Their advance was unopposed by the powerful Yorkshire trained bands whose mobilization was suspiciously delayed, and untroubled by Strafford's Irish army which had been equally slow to assemble. But can England's political revolution be attributed to the Scottish incursion? The Covenanters were as convinced of the need for English support as the dissident peers were of the reverse. And the English were far from passive. The most provocative piece of Laudian over-reach in England had been new canons the Archbishop's ecclesiastical convocation passed immediately after the dissolution of the Short Parliament; these convinced many of the imminence of clerical—and therefore Antichristian—tyranny over the laity. That summer, religious radicals in London were as eager to distribute Scottish propaganda for their own far from Presbyterian purposes as the Covenanters were to send it to them. The Covenanters and their army were a necessary condition for the unfolding of the English crisis, but scarcely a sufficient one.

The financial and political pressure of the troops in the north shaped English politics for nearly a year, and by no means only to one pattern. Assured by the dissident English peers that a parliament was the only way to raise the payments for the armies required by the humiliating Treaty of Newcastle that had followed Newburn, Charles met what became the Long Parliament on November 3. Scots promptly demanded the arrest of Laud, whom they blamed for the onslaught on the Kirk as much as most Englishmen blamed him for ills of every kind, and of Strafford, who was a more immediate danger to the Covenanters and their English allies alike. The pressure continued, though in an uncomfortable lockstep. Eager to hearten their godly English allies, in February 1641 the Covenanters urged a divided parliament to speedier reform of the Church, and shortly afterwards appeared complicit in a threat from London radicals that, unless Strafford was executed, the City would withhold the loans that kept the soldiers quiet. They thus opened a fissure that allowed a civil war to be fought. Even some of those who had been in the forefront of the previous year's protests against royal policy recoiled at what Lord Digby—who was to become a wartime royalist secretary of state—cast as an unholy alliance of social disorder and Scottish interference. The anti-Scottish backlash is palpable, and especially in the occupied north-east. Yet conservatives did not blame everything on the Scots, for they also noisily proclaimed their revulsion at massive English petitions demanding the downing of episcopacy 'root and branch', and at the demonstrations in London's streets.

The relationship between the Scottish presence and English partisan politics was indeed both central and deeply problematic. The Scots had not pressed in a vacuum. There were thousands in the capital and beyond as radical in their different ways as the most apocalyptic Covenanter (who was surely the lawyer and organizing secretary, Archibald Johnston of Wariston). But the English political community as a whole had been defined as much by common law as by religious struggle. Loyalties therefore divided, for the number of those—clustered especially in London—who thought the hour of the Lord at hand was dwarfed by the number who looked back to a pre-Laudian Church 'by law established'. As the more tangible English grievances were resolved or dissipated in 1641—Strafford was executed in May, Laud stayed in gaol, the privy council and the Church lost key disciplinary powers, ship money was abolished—many in England found less reason to see the Scots as saviours, and abundant reason to resent the mounting tax burden and the mood of insecurity. Polarization set in fast. Among those impatient of the Scots were some of the idled officers of the English army, and as evidence appeared in early May 1641 that Charles had listened to their talk of a military coup against the temporizers at Westminster, those who had long suspected a popish plot concluded that the King himself could not be trusted. Those who had conspired with the Scots in 1640 now had reason to fear for their heads, and to go to extremes if that seemed the way to save them.

Scotland was showing its own signs of strain. The Covenanters had gone quietly about a constitutional and ecclesiastical revolution that deprived the crown of much of its executive power—in the process providing a model for Westminster's 1641 Triennial Act that required regular parliaments in England—and had already cemented an anti-episcopal

Kirk. But the achievement concealed some potential divisions. Ancestral loyalties to the Stuarts ran deep, most Scots yearned for a return to order, and by no means all were Presbyterians. As early as August 1640, Montrose and eighteen other nobles secretly signed the Cumbernauld Bond to oppose Argyll's growing dominance. Charles saw hope of profit in such noble rivalries and in the return home of several leading Scottish courtiers, who might yet rally their regions. A formal Anglo-Scottish peace would enable him to go north in state and rebuild. Peace would disband the armies and thus remove his English critics' financial leverage over him. It would also allow other political sentiments—sheer loyalty, resentment at taxation, fear of disorder, and (in England) anxiety about the traditions of the Church—to come to the fore. Charles had everything to play for.

Yet once the peace was signed in August 1641 the crisis did not ease, and nor did the King regain power. The terms of the Treaty of London went some way towards the Scottish goal of security and economic access through a quasi-federal linking of equal kingdoms: mutual hostilities and mutual trade barriers would require the approval of both parliaments; tellingly, Ireland was for these British purposes folded into England and its parliament. But what concerned England in the short term was the domestic fall-out of the Treaty. As Saye, Pym, and their allies confronted a future without the guarantees the Scottish soldiers had provided, they turned in September to more radical attempts to seize parliamentary control of the executive and to reform the Church from below. In so doing, they speeded the polarization already under way in the provinces as well as at Westminster. But it takes two to polarize. While during his Scottish visit in the autumn Charles peacefully signed away royal control over Scotland's government, he also acquiesced in 'the Incident', an attempt to assassinate Argyll—whom he had just tried to win over by promoting him in the nobility to a marquessate—along with Hamilton, whose blood-ties to the Stewart line rendered his often-inscrutable politics dangerously suspect with some of Charles's Scottish supporters. This was a king as prepared to use force to recoup his position as he had been in England in May.

Perhaps to Pym's relief as well as his horror, the outbreak of rebellion in Ireland on 22 October re-established the fundamental condition of the previous year: rebellion had to be suppressed, so money and therefore a parliament were needed. There could be no quick dissolution, nor a speedy reassertion of royal power.

The implications of the Irish kingdom's subordinate status proved devastating as political revolution unfolded in Britain. In their complaints against Strafford, the Old English elite had eloquently claimed their rights under Magna Carta, but the rhetoric of English law and liberty was increasingly drowned out by a different excitement spreading from Edinburgh and Westminster. Apocalyptic notes resound in Scotland's National Covenant, and the dramatic collapse of Laudianism against the long background of anxiety about the fate of protestantism abroad and at home brought many in England to a similar pitch. Irish Catholics suddenly found Ireland's subjection to English law a matter of urgent concern: was Ireland, a kingdom, subject merely to the English crown, or as conquered territory subject to crown and parliament? Old English lawyers like Patrick Darcy quickly argued that English statutes bound Ireland only if they were confirmed by the Irish parliament, but the Treaty of London seemed to tell a different story. Indeed, the English parliament's main apologist, Henry Parker, was soon to insist in his *Observations* (1642) that 'England and Ireland are one and the same dominion... [with] as true and intimate an union betwixt them, as betwixt England and Wales'. Would any new anti-popish measures halt at the English ports?

And was ideology the only commodity on the market? Strafford had built an army in Ireland, and it gave a king who had toyed with the thought of military action in his other kingdoms an incentive to look west. In Britain in the summer of 1641 the Scottish forces were about to disband. Charles clearly hoped that by reviving the two key Graces—those ending plantation in Connacht and giving security for tenures going back sixty years—he might gain enough Old English support to fund the Irish army so he could use it. Despite all their disappointments, the Old English were at least willing to participate in covert talks. They still prided themselves on their loyalty, they saw only danger in 'the puritans', and they hoped that collaboration against the King's enemies would earn them royal gratitude along with the Graces. The Irish army might yet preserve the royal prerogative which alone could shelter the

Catholics from the protestant establishment—and not only in Britain, for the intransigent protestants on Charles's Irish council insisted that, short of a total conquest, plantation remained the only way to make Ireland safe.

But there were too many integers for easy plotting, royal or otherwise. The fractiousness of the Dublin parliament drastically reduced the prospects for a significant tax grant that would permit the retention of the Irish army. The King may have covertly tried through the Earl of Antrim to hold on to some of the troops, but hard evidence is elusive; anyway, he was not the only intriguer. The Covenanters had shown that self-help worked. Catholic leaders, notably among the Old Irish, had been whispering since the winter that it was time to emulate them, and to improve their nation's condition while England was distracted and while—since many of Strafford's soldiers were Catholics—there were still Irish men in arms available. Furthermore, Catholicism in Ireland was gaining a new self-consciousness, and not just because of the Counter-Reformation loyalties formed in the 1620s. Around 1634 there had appeared a widely copied manuscript history of early Ireland, *Foras feasa ar Eirinn*, written in Gaelic by an Old English priest, Geoffrey Keating. It advanced what became an enduring account of nationhood: the peculiar excellence of the Irish was that, despite oppression, despite conquest, they remained the most loyal of all Roman Catholics. The new persecution in prospect in the summer of 1641, as English parliament-men called for full enforcement of the penal laws against priests and recusant laity alike, thus threatened a sense of identity and purpose hard won after so much else had been swept away.

In the ferment of Ireland in 1641, more than one Catholic political group was moving, and all sought a version of what the Scots had achieved: a revision of the terms of the multiple kingdom. The Old English of the Pale were happy to exploit the King's need for support: in their negotiations they sought establishment for their Church, non-partisan courts, a king's council of Irishmen, and an autonomous parliament secured by a revision of Poynings Law and clarification that Ireland was subject merely to the English crown and not to English statute. The Old Irish conspirators who tried to seize Dublin Castle aimed not at national independence but to bargain from a position of strength. Like the Covenanters before him, Connor Lord Maguire of Fermanagh—whose contacts in Pale society were as deep as his indebtedness—was in contact with co-religionists abroad, and most notably with Owen Roe O'Neill, an heir to Tyrone and a colonel in Spanish service. Some of Owen Roe's clerical contacts, in Flanders and in Spain, had hopes of a Catholic Ireland that went far beyond the more politic and negotiable goals of the Dublin conspirators. Given the complexities, the rising which broke out on 22 October was not what the conspirators had intended: the plans to seize Dublin Castle on the 23rd leaked, fatally, the evening before. But there had been another and overlapping plot, centring on Sir Phelim O'Neill, 'the chief of his name' left in Ulster. In the more inchoate cause of the 'defense and liberty of ourselves and the Irish natives of this kingdom', he moved on the 22nd to take a series of strongpoints in the northern province. From there, revolt spread sporadically across much of Ireland, eventually drawing in and quickly transforming the neighbouring kingdoms too.

The motivations of the Ulster rebels perplexed local New English commentators who had thought relations with the neighbours good. Just two months before the rising, the lords justices assured Whitehall that Ireland was quiet; indeed, the trouble began when Phelim O'Neill called on Lord Caulfield for dinner, and instead seized his castle. But conformity with English ways had proved a wasting asset for the native Irish, including both O'Neill and Maguire. As they showed their political conformity by following English fashions—in dress, drink, food, farming—they were drawn into unfamiliar practices and expenditures, and plunged deeper into debt to British commercial interests. As they surveyed shrunken landholdings in a disturbed economy that now faced another bad harvest, material grievances pressed hard on the surviving Old Irish elite: in Monaghan, which had not been part of the Ulster plantation, Old Irish landholdings had already fallen by one-third in the three decades before 1641. Below the landowners, farmers edged off the better land by British tenants experienced in commercial farming found themselves not only subservient to foreigners but forced to pay tithes and fees to an established Church of which they were not members. The frequent reports that winter from Ulster, from northern Connacht, and from the old centre of Gaeldom in the Wicklow mountains of rebels' carefully staged trials and executions of English breeds of livestock, along with the desecration of protestant Bibles, rendered harsh verdicts on Sir John Davies's confidence that commerce and plantation would civilize. They also shattered Phelim O'Neill's hopes of a controlled, Scottish-style, rising.

But an Old Irish uprising against the English still needed to draw in the Old English elite if it was to succeed. The palesmen now confronted in its most acute form their usual dilemma of identity, though they found little sympathy for it. Eager still to be loyal, in the weeks following the rising they approached Charles with offers to suppress the rebels if he would confirm the Graces and grant toleration to Catholics. But in Dublin the lords justices refused to help them arm, while at Westminster parliament denounced any flirtation with the Antichrist; Charles, who hoped above all to hold his English kingdom, could only acquiesce. The partisan judgement that this was a religious rising, and not the social rebellion that some Old English claimed, promised to make loyalism untenable. To make sure of this, Phelim O'Neill flourished what he declared was a commission from the King empowering loyal Catholics in Ireland to make a pre-emptive strike in defence of the prerogative and against the puritans who held Britain and its king in thrall—a declaration made all too plausible by Charles's machinations in 1641. By December the lords justices could accord something of a welcome to the emerging outcome, the co-optation of the Old English into the rebellion, since by it the productive and profitable areas of Old English settlement 'now lie the more open to his Majesty's free disposal, and to a general settlement of peace and religion by introducing of English'. The old dream of an English Ireland, now firmly redefined as protestant, might at last be realized, if the New English could squeeze out their local rivals.

The rebellion and the killings had two distinct though fatefully interconnecting histories. One unfolded on the ground in Ireland, where little was clear other than the suffering. Driven by hatreds that were cultural as well as religious, partisans on both sides settled into a grim approximation of ethnic cleansing, with the anti-popish rhetoric of one mirroring the other's no less harsh rhetoric of purification. Over the winter of 1641–42, the Old English, who had been left with nowhere else to go, drifted into the rising and soon helped channel and contain the violence. Nevertheless, early outbreaks in largely Gaelic areas, and not just in Ulster, killed probably 3–4,000 protestants. An unknown number of others died when, harassed and stripped, they struggled as refugees through a harsh landscape. There does seem to have been at Portadown in Ulster in November 1641 one clear and unprovoked atrocity—as opposed to haphazard violence—against protestants, but this was more than matched by immediate protestant reprisals, or indeed pre-emptive violence, which included the racking by New English officials of leading Old English lawyers. The elderly Sir Charles Coote—he who years before had probably spirited away the money for Connacht's land titles—fully earned his reputation as the 'terror' of the Irish. Not surprisingly, the counter-atrocities helped ease the scruples of the more moderate Roman Catholic clergy and Old English elite.

The other history of the violence played out in England, where Phelim O'Neill's claim of a royal commission and the early and outrageously exaggerated reports of hundreds of thousands of protestant dead spawned the most consequential myth of the war years. Long afterwards, Richard Baxter, a mainstream English puritan clergyman, testified that he and countless others had sided against their king because he had used Catholic Irish to kill protestants. It is in such terms, and not because an army became necessary, that the Irish Revolt generated the Civil War in England. Without it, the popish plot that Pym and his allies, 'the Junto', had anxiously identified since at least the Short Parliament would not have seemed credible to enough people. But in the winter of 1641–42 doubts diminished as atrocity stories blown to monstrous proportions sparked scares across Britain; they dominated the mushrooming press output in London, figuring in 17% of all English publications in that first year, fed the rumour mills, and shaped political debate and action. To focus and substantiate such stories, and to extract funding from Westminster for reconquest and for compensation payments, New English clergy in Dublin quickly set about collecting the 3,000 depositions of survivors that have proven a trove for modern scholars. To those clerical editors, the widespread reports of local calm before the storm, and the occasional reports that priests encouraged the rebels, were confirmation of an apocalyptic popish scheme to extirpate protestantism.

Fortunately for British solidarities, the editors failed to identify the rebels' initial efforts in Ulster to spare Scottish settlers in order to avoid Scottish vengeance, and the readiness of some Scottish settlers to collaborate against English neighbours they resented. The discussions among English planners in the early days of the Ulster colony about planting Scots on poorer land 'as a wall' against the Irish help explain the Scots' anger. In England and Scotland, the atrocity stories were immediately integrated, and to the long-term cost of the Old English, into an existing protestant narrative not of Gaelic incivility but of popish plotting. The unease Charles had long excited among the godly deepened sharply when, on 1 January 1642, he at last publicly condemned the rebels but made no reference to their Catholicism. Distrust, 'fears and jealousies', now dominated English politics.

Those 'fears and jealousies' required the construction of a novel framework for containing Ireland's rebels and victims. The emergency helped bind England's localities tighter to the centre, as press and pulpit campaigns for suffering Irish protestants generated substantial charitable contributions—though how much reached the desperate refugees trudging the western roads may be questioned. The crisis had significant constitutional repercussions too. Neither Charles nor the parliamentary leaders could trust each other with an army. The Covenanters, however, were eager to act against popery; they had no standing in an Irish kingdom subject to the crown of England, but since the recent Treaty of London they were not in dispute with Charles. Furthermore, in the mutual security provisions of that treaty they and their English friends saw an opening for joint action; in the swelling protestant outrage, they saw too a way to persuade the King to accept military action by someone other than himself in his kingdoms.

The Scots were not the only newcomers to allow themselves to be co-opted in the cause of the reconquest of Ireland. Since the financial crisis was deep, Charles in March 1642 agreed to the Irish Adventurers Act: private 'adventurers'—Scottish and soon even Dutch as well as English, provided they were protestant—were invited to contribute, and to be repaid out of 2.5 million 'profitable' acres (about 20% of Ireland's usable land area) that would be confiscated from 'rebels' in equal proportions through the four provinces. Speculators and zealots—the latter including

Oliver Cromwell—trickled in to invest. This was to be the great and final plantation and, the Earl of Cork put it to an English nobleman, 'a fit opportunity ... to root the popish party of the natives out of the kingdom, and to plant it with English protestants'. The alacrity with which Parliament had come to the conclusion, amid so much chaos, that confiscation—in other words, responsibility—could be equally apportioned through the provinces is noteworthy, as is the implication: the 'Irish' were all alike guilty. Catholics concluded they had little to lose from further resistance; vengeful protestants by now expected nothing less.

The British upheaval formed the crucial context for Ireland's troubles, in their beginning, in their continuance, and indeed in their ending. In April 1642, and with the King's agreement, the Covenanters sent the first of 10,000 men to Ulster, to be paid by the English parliament and led by a Scottish veteran of the German wars, Robert Monro; meanwhile, 3,000 hold-overs from Charles's northern army went to stiffen the loyalist contingent that the Earl of Ormond had scraped together to defend Dublin. By the summer of 1642, the main areas of revolt were close to containment; the rebels' supplies were running out, and Phelim O'Neill was contemplating flight. But the rebel leaders lived to fight another day because the Stuart kingdoms found themselves distracted by other wars. None of these was simply religious. In Ireland and in the Scottish Highlands cultural fissures complicated and intensified partisanship. Even in the King of England's dominions, culture and ethnicity could move men to arms: resentment at the Anglo-Saxon heartlands, as well as at aggressive puritans, helped fill royalist regiments in Wales, most of it non-anglophone and contentedly Laudian, and in Celtic but anglophone Cornwall too; Oliver Cromwell, MP, even feared another Ireland in Wales. Nevertheless, alignments everywhere were conditioned by religion. Not even in south-eastern England, or south-western Scotland, or western Ireland, was the religious map entirely of one colour, and everywhere there was fighting. While the most obvious misalignment, triggering the most intensive and extensive violence, was that between a largely Catholic Ireland and an overwhelmingly protestant Britain, another was shortly to become visible, as the gap between a Presbyterian Scotland and a non-Presbyterian England widened. Almost as consequential for the 1640s, and certainly for the long term, was the emergence of a fully

Presbyterian identity among the tens of thousands of Ulster Scots, with the establishment in 1642 of a formal synod in the area Monro protected. What was soon to be called 'the protestant interest' in Ireland became fissured, even as the meaning of 'the English in Ireland' became more complicated.

For a year or so after hostilities began in England in August 1642, the three kingdoms maintained separate trajectories. The return of Hamilton and other courtiers to Scotland had strengthened the conservative nobles who thought their constitutional revolution sufficient and had no wish to challenge further a Scottish king in a religious, and therefore potentially explosive, cause. Anyway, few at Westminster thought their plight desperate enough to ask the unpopular Scots for aid. But a divided England with its own war needs was in no condition to aid others: Westminster swiftly redirected the funds subscribed by the Irish Adventurers, and not for the first time England's parliament—most of whose members anyway grudged the Scots' presence in 'English' Ireland—failed in promised payments to Scottish forces. While Monro bloodily secured the Scottish regions of north-east Ulster—not coincidentally, it was a Campbell regiment that devastated McDonnell territory—he could do little more as his unpaid army dwindled. With the divided Scots unable to reinforce Monro in Ulster and with no aid flowing from England to Dublin, Catholic forces soon regained the initiative when Irish officers, led by Colonel Owen Roe O'Neill and the Old English Colonel Thomas Preston, arrived from Flanders in September. The clergy excommunicated Catholics who did not support the revolt and the lay elite came together at Kilkenny in November 1642 as the Catholic Confederacy, its forces divided among the four provinces. By the summer of 1643, protestant forces were confined to parts of Ulster, Ormond's enclave around Dublin, and a few smaller pockets in the south-west.

And by the summer of 1643, the parliamentarians' position in England looked to be shrinking almost as fast that of the assorted protestants of Ireland. At suburban Turnham Green, the City trained bands had managed to block the King's march on London in November 1642, but Wales and the west soon fell firmly into royalist hands, along with the major port of Bristol; the Earl of Newcastle consolidated the north, and it appeared likely that Charles would again sweep down on his capital.

Fearing annihilation, Pym in the summer of 1643 persuaded the majority in the two Houses they had no option but to renew ties with the Scots who had saved the day in 1640. But at what price? The Covenanters still hoped for religious union and a confederal structure that would allow Scotland both institutional autonomy and a joint British executive. The English parliament, loudly convinced of the excellence of English institutions and more quietly certain of Scottish inferiority, sought only a military alliance. The effort to find acceptable terms for Scottish aid proved as divisive in Edinburgh as at Westminster in 1643. As so often, Charles helped his enemies to a resolution.

Parliament's needs, and the eagerness of some in Edinburgh to meet them (if for an ecclesiastical price) were well known to the King. Charles also needed soldiers, and he would need more should the Covenanters march south again. He therefore turned to Strafford's pupil Ormond in pursuit of Strafford's old dream of Irish troops for English purposes. A truce with the rebels would permit the diversion of resources from Ireland, and Ormond, a protestant royalist himself but with many Butler relatives prominent in the Confederate Catholic camp, seemed well placed to pursue it. The Butler cousinage did indeed suggest that the traditional model of magnate governance under the crown still had possibilities. Catholic pragmatists like the Earl of Clanricard—Old English royalist and half-brother to the parliamentarian lord general, the Earl of Essex—looked to the crown to defend them against the Calvinist juggernaut; as well, Catholicism's appeal to tradition, and the bardic tradition's appeal to kings, led Old English and Old Irish alike to favour the royal cause. But Ormond exemplified the flaws of enforced civility as a political programme for the peripheries. Brought up by royal command in England in order to break Catholicism's hold on the earldom, his ties to the Butler affinity were already weak before he joined Wentworth in an attempt to restore the family's estates that the crown had devastated in the previous, Catholic, generation. Ormond's commercial landlordism magnified the damage done locally by his support of Wentworth. It was no accident therefore that his own town of Kilkenny became the headquarters of the Confederacy, or that many of those who assembled there took an oath to kill him. And the alienated could turn to exiles too for guidance. Even before the war broke out, the historian and polemicist Philip O'Sullivan Beare in Madrid had urged the Habsburgs to become champions of the true Gaelic and Catholic Ireland, and denounced any collaboration with the heretics and the English. The negotiations for aid were therefore complicated, and outcomes as questionable as Ormond's own achievements. He eventually secured a year's truce, the 'Cessation', in September 1643. It would probably have been wiser for the Confederacy to consolidate its gains while it had the chance: instead, it marked time while the King, France, and Spain looked to Ireland for recruits for their own wars. Many in the Confederate Assembly had hoped a desperate King would agree to full toleration for Catholics, but the most Ormond would concede was *de facto* accommodation; even this split the Irish protestant camp. Monro, who was just hanging on in Ulster, recoiled from Charles's plans not just to divert protestants among Ormond's troops to England but—he knew from capturing Antrim—to revive Antrim's pre-war scheme to send Catholic forces into the Highlands in an attempt to distract the Covenanters from England. Only able to deliver a partial Cessation, Ormond sent Charles a mere 7–8,000 troops, whose military contribution was slight: the largest contingent was destroyed at Nantwich in Cheshire the following January. Their political significance was far greater, for they seemed to confirm the panic of the winter of 1641–42. Although conventions of reciprocity quickly moderated the initial parliamentarian instinct to execute out of hand 'Irish' prisoners (even when they were English- or Welsh-born protestant veterans) taken in England or at sea, parliament's living allowance for 'Irish' prisoners in England—just half that for English royalist prisoners—declared its aversion.

Far more significant than the Cessation, militarily as well as politically, was the Solemn League and Covenant agreed by the King's foes in August–September 1643. The awkward title reflects the divergent goals: parliament wanted a military alliance, the Covenanters a religious union. Each eventually got part of what it wanted. In Edinburgh, even after careful strengthening of non-noble representation in the Covenanters' counsels and with the turbulent Montrose absent in England, it took nine months of bitter argument before Argyll and Wariston could overcome noble scruples about fighting their king in England. What tipped the balance was the Scots' sense of vulnerability to Catholic assault: less as yet from Antrim's Irish clansmen than from the many 'popish' officers in the army of the royalist Earl of Newcastle that in 1643 dominated northern England. And in Presbyterians' eyes there were in this apocalyptic moment other possibilities of godly union with England that might yet reform the world. To encourage such hopes, and to live up to its own languishing promises of reform, parliament in June 1643 at last established a clerical synod, the Westminster Assembly of Divines, and invited the eager Scots to send a delegation. But giving substance to Scottish hopes was another matter, for most in parliament were nervous of the Covenanters' Presbyterian imperialism. To soften the Scots' insistence on their own binding model, the brilliant young Sir Henry Vane, parliament's chief negotiator, deftly inserted the phrase 'according to the Word of God' into the treaty's clause on Church reform, thereby creating a mere 'politic engine', as Wariston later lamented. Nevertheless, there was much to gratify the Scots: the treaty pointedly contrasted the duty to 'preserve' the Scottish Kirk with that to 'reform' the English and Irish Churches (the text explicitly yoked all three kingdoms), and parliament instructed the Westminster Assembly to work to bring England into 'nearer agreement with the Church of Scotland'. Parliament thereby gained its military alliance: indeed, the Covenanters agreed to send twice the number of troops that the dying Pym had anticipated, and a disheartened Hamilton returned to his king at Oxford, only to be jailed until the war's end for his failure. For their part, the Scots gained more than a two-kingdom godly 'covenant'. Most immediately, the reaction against Ormond's Cessation in Ireland ensured agreement that reconquest there would be a British affair. Indeed, since Monro's was the only viable protestant force left fighting, reconquest would for the moment be under Scottish command—Elizabeth Tudor must have turned in her grave at this surrender of English sovereignty. British coordination went further, since the alliance was soon coordinated in London by a Committee of Both Kingdoms[1]. Although the Committee's members,

---

[1] In a rare English venture into forward planning, the well-placed parliamentarian apologist Henry Parker had, in *The Generall Junto, Or The Councell of Union* (1642), called for a supreme advisory 'council of state' drawn from the (protestant) elites of England, Scotland, and Ireland. The new wartime needs of 1643–44 at last brought action, but on a narrower front.

twenty-one English and four Scottish, did not adequately reflect the Covenanters' troop contribution—the Scots were supposed to be paid cash as well—it was a massive step towards their goal of confederal association.

The Covenanter army of 20,000 that crossed the border on 19 January 1644 effected the biggest strategic shift of the war, for in tying down Newcastle's army it ended all prospect of Charles's separate armies uniting to march on London. But collaboration left parliament and its Scottish ally alike both disappointed and anxious. The Scots were once again not properly paid for their services. Nor did they gain the ecclesiastical unity they sought: a Presbyterian structure was slowly put in place in England, but to the dismay of Wariston's friends it was a Church firmly under parliamentary rather than divine control. Worse, they saw in London, in the flood of print that poured off the presses and in some of the parliamentarian forces too, signs of a continuing search for godly reformation that disparaged their own discipline. Samuel Rutherford, one of the Scots' clerical commissioners to the Westminster Assembly, in 1644 published *Lex, Rex*, a brilliant defence of war against an uncovenanted King; in London, he busily compiled an apocalyptic exposition of *The Due Right of Presbyteries* (1644), and took as his target the Independents (or congregationalists) and erastians, the advocates of lay—and especially parliamentary—control of the Church who flourished at Westminster. Before the year was out, he doubted whether true Christians were any more plentiful in London than in Spain. Those who had invited the Scots south grew as sceptical as he of the bargain.

The Solemn League and Covenant therefore changed the politics of the war as well as the military balance. New tensions appeared: as military success steadily eluded the Covenanters, resentment grew at the burden of their financially neglected soldiers on the northern counties. More importantly, the Scots brought the religious issue to the fore, since it was to reassure them that parliament began to institute a Presbyterian framework for a national Church; that, intended to unify Britain, proved increasingly divisive in England. And as a new actor on the English stage, the Covenanters provided opportunities for manipulation. Some MPs had warned that Scottish entry into the war would complicate the making of an English peace, and war-party leaders were indeed happy to see the Scots urge new overtures for peace in the spring of 1644. The Scots' presence was already offensive to Charles and his English supporters; their Presbyterian demands outraged his Anglican pieties, and peace prospects soon withered—as Saye and other war-party leaders clearly intended. The next three years abounded in similar episodes in which English politicians lulled or misled the Scots for their own purposes while the Scots laboured to advance a programme of confederal and Presbyterian association in which the English were fundamentally uninterested.

It was not only at Westminster that Covenanters opened divisions. In March 1644, Oliver Cromwell, commanding the cavalry of the Eastern Association counties, clashed with the Association's infantry commander, a Scots professional who had arrested a Baptist subordinate for refusing to take the Covenant. Cromwell's famous rebuke, 'The state, in choosing men to serve them, takes no notice of their opinions', helps explain why the Scots quickly reconsidered their initial affection for war-party men like Cromwell. When in July the London press credited him with the great victory at Marston Moor outside York over the combined royalist armies of Prince Rupert and the Earl of Newcastle, a battle they were sure their men had won, the Scots felt still more aggrieved. And when in September Cromwell and his cousin, the lawyer Oliver St John, pushed through parliament the 'Accommodation Order', urging the Scots commissioners and the Westminster Assembly to find some way to accommodate 'tender'—godly but non-Presbyterian— consciences, the Covenanters recognized that the war party was not their friend.

The insistent Scottish demand for Presbyterian reform quickly refashioned alignments in the parliamentarian camp. The identity of friends and foes was by this stage in England's civil war often a matter of perplexity as the Scots imposed their own interpretive grid. Since the anti-Presbyterian Cromwell was the favoured war-party general, the Covenanters concluded the enemy of their enemy must be their friend; in the late autumn of 1644 they began to work with the conservative Lord General Essex, whose supporters had earlier opposed Scottish entry into the war. However lacklustre the combined military records, theirs was a potent political alliance. When the Scots primed Essex and his friends to attack Cromwell as an incendiary, they provoked the war-party leaders to propose the general remodelling that was to become the Self-Denying Ordinance. But though the war party's rhetoric became increasingly anti-Scottish in 1645, the peace negotiations that opened at Uxbridge in January paradoxically enough marked a high-point in British moves towards federalism, since the negotiators sought to build on the 1641 Treaty of London to allow both British parliaments a continuing involvement in the military affairs of all three kingdoms. A cynic might suspect that the war party encouraged the Scots to urge strict Presbyterianism and a British programme on the King in order to distract them from the military and financial remodelling that was simultaneously under way and that was gravely to undermine what passed as a British executive, the Committee of Both Kingdoms.

Alignments in the other Stuart kingdoms were as volatile. As the Cessation failed either to halt piecemeal Catholic encroachments or to provide supply, fissures opened in Irish protestant ranks. Murrough O'Brien Lord Inchiquin and Roger Boyle Lord Broghill, commanding in Munster, defected to parliament in the summer of 1644, and soon protestant royalism in Ireland was confined to Ormond's circle in the Pale. Disarray on the protestant side was matched in the Confederacy, where in the late summer feuding between Owen Roe O'Neill, commanding in Ulster, and Thomas Preston, his former subordinate in Flanders now commanding in Leinster, wrecked what had seemed a good chance to destroy the Ulster protestant forces; instead, it ushered in a long period of fractiousness. All that the Confederacy managed to achieve in 1644 was the dispatch of fewer than 2,000 of Antrim's clansmen in support of his recurring plan to aid the King and advance his own interests by attacking the west Highlands. The Confederacy's hope was that Monro would be drawn back to Scotland, thus allowing the Catholic cause at last to sweep Ireland. This time, Antrim's plan almost worked. Monro was not drawn away, but a distracted Covenanting regime could not reinforce him.

Antrim's counter-stroke—Scotland's civil war of 1644–45—was a proxy war not just for Ireland's Confederate Catholics seeking to clear the Scots from Ulster, but for the King who hoped to draw the Covenanters out of England. For the protagonists on the ground, the fighting was for the most part bitterly local and ancestral. The assault on the Covenanters wreaked havoc because a brilliant battlefield commander, Antrim's kinsman Alasdair MacColla, encountered a charismatic Scottish royalist, Montrose, who was in the late summer of 1644 footloose in Scotland seeking an army to lead. Saddled with incoherent objectives, their campaign contributed little to the wider royalist cause. Montrose's decision to sack Aberdeen—the centre of Scottish royalism—appalled Scottish royalists, his alliance with Irish Catholics proved deeply unpopular throughout Scotland, and his McDonald and McDonnell contingents refused to leave the Highlands. But Montrose did seize brilliantly on the opportunity presented by the absence in England of the Covenanters' army. Plunder was a large attraction to the clansmen, but much more powerful was the urge to destroy the Campbells who had driven them from their lands in Kintyre and the Isles. The Covenanters showed an impressive refusal to turn from their wider objectives to remove the burgeoning embarrassment in their rear, but in the summer of 1645 the war became local for them too when Montrose threatened Glasgow and the Covenanting heartland in southwestern Scotland. The Covenanters' reluctant decision to divide their army in England at last ensured Montrose's defeat, at Philiphaugh in September 1645—the accompanying massacre of McDonnells requited the earlier massacres of Campbells at Inverlochy and Auldearn—but the division came too late for Charles's purposes in England. He had effectively lost that war at Naseby in June 1645.

Montrose's Scottish victories did not have the effect his sponsors had hoped in either the Irish or the English theatre. But they did slow the momentum of what might have passed for a British cause. His opening blows to Covenanter reputations made it easier for parliament-men to slight the Committee of Both Kingdoms as they proceeded in early 1645 to remodel parliament's forces and establish the New Model Army. The Scots commissioners in London, frustrated and resentful, identified their critics and their New Model Army rivals with their ecclesiastical bugbear, the decentralized Independents; they thus laid a religious grid on politics (since they and their friends were promptly labelled 'the Presbyterians' to match), though parliament was not in fact seriously divided in religion. Most members were erastians. Most would have been happy with a limited episcopal frame, but in default of that they proceeded in 1645 to establish a limited Presbyterian national settlement. And what is striking is the readiness of the Scots to accept this. There is perhaps no greater tribute to the genuine commitment of the Covenanters to a British ideal than their acceptance in 1645, and indeed their imposition on Scotland, of the Directory of Worship and the Catechism thrashed out in a Westminster Assembly in which they were inadequately represented. Indeed, however much they lamented the insufficient rigour of the Presbyterian structure the English parliament elaborated in 1645, they accepted England's entitlement to differ within the common anti-episcopal and doctrinal frame that both nations possessed and that provided in their eyes a foundation for Britain. But when their commissioners in London tried to alert their neighbours to the sectarian indiscipline that might spread from England to the other kingdoms, they found their credit as doomsayers undercut by their drubbing in the Highlands.

The god of battles spoke clearly in England by the summer of 1645. When the New Model won at Naseby and cleared the south-west at Langport and Bristol, some—including Oliver Cromwell, along with future Levellers—read there God's favour to an army largely devoid of intolerant Presbyterians, and they read there too God's 'owning' of a non-disciplinarian godly cause. The Scots, appalled, concluded that if such an army won the war, the religious settlement that emerged in England would be dangerously unstable, and would threaten their precious Kirk perhaps even more than Archbishop Laud had done, not least since the New Model represented a power greater than any Laud had possessed. With the help of the French ambassador, who was eager to succour the French-born Queen and to recruit troops for France's wars, the Covenanting leaders opened secret talks with some of Charles's courtiers.

The imminent parliamentarian triumph in England cast its shadow over Ireland as well as Scotland. One casualty of the battle at Naseby had been the royal baggage-train, and when parliament published a careful selection of Charles's captured letters it exposed to public outrage not just his devotion to his Catholic wife but his determination to raise troops in Ireland, and the readiness of some there to work with him. The nearness of defeat made the King's efforts more desperate and more devious. Both qualities appear in his dispatch of the Roman Catholic Earl of Glamorgan in the summer of 1645 to find terms that would persuade the Confederacy to send 10,000 troops to England, even as he issued strenuous counter-assurances to the protestant Ormond designed to maintain royal deniability. Glamorgan quickly promised a royal administration of Ireland run by the Irish-born, and abolition of the penal laws against Catholics. It was his undertakings to the Roman Catholic bishops that the protestant Ormond found most objectionable: restoration of their episcopal jurisdiction and, worst of all, retention by the Catholic clergy of the Church lands and buildings that the Confederates had seized in the Rising.

Ormond and Glamorgan were here contending for aid from a Confederate cause that was increasingly divided between clerical and lay elites. The King's growing military difficulties added urgency to the royalists' argument that it was in the Confederates' interest to make a deal before a 'puritan' victory presented a much bigger challenge. The so-called 'Ormondists'—largely members of the pre-war Old English landholding elite—could see the point, and were willing to settle for amelioration of the conditions for Catholics: repeal of the penal laws, guarantees of political influence, and security for lands held before Strafford's onslaught, all within the familiar frame of a Stuart monarchy held together by royal prerogative, which their troops would sustain. But the bishops, schooled in Counter-Reformation principles, convinced that it was they who had filled the Confederates' ranks, and rightly sceptical of Charles's military prospects and informal guarantees alike, saw this as the moment to consolidate a Catholic Ireland: they demanded formal recognition for their Church and a restoration of its material base. They had little concern for the predicament of a king who ruled kingdoms divided from one another in religion; and in the dispossessed Owen Roe O'Neill—with his hopes for some kind of Gaelic restoration in Ulster—they had a general with his own inclinations to intransigence. Glamorgan's willingness to give ground to the clericalists was made painfully clear when his letters were captured and published in October 1645, but he was himself over-reached when a hard-line papal nuncio, Gianbattista Rinuccini, arrived in Kilkenny that November. Rinuccini's suspicions of Glamorgan were vindicated in December when Ormond charged him with treason for his dealings. The Ormondists in the Confederacy quickly built on Ormond's coup and, concealing their workings from the nuncio, made an awkwardly provisional agreement—the first so-called 'Ormond Peace'—with the Lord Lieutenant in the spring of 1646. Before this could become fully operational, Owen Roe O'Neill mauled Monro's army at Benburb on June 5. Rinuccini had brought the equivalent of £20,000 with him, when the Confederacy's revenues had been running at about £30,000 p.a.; dissuaded from mutiny by this new funding, Owen Roe's usually unpaid forces at last moved determinedly to war. Benburb was the Confederacy's biggest victory of the war, and it disrupted Ormond's revival of Strafford's strategy of deploying Ireland in the King's interest.

Implementation of the Ormond Peace was doubly pre-empted, for Charles had surrendered at Newark in May. The troubles of the 1640s had begun in Scotland and in Ireland, and there was some symmetry in the King's decision to end the fighting in England by surrendering to the Scots with an outcome in Ireland very much unresolved. But Charles's aim in surrendering to the Scots was of course not to put an end to the troubles. He sought only advantage in his politicking.

Map 5 Constriction of Catholic Landownership 1641–1688

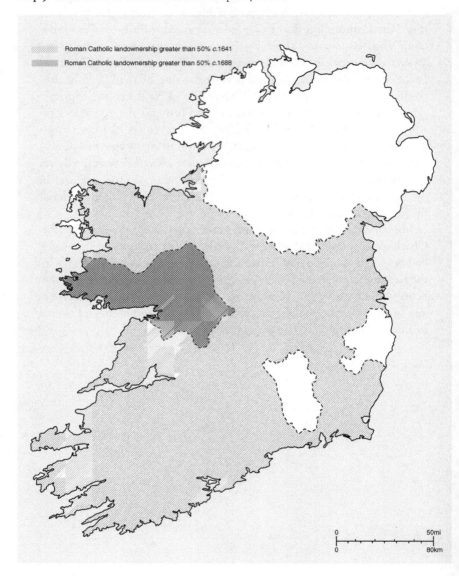

Roman Catholic landownership greater than 50% c.1641
Roman Catholic landownership greater than 50% c.1688

0   50mi
0   80km

CHAPTER 9
REVOLUTION AND CONQUEST
1646–1660

The King's surrender settled little in any of his kingdoms. Only in Scotland did one group exercise overwhelming control, and that group would only feel secure if significant changes occurred in the other two kingdoms; in England and Ireland all was still in flux. A captive Charles could easily recognize seeds of division in the tensions between Independents and Presbyterians in England, and between the former and the Scottish leadership—and see in the war-weariness so evident across the British mainland constraints on whoever controlled Westminster and/or Edinburgh. In Ireland, open war continued. What makes these years so remarkable is the degree to which all parties marched to the beat of multiple drums: none could turn single-mindedly (though some tried) to the work of consolidation and settlement in one nation. Just as the Covenanters sought to build a British Zion and to lay some foundations in Ireland, Ormondists saw the only hope of security for Catholics in the eventual triumph in England of a king indebted to Irish aid; and while most English thought of Scotland as little as possible, few could resist wishing destruction on the Irish rebels.

Power and pacification were not the only concerns; ideology and commitment complicated agendas dislocated by many-sided wars fought in worsening conditions. Among Ireland's Catholics, clericalists determined to vindicate the Church challenged the efforts of a lay elite to gain some easing of conscience along with some security for property-owners, subverting any attempt to build fortress Ireland. In Scotland, confidence in Presbyterianism's inexorable outward spread had lessened by war's end, for—so the Scots commissioners in London and the news-books they sent home reported—in London's alleys and in the New Model Army too the radicalizing work of war was becoming all too clear. English royalists were divided between the pragmatists who urged a French-brokered deal with the conservative English Presbyterians and with politically though not necessarily ecclesiastically flexible Scots, and determined traditionalists like Sir Edward Hyde, who would have no truck with anything foreign; the King himself seemed to oscillate between a frantic quest for aid from any quarter and an adamantine commitment to episcopacy. Meanwhile, at Westminster growing religious fissures—the urgency of godly reformation, the equal urgency of godly discipline—complicated the fundamental question of whether Charles could at all be trusted.

And could the members of the Anglo-Scottish alliance that had won the war trust each other? The King's surrender to the Scots at Newark gave them the opportunity to shape the peace, perhaps to impose it on Britain as a whole. They quickly showed their distrust of their allies by escorting Charles north to Newcastle for safer custody, a move that only intensified the dissension at Westminster. The peace terms that the Independent coalition sent to Newcastle in July 1646 were as intransigent towards the Scots—insisting on English military autonomy and control over Ireland—as they were towards the King. But the end of fighting was already tilting the partisan pendulum in England away from the Independents and towards the old peace party, the Presbyterians. Their advocacy of order was aggressively seconded by London preachers and publicists who denounced religious Independents and the more radical sectaries as a 'gangrene' that would destroy the whole. Such antipathy was reciprocated in some of London's gathered churches. Conventional boundaries were breaking, and Presbyterians and Independents alike castigated their enemies for playing the royalists' game, and royalists thought not unrealistically of a new war. All this would have meant little if the Scots at Newcastle had been able to persuade Charles to take the Covenant—so widespread was the desperation for peace, lower taxes, and the disbandment of the armies, that almost any terms could have held if the King would accept them. But though the Covenanters barraged their captive with Presbyterian homilies, and though they steadily eased their political conditions, Charles was firm in his insistence on episcopacy and his conviction that Presbyterianism and monarchy were incompatible. By the autumn of 1646 the Covenanters were eager to turn the task, and the King, over to their Presbyterian allies in England. Before that could happen, Thomas Edwards, London's leading Presbyterian heresy-hunter, had in the third part of his *Gangraena* (December 1646) identified the New Model Army as a major site of contamination.

There were more immediate reasons for Presbyterians English and Scottish to wish the New Model gone, for the war was over. If the problem of the King was one pole of post-war politics, the presence of the army was the other, and the two were inseparably connected. The Independents' hard-line demand at Newcastle that Charles be permanently deprived of the sword carried weight because the New Model was 'their' creation. Getting rid of it would reduce their clout, and ease compromise with the King. The Covenanters' readiness to withdraw thus made political sense, since withdrawal would remove a powerful argument for retaining the New Model. But every move had consequences. When the Covenanters handed over the King to parliament in February 1647 they marched home with £200,000 in partial recompense for their service in England. They thereby incurred the wrath of English royalists for appearing to sell their sovereign—an anger that turned visceral after Charles's execution. They also added to the mountain of parliamentary debt, and thus to the urgency of disbandment. Here the geographic frame widened. The simultaneous need to rebuild a protestant Ireland— and to respond to the demands of the Adventurers who had in 1642–43 lent money that was to be repaid in Irish lands—allowed the peace-hungry majority at Westminster to make a virtue of necessity. Those soldiers who agreed to serve in Ireland would gain some of their accumulating arrears of pay, the rest—apart from a small security force— would be sent home.

The conservative parliamentary majority surely had a wider public on its side, but it was on dangerous ground. The army possessed a sense of self-righteousness—it had after all fought and suffered at parliament's behest, and deserved to be paid—and a sense of righteousness too, hardened by victories won in a cause that was God's as well as England's.

When the Presbyterian leaders in the spring of 1647 sought to hurry them off to Ireland or to penury, and denounced and dishonoured their officers' attempts to petition on their behalf, angry soldiers could only conclude that corruption and faction went hand-in-hand with Scottish-style persecution. Radicalization proceeded apace, in the name of the army's honour, and soon of 'England's Freedom' too. London's oligarchy in reaction purged the militia to secure a conservative counter-force, but London could not alone resist the New Model: would there be Scottish support? Hamilton's return to Edinburgh in 1646 strengthened the conservative nobles there, and Montrose's bloodletting had weakened the Covenanters, but there was little eagerness for another southern venture. These were for the moment to be England's troubles.

And yet they were not only England's, since Presbyterian plans hinged on diverting the New Model to Ireland where, despite Rinuccini's efforts, fortress Ireland was conspicuously not being built. True, relations among the surviving protestant forces were frigid: the remnants of Monro's British army in Ulster scowled impotently at royalist Ormond in Dublin; the Old English command of Murrough O'Brien, Lord Inchiquin, in Munster vied with that of his bitter rival, the New English Roger Boyle, Lord Broghill. But Catholic divisions ran as deep: though Rinuccini's threat of excommunication effectively destroyed Catholic support for the Ormond Peace, O'Neill in Ulster and Preston in Leinster were almost as ready to fight each other as the enemy. In the autumn of 1646 the nuncio resolved his feud with the Confederacy's Ormondists by having their leaders arrested, and then stirred the two quarrelling generals to march on Dublin. Their campaign, futile and destructive, pushed Ormond into negotiations with Westminster to hand over the isolated city and its devastated region to parliament, thus offering the prospect of a landing-place in Ireland for an English force.

The character and purpose of such a force raised remained in question. The Presbyterians in 1646 leaned towards working with Ormond as well as the Scots, maintaining the frame of the 1641 Treaty of London for the three kingdoms though further reducing the King's role. The Independents had their own, firmly English, design: not just the termination of Scottish involvement in England and Ireland alike, but a thorough anglicization of Ireland. Sir John Temple's *The Irish Rebellion*

(1646) was pitched disruptively into this moment when a strategy for Ireland was in question. Temple, a New English lawyer and long-term client of the Sidney family, had his partisan sights set on Ormond as well as the Catholics when he classed everybody but the New English as the enemy. Systematically aggravating the violence and selecting the slurs of 1641, he insisted that Catholics sought to make their 'war for religion' a war against the English nation; and soon Inchiquin, despite his protestantism and his long service against the Confederacy in Munster, had to defend himself in England against the charge that he was 'an Irish general'. The horrific story Temple wove from the depositions taken after the revolt renewed a protestant outrage in all three kingdoms that had been jaded by too many subsequent atrocities. His story had a clear argument: there must be no deals with the Old English, for Ireland could only be secured by eliminating the Catholics' power to do harm. Safety meant total conquest, confiscation of Catholics' land, and the erection of a 'wall', as Temple put it, of English settlement against them. The 1641 assaults on 'English' settlers had cemented land, religion, and nationality together as the destructive fundamentals of English thinking about Ireland.

But as English would-be reformers in Ireland had found so often, programmes had to give place to politics. In the spring of 1647 the Presbyterians polished their plans to reduce the English army and Irish enemy on the cheap, but they were soon overwhelmed in the revolt of the New Model. At one level, England's accelerating political crisis that summer played out along insistently domestic lines. When the army seized the King, worked out an ideology at Newmarket, and drove the Presbyterian leaders from parliament, neither time nor resources could be spared for Ireland. On the other side, the King—smarting still after his Scottish hectoring at Newcastle, eager to exploit further political disintegration in England, and surely aware that any Scottish incursion would only unify an angry English nation—dissuaded Hamilton and his noble supporters from intervening to protect him. Nevertheless, the crisis was contained neither geographically nor ideologically: the army's anger and the parliamentary Independents' frustration built to revolution because the King after 1646 was able to play the Scots and the English and the Irish against each other. So when the King escaped from the army's hold at Hampton Court in November to the Isle of Wight, he changed the dynamic in more than one kingdom. Invigorated, Hamilton and the Scottish nobles sent emissaries to the island. Infuriated, the Independents and the New Model prepared for a new war, and made harsher judgements of blame than they had in the past. Meanwhile, the soldiers' arrears of pay mounted, and the intensifying economic depression made it unlikely that English taxpayers could bear the burden. The Irish lands on which the Adventurers had set their sights in 1642–43 were soon to acquire a more urgent significance.

Polarization in England paralleled deepening divisions in Ireland which steadily fractured the Confederacy. When Ormond prepared to surrender his Dublin command to Westminster in the spring of 1647, Rinuccini and his advisors saw opportunity; but since the Old English could not stomach the presence of Owen Roe O'Neill and his Ulster army in Leinster, the less competent Preston set off once more to attack the capital. One small fruit of the English Presbyterians' reorganization that spring was the dispatch of Colonel Michael Jones, a New English professional soldier who had been serving in Wales, to take command in Dublin. Jones arrived in June with 2,000 English soldiers and more resolution than Ormond; reinforced by the 3,000 troops left from Ormond's hard-pressed garrison, he crushed Preston at Dungan's Hill outside Dublin in August. The massacre of thousands of Preston's men seems to have been at least begun by New English hold-overs rather than of newly arrived, and potentially vindictive, English regiments, but Jones did not stop the killing. It was soon echoed in Munster, whose demoralized Old English Confederate army had been trying to transfer to French service; a newly galvanized Inchiquin, anxious to vindicate himself and thus secure funding from the Independents now dominant at Westminster after the New Model army's revolt, caught the Confederate force at Knocknanuss in November. Once again, thousands of those who surrendered were massacred, including Alastair MacColla and the remnants of his McDonnells, as the unexpectedness of sweeping victory amid devastated landscapes and political chaos lessened inhibitions. Unmoved by Inchiquin's anti-Catholic zeal, the Independents dispatched funds instead to his local enemy, Broghill. Angry and desperate for supply, Inchiquin found himself with other prospects as civil war flared again in England. Fearful of what an Independent political victory there might mean, in the spring of 1648 Inchiquin made a truce with what was left of the Ormondists in the Confederacy. His distaste for the Independents now overwhelmed the distaste for the Catholics that had driven him to break with Ormond after the Cessation. But what could such a truce achieve? Perhaps Rinuccini's contempt for the idea of a royalist Ireland secured by Catholic arms was the sounder political vision.

The King and his crown had held the three kingdoms together, and the Irish combatants were not alone in facing hard choices after he was made captive. In the spring of 1648, Hamilton persuaded the Scottish parliament to accept the 'Engagement' for military aid that the aristocratic emissaries had agreed with Charles on the Isle of Wight. It was not easy work, for many Covenanters, especially in the zealous south-west, would not fight for an uncovenanted king. Resentment at English (mis) treatment of Charles Stewart, Scotland's king, and fear of the radicalism of the English sects were widespread, but so was unease at Charles's very conditional undertakings. The three years of Presbyterianism in England he promised pending a final settlement left open the possibility that a king wielding an English episcopalian sword might return to threaten Scotland's Kirk. The Engagers therefore had to deal in 1648 not just with the English enemy but a divided Scotland: indeed, the previous winter Covenanting forces had still been brutally mopping up royalist remnants in the north and north-west. Not until past midsummer did the Engagers invade England in 1648, when the New Model had all but finished suppressing resurgent English royalism. The Scottish parliament had ordered the levy of 30,000 men for the cause, but the Kirk's protests, English lobbying, and the ruin of the Scottish economy by years of war and plague hampered the work. It was with a paltry 9,000 that Hamilton marched south in July; the half-year's delay since the Engagement had given the English regime time to prepare.

There had been something of a royalist design for Britain in 1648, courtesy at least in part of French brokerage (Charles's queen was French, Scotland was France's customary backyard, and France feared the Dutch or Spain might profit). Assault from Scotland was to coincide with risings in England while mutinous elements from parliament's navy threatened a London still yearning for prosperity and the return of the King. And there was cooperation: hundreds of English cavaliers joined Hamilton in Scotland, and perhaps 3,500 northern royalists linked up with his slow, rain-sodden advance south through the Pennines. Nevertheless, disorganization was the main story in England just as much as in Scotland. The parliamentarians' heavy hand created dissidents aplenty, but they were hard to coordinate. Widespread protests broke out in the south-east in the spring of 1648 before the Scots could stir, and the New Model's commanders were as a result able to stabilize London quickly. Resentments among the royalist gentry of south Wales at the intrusiveness of 'mechanic' puritans, compounded with the anger of unpaid provincial soldiery, flared up next, at St Fagans in Pembrokeshire on 8 May, as regular New Model regiments marched in. Some of the 3,000 Welsh royalist prisoners taken there experienced a new construction of empire as they were dispatched to servitude in the Caribbean plantations. This harder line strengthened as the bloodshed continued, first in Kent and then in the long and harsh siege of Colchester, the strong-point royalists had seized in Essex. Had Hamilton's generalship been better and Scottish support fuller, had hostility to the Scots in England's disgruntled north been less, the threat to the English regime would have been serious, for a significant part of the army was tied down at Colchester. But decisive manoeuvring by Cromwell around Preston in Lancashire in atrocious weather in mid August destroyed the hapless Scottish forces as nativist English rhetoric rolled off the more radical printing presses. General Fairfax at Colchester summarily executed royalist commanders and sent some of their followers to the Caribbean, and the army and its supporters in parliament prepared to do justice on the King as the author of this latest—and in the soldiers' eyes wholly unnecessary—spilling of blood.

The New Model soldiery angrily claimed the finality of God's verdict, but the divine jury was still out in the three kingdoms. However comprehensive royalism's recent failures, England's soldiers and parliamentary Independents held power as an embattled and insistently English minority in a single kingdom; something might yet cause discontent to snowball. If Ireland could be united, it might present too big a challenge to an unsteady English regime. So Ormond returned from France in late

September 1648 in hope still of rescuing the King, and if need be of building a base for Charles's son. Here lay Ireland's misfortune. The developing crisis in England had once more diverted resources from Ireland, so Michael Jones had not followed up his success at Dungan's Hill. Concerted pressure on Dublin might therefore have had some effect. But just as Ormond's Cessation had prevented the Confederacy from consolidating its hold on Ireland, so now the renewed royalist agenda split the Catholic camp. The desperateness of the King's position encouraged the Ormondists in the Confederacy to push forward with Ormond's familiar assurances of royal goodwill towards Irish Catholic worshippers (though not to the Catholic Church) and towards Catholic landowners (those of Connacht were to be freed from Wentworth's plantation design): the Inchiquin truce was therefore followed in January 1649 by the 'Second Ormond Peace'. But O'Neill scorned Ormond and his commitment to a royalist cause whose centre lay beyond Ireland, and welcomed Rinuccini when the outraged nuncio fled to his army—on which Inchiquin, the Ormondists, and the Catholic royalist Clanricard converged in the Confederates' own civil war. Alignments fragmented, such that by mid 1649 Owen Roe O'Neill was collaborating with English parliamentary commanders in Ulster against the Ormondists, while at the other extreme Inchiquin's protestant officers were in a state of intermittent mutiny against collaboration with Catholics. When Ormond himself finally moved against Jones, the catastrophe at Rathmines outside Dublin on 2 August 1649 showed his ineffectiveness as a commander. Rinuccini had by then returned to Italy in despair. The nuncio and the clericalists can be faulted for refusing to accept anything less than full establishment for the Catholic Church in Ireland, but surely not for believing that Ireland could only lose if it tried to fight England's battles.

Scotland's civil wars, like those of the Confederacy, ended in English conquest. In Covenanting eyes, the destruction of the Engagers reinforced the message declared in plague, bad weather, and economic collapse: God was judging the nation for its breach of Covenant. As survivors straggled home from Preston, thousands of rigorous and often humble Covenanters from south-west Scotland marched on Edinburgh in the 'Whiggamore Raid'. What was left of the aristocratic Engager regime fled north as Cromwell followed up his victory. They left power to the Kirk, which was by now towing Argyll in its wake, for the English regime had no desire to extend itself further. Cromwell thought a conquest 'not very unfeasible but...not Christian', and he was happy to quit Scotland in early October on the assurance that Argyll would suppress their shared enemy, the Engagers. The Independents had less common ground with the Kirk party than Cromwell thought. Nevertheless, he did learn something from his visit, for he remarked admiringly at the Covenanters' ability to establish a minority regime by purging a parliamentary majority: 'Think of the example and of the consequences'. For the Scots, this was of a time of trial, but also one that sharpened and narrowed the Covenanters' claim on Scottish nationhood. The Kirk-based government turned its schema of guilt, the Act of Classes, above all onto the many nobles who had supported the Engagement, and purged the localities as well as parliament. To avert God's wrath it sought out God's enemies, fornicators and witches alike: hundreds of Scottish witches were executed over the following two years. And when news came that on 30 January 1649 Charles I had been executed at Whitehall, the new Scottish governors—in grim consciousness of what might follow—proclaimed the younger Charles Stuart king not just of Scotland but of 'Great Britain' and Ireland too. That they did so, despite their hostility to the older Charles as an uncovenanted king, speaks to their outrage that a monarchy which had given Scotland its historic identity should be so slighted. It speaks too to their continued commitment to a vision of Britain.

Few in England shared that vision. In English eyes, the kingdoms had been united since 1603 only in the crown; with the monarchy gone, union went with it. True, few of the Independents and the army officers who at the beginning of December 1648 followed the Covenanters' example and purged parliament and then put the King on trial were doctrinaire republicans. Most thought they were where they were by necessity, or divine providence. They were pragmatists, alarmed by Ormond's creation of a royalist Ireland and the reports of the King's confidence in it; they were determined to punish Charles for so impenitently dragging his people into blood, but punishment might not mean regicide, and nor might a republic be the outcome of a trial—unless no member of the Stuart family would collaborate. But they knew they were English, not British, and that the Scots had no business with England's proceeding against Charles Stuart. As a corollary, the new English Commonwealth (that was only later to be called the Rump) insisted it had no quarrel with the Scots and was ready enough to call the young Charles Stuart, after his Scottish proclamation, 'King of Scots'. Nevertheless, the English Independents certainly possessed a sense of England's priority. After the Scots proclaimed Charles II, there was talk in the press of annexing southern Scotland as a barrier; when Ulster Scots joined Presbyterian clergy throughout the islands in denouncing the Rump for the monstrosity of king-killing, John Milton in the name of every 'true born English-man' leapt to put them in their place, trumpeting England's generosity in allowing them to be in Ulster and denouncing the ingratitude of 'a generation of Highland thieves'.

The claim of English right to Ireland helps explain why that was the direction in which the new English republic first turned. Scotland was a separate polity with which England had in late 1643 covenanted amity, whereas the 1641 Treaty of London had acknowledged Ireland as a dependency of England and its parliament: indeed, of the nation and not just the crown. So from 1649, the Republic's coinage pointedly coupled the Irish harp with England's cross of St George. This was no mere titular claim. Milton, one of the young republic's chief spokesmen, fantasized when he insisted early in 1649 that English settlers in Ireland 'had us'd their right and title...with...tenderness and moderation' as they helped the Irish 'to improve and wax more civil by a civilizing conquest'. But it was not fantasies of profit that drove the conquest and overcame the usual English unconcern with Ireland. The Second Ormond Peace declared royalist intent. Further, there was the matter of punishment for what Milton called the 'merciless and barbarous Massacre' of 1641, and rebellion against the very nation of England.

If the regime was to survive, Cromwell's Irish invasion must not fail. Everywhere, the Rump's enemies were running together: Presbyterians and royalists, Levellers and mutinous soldiery, and in Ireland Catholics and protestant royalists under Ormond. Political challenge, therefore, as well as the scale of the military task conditioned Cromwell's decision to delay embarkation until he had ensured adequate supplies and transport for his 12,000-strong force—a precaution Essex had omitted in 1599. Indeed, Cromwell refused to sail without sufficient cash in hand to persuade his troops not to desert: the Rump's sale that year of the confiscated lands of the crown and of the English cathedral clergy was thus part of the price of Ireland's reconquest. But Ormond made Cromwell's task easier by delaying his own advance on Dublin, enabling a newly reinforced Michael Jones to take him by surprise at Rathmines on 2 August. The rout cost Ormond thousands of his troops, and not only as casualties, since many of Inchiquin's protestant contingent defected after the battle; more importantly, it secured Dublin and gave Cromwell's army a safe landing-place. The delay had other consequences. The lateness of his landing probably helped prompt Cromwell's harsh order while storming Drogheda, his first objective, that the garrison be put to the sword: with winter coming, examples, deterrents, would be valuable.

The massacre at Drogheda introduced Ireland to the new English rigour. The laws of war left to the attacker's mercy defenders of a town that had to be stormed, so while Cromwell's harshness is undeniable, such harshness was familiar. Less familiar was the number of civilians among the thousands dead. Cromwell always insisted that he had not had civilians killed, though his own report on the engagement acknowledges many civilian deaths, if not at his direct command. More striking is his fixing of blood-guilt onto a mixed—Ormondist and English royalist—garrison that was but lately placed in Drogheda, and that he almost certainly knew had had nothing to do with the massacres of 1641–42. Perhaps he was disingenuously extenuating violence he realized had been unjustified—his career certainly had its moments of disingenuousness. But like Spenser before him and like Fairfax recently at Colchester, he was a fierce providentialist and he blamed those who should have known better. English royalists who entered the Irish war despite God's clear and repeated verdict in England had condemned themselves. Accordingly, the severed heads from Drogheda that Cromwell—uncharacteristically for him—sent for display on Dublin's gates belonged to English officers. Likely enough, though, many of his soldiers thought their victims Irish, and blood-guilty in a quite different way.

The question of Cromwell's—and, by extension, English—motivations in Ireland is complex. In the council of state that spring Cromwell had insisted that the Irish were worse than the royalists because of their 'barbarism—not of any religion, almost any of them, but in a manner as bad as papists'. Here was not fundamentalist protestantism but conventional cultural prejudice against the Irish as 'ethnics' in the contemporary meaning of that term: heathens, barbarians. He harboured similar prejudice against the benighted Welsh, who 'had not forgot their mountainous qualities'. Yet Cromwell's progress from Drogheda to a second massacre at Wexford has shaped a compelling narrative of religious prejudice. Civilians were slaughtered; Catholic clergy were summarily executed in some garrisons Cromwell took. But it is clear that in the confusion of Wexford's mishandled surrender negotiations Cromwell lost control of his troops, though—providentialist as he was—he accepted the fact of the killings as God's judgement; it is also clear that during the subsequent campaign he and his subordinates managed to do deals with the most Catholic and 'Irish' of their enemies, like Owen Roe O'Neill, for these were the least royalist. The executed priests were, arguably, animating obstinate defenders, and thus the very epitome of popery, of political Catholicism. When, early in 1650, an assembly of Catholic clergy at Clonmacnoise called on all Catholics to resist the extirpation that confronted them, Cromwell self-righteously denied acting against anyone's conscience, though he had no qualms about prohibiting the public exercise of the mass, the symbol of the institutional Church and thus once again of popery. Like Milton, he trumpeted the English 'right' to be in Ireland, to hold land in Ireland, on grounds of history and written record—a record which, of course, the English had written and interpreted. And as an Adventurer of 1642–43, he now had record of his own.

Maintaining such rights was costly. Parliament had initially anticipated £20,000 a month for a campaign of less than a year, but Cromwell—alert to the dangers of a war of attrition in Ireland's fragmented political and physical landscape—wisely held out for £90,000 a month. Had he projected six years rather than six months at that level he would have been right: when, in the mid 1650s, resistance was finally ground down, reconquest had cost close to £7 million. It was the worst kind of war. Within two months of landing, sickness had reduced Cromwell's effective force by half, and Ireland continued a graveyard for officers and men far into the 1650s. The costs to the defeated were of course immeasurably higher: the wars of the 1640s and the reconquest are estimated to have reduced the Irish population by almost one-third, and certainly blighted the lives of those who survived in a devastated economy.

The reconquest blighted the finances of the Commonwealth too, but it scarcely did that work alone, since the defeat of Ormond and the disintegration of the Irish Catholics' forces had cleared the way for quite another challenge to the Republic. Though incessant campaigning through a miserable winter left Cromwell 'crazy' in his health, he hurried home in the early summer of 1650 not to recuperate but to confront the Scots. His one consolation was the distractions of England's European neighbours, with France torn by the civil wars of the Frondes, the Netherlands entering its own republican phase on the death of the Prince of Orange in 1650, and Spain newly recovered from its own convulsions and eager for help against France. There were worse moments to establish a pariah regime.

The young Charles Stuart—Charles II in Scottish title and an exile even before his father's execution—was thus left to undergo unaided the contradictions of three nations notionally conjoined but divided in religion. A two-pronged attack on an isolated English regime might have worked, but a Catholic-royalist alliance in Ireland could not combine with an intransigent Kirk regime in Scotland. Anyway, only in the summer of 1650 could Charles swallow his own distaste for the Scottish Presbyterians—all his other options had expired then with Ormond's collapse and the collapse too of the hapless Montrose, who had invaded Scotland separately and futilely from the north. The Kirk's insistence that it would only invade England if the King took the Covenant and disavowed the Ormond Peace explains his reluctance. Worse was to come, for once Charles was in the Kirk party's hands it insisted that he condemn his father's faults, his mother's idolatry, and his own youthful failings; even this he did in August. He had presumably hoped that once in Scotland he would capitalize on the popular royalism that greeted him, but Johnston of Wariston and his allies guarded ferociously against this. Charles struggled to maintain some freedom of action, as the Kirk party purged his entourage of Scots with any royalist leanings.

A bitterly divided Scotland provided an unsteady base for a semi-captive king trying to regain his other kingdoms. With its ideological flank secured by Charles's familial confession of fault, the Kirk purged remnants of the 1648 Engagers from the Covenanting forces the Scottish parliament raised. Cromwell's pre-emptive invasion in July with an army of 16,000 eased the Scots' recruitment problems by making the confrontation a national cause. That pre-emptive move caused problems too in England: Lord General Fairfax resigned his command, and Presbyterian clergy preached against the attack on co-religionists. Cromwell needed a speedy victory to avert further disarray, and dispatched godly appeals to unimpressed Scots secure behind their defensive line to Edinburgh's south-east. Had they stayed there, the English army would have wasted away in the cold and rain, bringing disaster on the Republic. But the Kirk's pulpit-warriors were confident both of God's blessing and their larger army. Purging the officer corps one more time, they urged their general, the very competent David Leslie, out to battle against his better judgement. The result was Cromwell's most spectacular victory, at Dunbar on 3 September, and further instability in Scotland. Wariston and other Kirk-party radicals sought to purge again in the name of the Lord, but Cromwell's follow-up victory over the extremist Covenanters of the south-west allowed Engagers and even some royalists to return to public life in Scotland. A sign of changing times was the young King's ability to secure a Scottish coronation on 1 January 1651, though it was humiliating enough with its long sermon on his faults. Once again, Scotland prepared for war, but though the King's cause was now broader it was not much more unified: in particular, the Presbyterian Leslie clashed with his fiercely anti-Presbyterian cavalry commander, John Middleton. When Cromwell in July finally broke through Leslie's defenses that had protected the main royalist recruiting-grounds in the north, he precipitated the King's rapid march on England ahead of him. The Scottish parliament's mistake in presenting Charles to England as a Covenanted and Scottish king then became clear, for Thomas Hobbes's *Leviathan* (1651) was far from alone in likening Scots to Judases for selling Charles I to parliament in 1646–47. Few English royalists rallied to Charles II and his Scottish cause as he marched south to disaster at Worcester on 3 September. The English county militias turned out enthusiastically for national defence, and country-folk harassed Scottish survivors as they straggled home. British solidarities had advanced little since 1603.

Yet the Republic now found itself master of Britain, indeed of all three former Stuart kingdoms: definitively so in the case of Scotland, where the message of Worcester was brutally reinforced by general Monck's sack of Dundee and capture of the entire Scottish government at Alyth. There were limits to the Commonwealth's aspirations to control. The royalist Earl of Derby would probably not have been executed for his presence at Worcester had he not refused to surrender his semi-autonomous Lordship of Man; nevertheless, instead of abolishing that jurisdiction the Rump promptly granted it to Fairfax. And control was limited in practice too, for guerilla resistance continued in Ireland, while in Scotland royalist revolt flared in the Highlands in 1653–55. But mastery acquired as practical necessity soon gained ideological projection as the regime developed an imperial posture in its dispatch of prisoners taken in its battles—at St Fagans, Colchester, Dunbar, Drogheda and more minor Irish engagements, and English rebellions alike—to toil in the Barbados plantations. In the Navigation Acts of 1650–51 the Rump built what would become an imperial frame for protectionist regulation of colonial commerce in England's interest. As the framework filled out, the Irish, deemed part of the 'Commonwealth of England' from its outset, found themselves within the navigation laws but the Scots had to wait until they were properly incorporated with England after the tender of union in 1652.

This was an English and not a British empire. In the English translation of Selden's *Mare Clausum* that appeared in 1652 as support for the naval war with the Dutch, sovereignty of what were announced as 'the British Seas' and a 'British Empire' was located firmly in England. After all, as the pamphleteer Thomas Jenner had noted proudly in *Londons Blame* (1651), the 'Commonwealth of England ... is now almost absolute commander of all the British Isles'. The assumptions of dominance were clear: the poet and former MP Edmund Waller, in his *Panegyric* of 1655, saluted England as 'the seat of Empire, where the Irish come, and the unwilling Scotch, to fetch their doom', and then went on to celebrate the wealth of England's foreign trade and the strength of its fleet. Still more explicit on the role of England's neighbourly conquests was James Harrington's republican master-plan, *Oceana* (1656). In Harrington's expansionist oceanic republic, the role of Scotland was to supply manpower and Ireland revenue to an English empire vindicated not just by its conquests but by the civilizing benefits it conferred.

Thinking beyond the immediate conquest took some effort. The Rumpers knew all too well the depths of the financial and economic crisis, and the English press in 1650-51 resounded with denunciations of Scots and lamentations at the financial costs of dealing with them. Slowly, though, the Commonwealth concluded that the only way to contest the Stuart challenge through Scotland was by incorporating, though not quite on the Welsh model, what was after Alyth a decapitated nation. Although the union the Commonwealth held out in 1652 did not impose English law on the Scots, it offered no concessions to Covenanting confederalism. It promised a parliamentary union, law reform at least to eliminate the 'vassalage' of feudal tenures and feudal courts, and, to the Kirk's horror, an end to religious coercion of protestants. The Rumpers congratulated themselves on their magnanimity in extending English benefits to an oppressed people, and the more radical assumed that Scots would rally to them once the tyranny of Kirk and nobles was removed. And even if the Scots failed to understand their own interests, the apocalyptic imperialism of the Kirk that had subjected England to repeated invasions had to be countered; so, in 1654, some 18,000 English troops were quartered in Scotland. Since this was not to be a conquest, the 1652 'tender' of union entailed some show of local consultation, though the element of choice was limited, and designed more to reassure English than Scottish doubters.

The Commonwealth of England, Scotland, and Ireland—no collective term appeared—took shape piecemeal in 1653-54. There were some continuities between this work of conquest and the earlier English conquest of Ireland. The aim of the English commissioners with civil powers who worked in Scotland alongside the army was 'civility', through the dispensation of regularized, non-hereditary justice, as well as security. One clergyman dismissed as 'kinless loons' the English officials who boldly came to reform a society that in some of its outer reaches was feuding as well as feudal. The nobles—the Engagers' backbone—were the chief target of English policy, as they had been once in Ireland. Since many of the Scottish nobles were already suffering from the long-term effects of inflation alongside crippling wartime expenses and fines, and now faced the threat of confiscation and the end of feudal superiorities, resentment quickly became resistance. Straggling English soldiers were not the only victims. Civilian officials were picked off even in Argyll's territory, and in the Highlands rebellion flared under former Engagers, the Earl of Glencairn and general John Middleton. But the return to Scotland in 1654 of George Monck as army commander with expanded powers shifted policy away from reform. Monck, a pragmatist who had learned to despise Scots Presbyterians after serving against them in Ulster in 1647–49, had few qualms about making concessions to enemies of the Kirk. As he eased the pressure on private justice and backed away from confiscation, even while scorching the earth of the central Highlands, the revolt subsided. At his prompting, the government thereafter concentrated on stability and reducing costs, not reform.

English administration in Ireland underwent a similar transition, and for similar reasons of financial stringency and dwindling hopes. In Ireland, the hopes had briefly run higher. Scotland's Presbyterian clergy, however intolerant, could not be displaced because they were at least godly; in Ireland, conquest promised to permit the elimination of the Catholic clergy and thus eventually of Catholicism. Civility too seemed at last in prospect, for this new conquest left Ireland 'as a clean paper', in Cromwell's words. With reformed laws, cheap, speedy, and equitable justice, and the tyrannies of the great suppressed, the people—or what was left of them, for the wars had killed off close to one-third of the population—might at last be won over and English values spread. In that spirit, John Cook, reforming lawyer and solicitor at Charles I's trial, in 1650 accepted the chief justiceship of Munster, while the papers of radical reformers in England filled with proposals for the transformation of Ireland's economy and society.

But reform in Ireland was blocked, and most of all by the urges to punish and to survive. The basic principle of English justice in Ireland, retributive now rather than equitable, was declared in the Rump's ominous promise in its 1652 Act for the Settlement of Ireland: it would judge the Irish 'according to their respective demerits'. The main charges levelled against them were political rather than religious. Various grades of punishment were to be meted out to those involved in the revolt or the Confederacy, or resisting—or inadequately assisting—the parliamentary forces. Protestant royalists who had fought with Ormond as well as Ulster Scots who had sided with the 1648 Engagers were guilty, not just Catholics who rebelled in 1641–42. But there was an underlying, and not merely political, discrimination here, since such punishment was not applied in Scotland. Indeed, the Act reserved the sternest punishment for the massacres of 1641–42, and thus for Catholics. Had it been strictly applied, perhaps half of the Catholic Irish adult males would have been executed for treason. Only a few hundred went to the gallows, but 34,000 left Ireland for military service abroad, and thousands more deemed socially as well as politically dangerous suffered transportation to indentured servitude in the Caribbean plantations.[1]

The Rump's survival was bound up in its swingeing definitions. Not all of the conquering army had intended such a harsh outcome: many had distinguished—as in Scotland—between the guilty elite and the peasantry to whom clemency should be shown; additionally, the terms Cromwell had offered to surrendering Catholic forces often promised protections, and thus engaged the honour of the army. Yet during 1651–52 the Rump's commissioners in Ireland concluded that the land available would not cover the Commonwealth's obligations. Like their masters, the all-but-bankrupt regime in London, they were painfully aware of the financial burden that the long-drawn and underfunded wars in England and now in Ireland had generated: the Adventurers' initial loans had acquired interest charges, and the arrears of the 35,000 English soldiers sent to Ireland had grown. The commissioners' needed maximum land-clearances, but they suffered from an 'aptness to lenity', as they piously reported. From this affliction they were delivered by the

---

[1] In the late 1660s there were reported to be 12,000 Irish in Caribbean servitude. Since mortality for those sent to the plantations was close to 50% in the first year, large shipments must be presumed. The time-limit implicit in indentured servitude would have been for many a merely technical extenuation of what was in practice a death sentence. Many poor English youths were also forcibly 'spirited' by freelance contractors into Caribbean servitude, though that is no defence of English conduct in Ireland.

New English, who wanted vengeance, further confiscations, and further English settlement. Henry Jones, the Church of Ireland clergyman who had coordinated the depositions taken in Dublin after the 1641 Rising, carried an abstract of these with him to headquarters in 1652, and that did its persuasive work. The commissioners fully endorsed Jones's sweeping anatomy of guiltiness as they forwarded it to an attentive parliament.

The land settlement was thus a New English settlement, a hungry officers' settlement, even, in a way, an English taxpayers' settlement. It was not so much an Adventurers' settlement, since most of them sold out: only about 2% of those who had adventured emerged in the mid-1660s with estates intact. Nor was it Cromwell's settlement, though his name is probably indelibly associated with it; the Rump sent him about other business when the Act was in debate, and then removed him from the lord lieutenancy of Ireland to which he had been appointed in 1649. But whatever Cromwell's misgivings, the Rumpers—most of whom were more anti-Catholic than he—needed to ease the pressure of a discontented army, and they were happy to remove part of it by settling it in Ireland. Although English journalists pointed to the blood-guilt of the Irish, the main impetus of the settlement was unquestionably fiscal. Still less in doubt is the outcome. The Adventurers' Act of 1642 had promised to confiscate about 20% of Ireland's productive land-area; the actual settlement effectively tripled that. And in its land-taking, the Act did apply a religious test. Protestant royalists might be fined 20% of the value of their estates, but Catholic landowners faced confiscation of two-thirds for supporting the Confederacy or, at best, one-third for insufficient support of England; the portions left to them were to be held in Connacht, in the west, safely distant from Dublin and the crossing to England. The objective was protestant settlement across the land and protestant monopoly of corporate towns and trades, from which Catholics were to be excluded. And the big winners were the existing 'old protestant', or New English, planters (to be distinguished from the 'new protestant' settlers of the 1650s), who eagerly bought up from hard-pressed soldiers, and at knock-down discounts, the debentures for pay arrears that enabled them to purchase land.

What emerged in Ireland in the late 1650s was a precocious exercise not just in English partisanship but in state-building. An imperial mindset—on which anglicization and evangelization seem mere window-dressing—appears in the instructions of the relatively humane Henry Cromwell, the Protector's younger son and soon to become lord lieutenant of Ireland, for the dispatch in 1655 of 2,000 Irish boys to newly conquered Jamaica: 'It may be a means to make them Englishmen, I mean rather Christians.' Conquest and plantation had sharpened some of the tools of the assertive state, most obviously in two generations of sophisticated map-making, from c.1565 to c.1615; now the Commonwealth settlement prompted a landmark in spatial measurement too. The 'down survey'—'down', as in on the ground—was carried out by the army physician and mathematician, William Petty, who was commissioned in 1654 to establish Ireland's acreages and entitlements. His calculations were not impeccable, but recent research has given them high marks. Watching from exile that year the forcible creation of large estates that could be readily commercialized, Charles Stuart's advisor Sir Edward Hyde could only express admiration: 'We shall find difficulties removed which a virtuous prince and more quiet times could never have compassed.' Local opinion was less impressed, and Petty's surveyors were frequent targets of reprisals by disbanded but hardly pacified Catholic fighters, or 'Tories'.

Even without Tory resistance, the execution of this venture in social engineering was flawed. The confiscations and the allocations Petty delineated changed Ireland's political map, both urban (fast reshaped into a protestant redoubt) and rural. In 1641, 66% of land was owned by Roman Catholics; in the 1650s settlement, Catholics received allocations of about 6%. Some 40,000 new Scottish and English families settled in the more securely 'British' landscape of Ulster in the 1650s. Elsewhere, immigration was thinner. In the interests of remodelling, the planners refused to allow adventurers from individual English regions to cluster together in Ireland, and that diminished solidarity. Only one-third of the soldiery entitled to land actually settled: they resented their treatment, since they had to accept Irish land rather than cash for their dues, and most sold out at a discount to their officers or to existing New English settlers. Catholic landowners who made the chaotic trek to Connacht in search of their allocations in an already-inhabited region of course fared far worse. By 1655, weary of radicals' disruptions in England

and Ireland alike, Cromwell, now Lord Protector, was ready to call a halt. His dispatch of his son Henry to Dublin signalled his willingness to listen to some of the 'old protestants'—the pre-1641 settlers—who were alarmed at the economic implications of relocating the Irish labouring population westwards when so few English labourers came over. Transplantation was to be limited to the Catholic landowners, perhaps 3,000 households in Petty's estimation. Otherwise, the disputes went on, and adventurers and representatives of the army were still contesting their acreages and apportionments as the Protectorate fell.

Where the Protectorate failed most thoroughly was in the religious mission that had seemed to shape its purposes. All three nations now had protestant political establishments that were more or less erastian— that is, under the control of the secular power: less erastian in southern Scotland, where it proved difficult to dispense with the social discipline of the entrenched local presbyteries, more in England and Ireland. Union brought other symmetries. England's harsh Elizabethan laws against priests and recusants were at last extended to Ireland; the displacement and political exclusion of propertied Catholics was therefore accompanied by the exile or execution of well over a thousand priests, and the near-obliteration of the Catholic ecclesiastical structure built up since the 1620s. But protestantism did not spread in the years available to it. In 1657 Henry Cromwell gestured towards reformation by preserving the manuscripts of the newly deceased Archbishop Ussher—whose researches into the antiquity of a pre-Catholic protestant Church in Ireland provided hugely learned reinforcement for all those who would connect modern England to ancient Britain—and by yet another small attempt to fund the training of native Irish protestant clergy at Trinity College, Dublin. But the regime was maintaining rather than spreading the Word. Protestant energies as a whole were dissipated in sectarian feuding, each blaming others for turning God's providential hand against the godly because of the backsliders among them. The government itself spent what gospel money it had on salaries for 276 trained clergy ministering to existing congregations, who were to maintain orthodoxy and political goodwill against the challenge of sectaries or against Scots Presbyterians in Ulster. And though Cromwell trumpeted the efforts of the itinerant preachers whom the Rump's Propagators of the Gospel had sent into such 'dark corners of the land' as conservative Wales to fill the clerical gaps opened by purge and war, the main effect of these was to entrench anti-sectarian zeal in the Principality.

In its unmistakable protestant zeal the Protectorate might have found sufficient common ground with Scotland's Presbyterian faithful to advance the work of reform. But the Kirk disputes—between the so-called Resolutioners, moderate Covenanters many of whom had aligned with the Engagers in 1648, and Remonstrants, the likes of the Whiggamore Raiders of that year, who insisted on a hard-line application of the vision of the Covenant and no cooperation with the ungodly—were unremitting and all-consuming. The English authorities had at first welcomed the Remonstrants as anti-royalist, which they indeed were, but soon grew frustrated by their intolerance of any Scot who had in any way compromised with an uncovenanted king. In the mid 1650s, Cromwell sent the deft Lord Broghill to Edinburgh, and he managed to extract from the Resolutioners an agreement not to pray publicly for Charles Stuart, and thereafter directed patronage their way, but the broils wearied and frustrated all parties.

There was not much else to show for English rule in Scotland. Criminal justice became a little more standardized, thanks especially to the presence in Scotland of English officials acting on circuit courts and as JPs in newly invigorated quarter sessions. And there were even some economic benefits. As England's dependency, Ireland had been included within the 1651 Navigation Act (though its exhausted merchants were at first in no condition to profit), but Scotland—then a hostile neighbour—was not. Now, and as long as the Republic's union lasted, Scotland was brought within the Act, and Scottish cattle, coal, and salt faced fewer obstacles in the English market. In the figure of Britannia, introduced fleetingly in a 1654 medal, the Protector found an enduring emblem for something that transcended England.

However pragmatically, Cromwell had arrived as well at what seemed like an imperial solution to problems of multiple-kingdom governance. Scotland and Ireland in the mid 1650s became the sites of vice-regal courts, offshoots of Whitehall, as the Protector tried to balance the soldiers and at the same time rationalize government where so much of his army was stationed. Henry Cromwell's establishment in Dublin from

1655 was matched in Edinburgh by that of the graceful pragmatist Broghill, brought from Ireland to preside over the Scottish council. Both nations were represented in the English parliament, each with thirty seats under the Protectorate's 1653 Instrument of Government. Although that total grossly under-represented their populations, and although some of the seats were occupied by English officials or officers, republicans eager to assert England's sacrosanctity and to challenge the Protector reacted angrily. The attempt of some of Ireland's MPs in 1657 to reduce Ireland's excessive tax burden relative to England sparked the proposal that they be sent to the Tower. The objections went beyond mere conduct. After the Humble Petition and Advice, making the protectoral constitution a little more regal, narrowly passed parliament in 1657 with most Scottish and Irish members voting in favour, republicans denounced as imperial a regime that used the subject provinces against England. But no more than other Englishmen could republicans think in general terms about the nature of this 'empire', and the parliamentary attacks on Scottish and Irish representation took place on different days. Nevertheless, the republicans were at least correct in complaining about Whitehall's dominance in arrangements. Apart from Broghill (who quickly withdrew after the failure of the 1657 attempt to crown Cromwell), Argyll—one of the walking wounded of this revolution— and the half-crazed Johnston of Wariston, few Irish or Scots were seen there. And Whitehall dominated over those subsidiary courts too as it had in Elizabeth's day, for the jealous generals at the centre repeatedly paralysed the civilian reforms of Henry Cromwell in Dublin and Broghill in Edinburgh.

The practical meaning of the imperial English republic was therefore soldiers and taxes. Although the number of soldiers stationed in Scotland had been reduced to 10,000 by the close of the Protectorate, Scotland was by then paying close to £150,000 p.a. in taxation, and even this only covered half its costs of government; Scottish tax payments in the Caroline peace had averaged £17,000 p.a. Ireland, with 16,000 troops on its soil, was at that point paying close to £240,000 p.a., and covering about two-thirds of its costs. Of course, Ireland and Scotland shared such burdens with England itself, and indeed in their shortfalls added to England's burdens. They might have derived some bitter satisfaction had they known how little the Republic gained from its empire. In England, that republic was very close to balancing its fiscal books, but in Scotland and Ireland it ran massive deficits to the combined tune of well over £250,000 p.a.; as a result, it was forced to send subsidies from England, to turn to desperate and often coercive forms of borrowing, and to rely on the army even in England for political control. Extraordinary and unpopular courses helped drive the regime into political paralysis. Between 1637 and 1641, Scotland and Ireland brought down the rule of Charles I, and in the following years played a crucial part in his ruin. In their surly silence, they were no less instrumental in the failure of the English republic.

There was another condition that all three nations shared and that was news, and an unavoidable sense of being somehow and however unwillingly part of a common political environment. The still-vibrant printing presses of the 1650s and the army couriers who carried the newsbooks in all directions, even into the Scottish Highlands, enabled the provinces to share in the alarm as the shakings at the centre grew after Oliver Cromwell's death in September 1658, and share too the fear that the radicals threatened all ancient landmarks. The availability of news proved crucial in the demise of the Republic, and in allowing local bosses to respond to or even anticipate events. In Scotland, a watchful General Monck managed to hold on to his command and to maintain stability by tampering with correspondence and then purging the radical officers who were wished on him by the restored Rump parliament in May 1659; the purges in the Irish army went the other way, and they drove apprehensive less-radical officers into the arms of the Old Protestant elite. Together, these mounted a coup in Dublin in December 1659 as the army command in London wavered. Thoroughly briefed, General Monck did not have to work very hard to persuade a demoralized Scottish elite into quiescence as he crossed the border to march south into an increasingly royalist England on New Year's Day 1660. He would not have dared to do so had he not known that the army in Ireland had already been neutralized. The Irish coup thus began the Restoration.

CHAPTER 10
RESTORING CROWN AND CHURCH
1660–1686

By the summer of 1660 anxious clerics could once again descant on monarchy as destiny, now divinely inscribed in the blood of Charles the Martyr. The poet John Dryden's Virgilian and imperial echoes in *Astraea Redux* (1660) made much the same point: 'time's whiter series is begun'. But there were no clear signposts to that regnal future, and none that pointed across the national boundaries. Amid all the excitement, those who gave thought to the matter expected the multiple kingdom formed in 1603 to be restored—the maintenance of the Commonwealth's union found support from few beyond Irish and Scottish merchants who had benefited from access to England's expanding trade routes. The public mood and the remarkably uncontested (miraculous, said the clerics) restoration of monarchy in the three kingdoms gave the new king some freedom to find allies and patterns of rule. Yet Charles II's kingdoms were also more knowing than they had been. They had become uncomfortably well acquainted with each other, and the printing presses spread news and views, not as fast or thoroughly as during 'the late revolutions' but faster than in the 'halcyon days' of Charles I.

Those days of Charles I represented at best a pious memory. Unlike his father and his grandfather, Charles II had been born in England, and humiliation in Scotland in 1650–51 had only reinforced natal loyalties; having determined never to return north, this king also ended the Stuart practice of maintaining a strong Scottish complement in the royal bedchamber within a plausibly British court. Few Scots were to be found at Whitehall in the Restoration. Although it was in Scotland that he had first been crowned in 1651, Charles II was even more than his father an

English king. If there was a grand design for the Stuart kingdoms—unlikely enough with this pleasure-loving king, whose relief at having at last gained the throne was clear—it was simply the priority of England's concerns. But, far more than in the early-Stuart years, there were common emphases in the crown's dealings with the three kingdoms, for the King and those around him had learned from the upheavals at mid-century that there were common problems: in particular, ecclesiastical disunity and the turbulence of 'the old leaven', the self-proclaimed godly remnant. Further, though he speedily disbanded all but about 11,000 of the troops he had inherited across the three kingdoms, and lent some to neighbours and allies to get them off his books—he had little financial alternative—this Charles was less reticent than his father about the military option.

Not all Charles's subjects were as pragmatic as he, and nor was he able to control the agenda. He had learned in the disillusion of exile to distrust those who professed principles, but war and suffering had sharpened passions. In England, his chief minister, Edward Hyde (now Earl of Clarendon after long service) was a traditionalist who urged the pursuit of political harmony through patronage of the old political elite; in the Church, he urged as eagerly a return to episcopacy and the Anglican Prayer Book. Charles had his own memories of Scottish Presbyterianism and was ready to believe that the Church of England and its doctrine of non-resistance were the essential prop of monarchy and aristocracy. But how firmly should he lean on that prop? Those who had collaborated with Cromwell had after all restored Charles to his throne, while his father had destroyed himself by determined royal churchmanship. A more inclusive policy therefore had practical appeal. From Breda in the Netherlands, before he sailed for England in May 1660, Charles declared his concern for 'tender consciences' among his peaceful subjects and on his arrival in London tried to secure an accommodation with moderate puritan clergy. But many of the ardent royalists who had served him in exile were high Anglicans; when these reaped their rewards at the Restoration, they furthered a Church politics that was not quite the King's. They also encouraged those who derided all that Cromwell and his supporters had stood for. On a rising tide of royalism, young Cavaliers pushed, piecemeal, through Westminster's 'Cavalier Parliament' of 1661–78 what has become known as the 'Clarendon Code': its hall-mark was the ejection in 1662 of some 2,000 mostly Presbyterian clergy from English parishes, over one-fifth of the total.

Whether Charles's Breda approach might have worked is unknow-able, but coercion did not quell discord. Stigmatizing as 'non-con-formists' even Presbyterians who had been royalists since the later 1640s, the bishops' supporters cemented a division into the English protestant nation. Recognition that there were dangers in such a divi-sion, rather than the sense of obligation to politically loyal Roman Catholics that has sometimes been alleged, surely accounted for the Declaration of Indulgence that Charles issued in December 1662, reas-serting his concern for tender and peaceable consciences. The Indulgence's immediate effect was to intensify the Anglican reaction of the Clarendon Code, and there was some reason for this beyond mere vindictiveness. The Cromwellian interlude had reinforced traditional-ists' conviction that religious unity was the pre-requisite for a harmo-nious society—it had, after all, taken an army to hold Cromwell's tolerationist polity together. In his Declaration, Charles accordingly disavowed any thought of military rule; by attacking Indulgence, the Cavalier Parliament in turn aimed to preclude any such thoughts. Some of what were to prove the defining issues of the new-old order were already in view: a king might rule by co-opting the prejudices of the political elite, or by force against them.

The initial royal prescription for Scotland followed the English pat-tern. Charles made his British horizon clear when in 1661 he declared his intention to restore episcopacy in Scotland because of 'its better harmony with the government of the churches of England and Ireland'. Nevertheless, and as in his other kingdoms, he aimed for inclusion, and appointed as his secretary for Scotland at Whitehall a moderate former Covenanter, the Earl of Lauderdale; another, James Sharp, he appointed to the archbishopric of St Andrews and leadership of a Scottish Church that, as in the reign of his grandfather, combined episcopal structure with Calvinist theology and informal liturgy. And Lauderdale duly gratified his countrymen by persuading Charles to get the much-resented English troops out of Scotland fast. But there was a more divisive as well as a more intrusive story. English royalists had harsh memories of the Covenanters of the 1640s, and Clarendon showed none of the old English unconcern with things Scottish when he established an English privy council committee to oversee Scotland. In Lord Middleton, the old royalist general, whom he nominated to be royal commissioner to the restored Scottish parliament, he promoted a bitter anti-Presbyterian. Charles too had an axe to grind, and avenged his 1650–51 humiliation at the Kirk party's hands with the execution of Johnston of Wariston. Middleton followed suit: the ceremonious burial of Montrose's body parts, dismembered by the Covenanters for public display in 1650, and the execution of the arch-Covenanter Argyll set a tone that the King's commissioner exploited to invalidate all the legislation and all the encroachments on episcopacy and royal power that had constituted the Scottish revolution of the past generation. Manipulating the nobles' anger at the Covenanters who had ruined them, and manipulating too their eagerness for hand-outs, Middleton restored and even enhanced the Scottish crown's traditional powers over parliament that it had exercised through the procedural committee of the lords of the articles. He used those powers systematically, even flouting parliamentary claims to free speech, as he restored episcopacy as well. Close to a third of the parish clergy—a much higher proportion than in England—departed in 1662 for refusing to abjure the Covenant and conform to the bishops. The massive Scottish witch-hunt of 1661–62, in which some 600 died, suggests the intensity of the recent dislocations that had been as much socio-political—not least in the tensions between the local nobility and the Covenanting clergy and townsmen—as religious.

Scotland's dramatic reversals at mid-century ensured it a troubled history in the Restoration. Nobles and people alike jubilantly declared their loyalty, and the Scottish parliament granted the King what was for the Scots a generous revenue of £40,000 p.a. But though the episcopal Church showed considerable resilience, especially among the nobility and in the north-east and the Highlands, an apocalyptic sense of covenanted nationhood survived in the old Covenanting centres of southern Scotland, and promised turbulence. Middleton's aggression duly delivered this. Clarendon's high hand certainly cannot be blamed for the return of division, but Stuart absentee rule allowed it to play out. In the

Highlands, where informal ties were fundamental, an unconcerned royal master allowed local magnates to repair their own fortunes through self-help, doing down rivals in the process. Royal absenteeism had national consequences too, and not only for morale. Charles himself was informal and approachable, but in an English Whitehall he had few Scottish sources of information; dominant Scots politicians thus had an incentive to try to monopolize royal favour by demonstrating their zeal. Middleton moved a little too aggressively, and when he attempted to destroy his rival Lauderdale early in 1663 he only upended himself; Lauderdale promptly took over the drive for control and—despite his own Covenanting credentials—conformity alike. Indeed, the Secretary proved as assertive a royal servant as Middleton, and in September 1663 he secured from the Scottish parliament an Act declaring Scotland's willingness to buttress its meagre 2,000-strong army with a militia of 22,000 for use—so the Act boldly avowed—against foreign invaders or domestic rebels in Scotland, or in England or Ireland too. More tangibly, Lauderdale's allies sent soldiers to harry dissident 'conventicles' in the militant south-west, and so opened an early gap between Scottish practices and Charles's English denial of thoughts of military rule. Archbishop Sharp's swelling rhetoric of 'rebellion' proved self-fulfilling, and in the ominous year 1666 south-western Covenanters marched on Edinburgh, only to be bloodily dispersed in the nearby Pentland Hills. The 'Pentland Rising' accelerated the polarization Middleton and Clarendon had initiated, for while it demonstrated to some the treasonousness of Covenanters, to others it gave new martyrs. Euphoria had swept over Scotland at the return of the King, but there was soon precious little to show for it.

The cross-currents of policy in early-Restoration Ireland suggest that there too Charles had no clear programme. The English governmental dream was, as always, to make the Irish administration self-supporting, even profitable, but amid Ireland's slow recovery from the wartime devastation silver flowed substantially—and far more than in James I's reign—from Whitehall to Dublin; only in the later 1670s did the growth of Ireland's customs revenues tilt the balance the other way. A more realistic governmental hope was peace. Security as well as economy demanded that Charles reduce the republic's 15,000 soldiers in Ireland by a half; although that total, the bulk of the crown's standing forces in the three kingdoms, remained much larger than the normal Tudor garrison, it was probably less significant as a peace-keeping force than Charles imagined—for Ireland's variegated protestants recognized their total dependence on English support and Ireland's no-less disunited Catholics were demoralized and weary.

The major challenge to peace in Ireland lay in the fate of the 1650s land settlement. However incomplete it was, the entire protestant population had a fierce interest in maintaining it, but the dispossessed Catholics—many with claims on Charles's gratitude for military service in his exile, and all with hopes derived from the assurances given in the second Ormond peace of 1649—clamoured for its overthrow. The King promised all good things, declaring his support for the protestant planters and settlers who had in the winter of 1659–60 re-established monarchy in Ireland, and promising grace and favour to deserving Catholics. His first appointments gave few pointers. On the one hand stood Ormond, now made a duke and firmly protestant, though his royalism covered extensive Old English and therefore Roman Catholic connections; on the other stood Broghill, made Earl of Orrery for his loyal services in 1659–60, and spokesman for a sterner New English protestantism with ties to the Cromwellian past. Charles's first lord deputy in 1660 was, briefly, Lord Robartes, an English 'Presbyterian' peer and advocate of Indulgence, whose appointment suggests Charles's pragmatism: not until 1662 did he commit to Ormond as lord lieutenant, and he balanced that appointment by making Orrery president of Munster.

Ambivalence marked the Restoration land settlement itself. Like the Commonwealth before him, Charles sought to reward or redeem too many from too little Irish land. While the 1650s had not fundamentally reshaped Irish society—only about 500 of the 1,000 Adventurers and 7,000 of the 33,000 English soldiers awarded Irish lands in the 1650s were still settled in 1660—they had certainly changed the protestant population. Only about 10% of Ireland's population were members of the Church of Ireland that was now re-established. But were the new settlers covert republicans, deserving deprivation? And what of those clamouring for their lands? Some of the pre-war establishment, like Ormond, simply must be restored. Catholic officers who had served in

Stuart regiments abroad, or Catholics who had lost land simply for their religion, had claims of different kinds; but so did settlers who had conformed in the winter of 1659–60. Charles's brother James, who gained a massive Irish estate, apparently had claims too—Ireland was as usual a land-bank on which favoured Englishmen drew. The Act of Settlement of 1662 gestured in every direction as it tried to reassure the protestant proprietors while yet solacing Catholics. It outlined procedures for adjudication of claims and principles for compensation, but the claims court was soon swamped with appeals and with political pressures—from Catholics with allies at court, from protestant plotters—and the adjudication process was terminated in late 1663. An Act of Explanation in 1665 then gave broad summary judgement: beyond the special cases, Catholics who had accepted land in Connacht in the 1650s were bound by their action, while protestant proprietors must disgorge one-third of their acquisitions (in practice, rather less than that) to facilitate a limited compensation. The outcome was that Catholic landholding, concentrated overwhelmingly among Old English with political contacts and the financial reserves needed to bribe them, crept back from 6% to close to 29%—still a sharp reduction from the 66% level of 1641, but a major rebound nonetheless. William Petty, the Cromwellian surveyor who had profited richly, defended the protestants' gains as gamblers' winnings that they were entitled to keep. Protestants' frustrations were as nothing compared to the bitterness of the Catholics—approaching 80% of the population—at sufferings inflicted and promises broken.

Anger at the land settlement and the internal divisions it fostered among losers and relative winners on both sides gave an added charge to more general anxieties about Ireland's ecclesiastical future. Both protestant and Catholic 'interests' frayed badly after the Restoration. The Church of Ireland, now largely run by Bramhall and other superannuated English Laudians and serving a minority among Ireland's minority protestant population, was equipped neither for a pastoral role nor to further the King's wishes for accommodation. War had hardened attitudes, and the bishops felt little charity towards the scattered remnants of the Cromwellian-era sects or to Ulster's Presbyterians—particularly since immigration from a Scotland hard hit by the wars meant that, in Ulster, Presbyterians outnumbered the Church of Ireland by two to one.

No more than their neighbours in Scotland did the Ulstermen relish the new rigours of episcopacy as enjoined by Bramhall, or the arch-ritualist Jeremy Taylor who purged Presbyterians from dozens of livings in his diocese in the province's north-east. The Ulster Scots, hard-bitten survivors of the 1640s, fast found themselves becoming second-class subjects in the 1660s, while elsewhere Congregationalists, Baptists, and Quakers were sporadically harried.

Roman Catholics were still more firmly excluded from Ireland's political community, though official harassment had ended. Freed once more from the reach of England's penal laws, a Catholic hierarchy and priesthood reasserted itself quickly. By 1665 there were about 2,000 Catholic priests in Ireland, nearly twice the number of forty years earlier, and Catholic merchants and tradesmen were returning to the urban economies. And after 1662, there was in Ormond the first Old English chief governor in a century. The sense that the Restoration might bring major change was clear in the very public efforts of one of Ormond's clients, the Franciscan Peter Walsh, to persuade him that Catholics were quintessentially loyal. Ireland's Catholics were in fact no more united than they had been in the 1640s and Walsh was widely abused, but not before he had plunged into a bitter dispute with Orrery in the London press about responsibility—puritan? Catholic?—for the catastrophes of the 1640s. The land settlement was the ultimate target of any Irish realignment, so the stakes were high; but the slow re-emergence of Ireland's Catholics and the harassment of protestants of various stripes had meaning elsewhere. Not for nothing did Orrery, playwright and novelist as well as politician, in the 1660s continue his story of the wars in several wildly successful plays for the London stage.

The London audience might warm to stories of Irish guilt, but its sympathies were narrow. The publishing sensation of the early Restoration was Samuel Butler's anti-puritan *Hudibras* (1663), which directed considerably satiric energy at the root of all ills, blue-bonneted Scots Presbyterians. Still more telling as an index of English thinking is Dryden's *Annus Mirabilis* of 1666, a work that soon earned him appointment as Charles's poet laureate. Responding to radical non-conformists' claims that London's 'great fire' of that ominous year gave the mark of the apocalypse to Stuart rule, Dryden spun a brilliant counter-prophecy

of a London-centred commercial empire. London as 'this fam'd empor-
ium' was a story Irish and Scots alike had cause to rue, since English
politicians had little desire to admit them either to trade or empire.
Ireland as dependent kingdom at least lay within the framework of
England's Navigation Acts of 1660–63, but English commentators and
legislators were more interested in protectionist barriers than in expanding markets. Had the economy been as robust as Dryden fantasized,
there might have been fewer jealousies, but English profits were badly
squeezed by the dislocations and taxes occasioned by the Anglo-Dutch
war into which Charles adventured in 1664. On all sides, England's
neighbours represented unwelcome competition—the French and the
Dutch obviously, but the Irish and the Scots also competed in primary
products as their economies responded to the metropolitan market.

England's so-called 'commercial revolution' that was now beginning
to get under way proved something of a mixed blessing for the other
Stuart kingdoms. There were gains: Scottish and Irish migrants trickled
into London (though far more went to the Continent and the Americas),
and a Scottish coffee-house and a Scottish hospital opened in London in
the 1670s. Scotland's trade with Newcastle and London grew slowly,
and—though still formally excluded from the trade—Glasgow began its
epochal growth as a tobacco port. The transformation of Ireland was
more dramatic, for when newcomers took over confiscated estates they
linked Ireland more firmly to the commercial economy, above all
through cattle-rearing. But as Ireland's shipments of live cattle for the
London market soared to tens of thousands a year, so did the complaints
in parliament—in 1663, and more seriously in 1666–67—at the damage
to the income of English farmers and landowners during an agricultural
recession. England's Irish Cattle Act of 1667 banned cattle imports
despite the damage this must do to Ireland's economy, and made clear
English expectations that theirs would be the advantage within the
Stuart empire: English goods must enter others' markets unimpeded,
but theirs must not compete in England against English products. The
King had hoped to protect his subjects in Ireland, and certainly some at
Westminster urged favour for the protestant 'English' there; but the
need to placate his parliamentary tax-base in a ruinous war with the
Dutch overwhelmed whatever good intentions Charles may have had.

Recent settlers in Ireland found themselves in the characteristic colonists' plight: convinced of their strategic importance yet all too conscious of their dependence on England for mere survival, and fast learning their economic expendability.

The lesson of expendability applied to the Scots too, and their resentments quickly challenged English priorities. The hopes of commercial benefit from regal union that the Scots had intermittently entertained since 1603 dwindled as the separate British kingdoms were restored in 1660 with their barriers intact. Indeed, Scotland like Ireland faced competitive pressure from England, and workers in the Scottish coal and salt pits were pushed into serfdom in these years as masters tried to keep costs down. More explosive were the effects of war. The Dutch war, which Scottish taxes helped fund—to the tune of over £80,000 p.a. in new taxes by 1667—was scarcely fought in Scotland's interest, for the Dutch were important trading partners and Holland the home of a significant Scottish merchant community. Scotland was now being ground between empires, for it found itself excluded from the trading system of its other old trading partner, an increasingly aggressive and protectionist France, as well as of England: by the spring of 1665 Scottish trade was reported to have already 'ceased universally'. It was England's war, and the glory-seekers around the King found support among London merchants who hoped to displace Dutch competitors, but no Scottish commercial interests shared their enthusiasm. Furthermore, war against a leading protestant power signalled the erosion of that protestant cause which had edged the two British nations together long ago in the 1550s, and Dutch efforts to exploit Covenanters' unease at this may have contributed to the Pentland Rising in 1666. Once Anglo-Dutch peace was made in 1667, a chastened king showed some sympathy for Scots' complaints that, during the first Anglo-Dutch war of 1652–54, union had at least given them access to England's oceanic trades, from which disunion and the renewed Navigation Acts now once again debarred them. Sir Thomas Clifford, a supporter of reform and soon to become England's lord treasurer, dismissed English fears of competition with a lesson in political economy as revealing in its assumptions about nascent economic imperialism as about the Scots: 'Manufactures they have few, because their people run most in clans, and the rest are slaves... Scotland is our Indies, as [the French minister] Colbert calls England the King of France's Indies.' It should be noted that English economic attitudes to Ireland were just as narrowly self-serving: when lord lieutenant in 1674 the Earl of Essex confided that Ireland must be managed 'as a plantation (for in reality it is little other)'.

The disruptions of foreign wars fought by what was a multiple kingdom rather than a tightly integrated empire could not be limited to the economy. For a moment after 1667, political union between England and Scotland seemed once again a possibility. When Scottish shipowners trading with the Dutch had sought compensation through regular Scottish channels for wartime losses, the Scottish admiralty court listened to their pleas for reprisals against the English: Charles suddenly faced the alarming prospect of his kingdoms in conflict. Accordingly, he nominated union commissioners from both nations, but he faced potent opposition. Scots were insulted by the proposal to allot them a mere thirty seats—the 1650s allocation—in a British parliament, and Lauderdale, determined to retain his hard-earned power-base, did nothing to quell their anxieties about sovereignty and identity. Scotland's politic Lord Advocate, Sir George McKenzie, urged the advantage the crown possessed in being able to play off the parliaments against each other in competitive displays of loyalty. Opposition came too from English bishops appalled at the prospect of closer proximity to Scotland's Presbyterians. As they pushed for further restraints on English dissenters in what they saw as a turbulent time, the bishops began to create new alignments. In his satire *The Loyal Scot* from 1669–70, the MP and poet Andrew Marvell savaged the bishops, and found in clerical tyranny an experience that English and Scots shared. Little of such cross-border sympathy had been heard since the early 1640s.

The casualties of the Dutch war included not just domestic good feelings but Clarendon, whose fall in 1667 involved as well the assumption that old ways in government could be maintained. What ways should be followed next was more than usually unclear, since the factionalism of the court was compounded as Charles decided to add a strategic dimension to his habitual deviousness. In face of Louis XIV's growing religiosity and aggression, much English opinion waxed as anti-French as it had been anti-Spanish a century earlier. Charles therefore needed to temper for public consumption his own pro-French leanings. But he also felt bound to restore the royal honour after the disasters of the Dutch war, not least since many of his anxious English subjects now hankered after the myth of Cromwellian glory. Action abroad seemed the answer, though parliament would never fund the French alliance to which he leaned for familial and, increasingly, ideological reasons. Thus began one of the most complicated episodes in seventeenth-century history, the so-called 'Cabal' period (named after the initials of Charles's mismatched ministers) which endured until another upheaval in 1673. Hedging his bets diplomatically, the King allied in 1668 with the Dutch and Swedes in a Triple Alliance against France, and loosened the reins on protestant dissent. But he did not warm to this northern embrace, and in 1670 his ministers signed the Anglo-French Treaty of Dover committing to a joint attack on those republican tradesmen of the Netherlands and secretly promising the King would at some point declare his own Roman Catholicism. To ensure funding for the war he sought, Charles bid for Anglican support by signing the draconian second Conventicle Act (1670), further outlawing dissenting worship. But, since Scotland's Pentland Rising had shown the dangers of fighting protestants abroad while repressing them at home, in 1672 the King issued a second Declaration of Indulgence, offering licensed toleration to peaceable dissenters. Such convolutions were too many for Westminster, and in 1673 parliament retorted by passing a Test Act requiring membership of the Church of England for full participation in English public life. When Charles's brother James, the Duke of York, then declared his own Catholicism, he created problems for the present as well as the future. He was that rarity, an adult heir to the throne who was almost as old as the king; unlike Charles, he was also stubborn, conscientious, and not very astute.

Convolutions at Whitehall necessarily implicated the other Stuart capitals. In Ireland, the stately Ormond—vulnerable in the protestant moment of the Triple Alliance to Orrery's charges of luke-warmness and corruption—did not long outlast his ally Clarendon. The aftermath showed how closely alignments abroad and among the three kingdoms were becoming yoked. As befitted that brief Triple-Alliance moment, Ormond's immediate successor was the dour Presbyterian, Robartes. In

1670, the new French alliance saw the appointment of Lord Berkeley as lord lieutenant. A client of the Duke of York and himself married to a Catholic, Berkeley extended favour and local office to selected Irish Catholics, while Catholic clergy operated openly. The hopes he generated in some Irish Catholic circles were profound, and in 1672 Richard Talbot, an army officer and favourite of the Duke of York, took to Whitehall a petition challenging the land settlement of 1662. Ormond's kinsman, the Franciscan Peter Walsh, returned to the fray too, and in 1673 sent a slew of pamphlets to the London press renewing his challenge to the political claims of the papacy and asserting the peaceful obedience of English and Irish Catholics save for a few of the 'rascality or kerns'—who, he insisted, were more than matched among protestants. The misgivings these initiatives inspired were no less profound. From this moment—and in one more instance of the way the colonization of Ireland drew England towards state-building—derived the discipline that was to become known as political economy, thanks once again to William Petty's precocious quantifying enterprise. Eventually published in 1690–91 as *Political Arithmetic* and *The Political Anatomy of Ireland*, Petty's labours represented a late foray into the history of plantation, and aimed at safeguarding English Ireland through the forcible miscegenation of the English and Irish poor.

The Irish—Catholic and protestant alike—looked to a king whose priorities of course lay elsewhere. Like many others, Berkeley failed to gauge Charles's fast-changing preferences, and was recalled in 1672 after imposing sanctions on protestant dissenters—a stance ill-suited to war with the protestant Dutch. He was followed as lord lieutenant by the protestant Earl of Essex, an efficient administrator, who licensed individual dissenters and Catholics to hold local office in accord with the Declaration of Indulgence, and seemed well-suited to implement in Ireland the anxious Anglican mood that dominated Westminster after the overthrow of Indulgence. In 1673 the Westminster parliament coupled the Test Act with an attack on Talbot, demanding the maintenance of the Irish land settlement, the removal of Catholics from local and municipal office there, and the banishment of Catholic clergy; Essex tried to comply but he was caught up in a continuing dispute between Ormond and his followers, who urged the advantages of the Irish army, and Orrery, who touted a militia that others suspected of Cromwellian sympathies. The complaints found their way back to London, feeding apprehensions about the meaning and direction of royal policy in England.

The lessons English observers learned from Scotland's troubles in the 1670s were more disturbing. During the union discussions the persecution of religious dissent had eased, as in England. Lauderdale, who had edged out all possible rivals, sought to isolate hard-line Presbyterians in 1669 by offering a limited indulgence to the peaceable—a move that allowed forty-two 'outed' ministers back into their old parishes without accepting episcopacy. In the same year, he detached himself from the Scottish bishops by pushing through Edinburgh's parliament an Act of Supremacy vesting control over the Kirk firmly in the crown: 'Never was king so absolute as you are in poor old Scotland,' Lauderdale told Charles proudly. But Lauderdale aimed to split dissent, not to indulge it, and in October 1669, even before the Supremacy Act, he began a new campaign against conventicles. Swingeing measures followed not just against conventiclers but against owners of the lands on which conventicles were held, culminating in 1670 in the so-called 'Clanking Act' making unlicensed preaching at a 'field conventicle'—one that spilled outdoors—a capital offence. That Act says as much about the crown's powers in the unicameral Scottish parliament as it does about the nobility's loathing for Covenanters.

Lauderdale was courting the English bishops, for—as Tudor deputies in Ireland had learned—an abrasive viceroy needed sure friends at Whitehall to protect his back. Accordingly, Lauderdale balanced a second royal indulgence for Scotland in 1672—under which eighty-nine more dissident clerics were restored, bringing the total number restored close to half of those first ousted—with fiercer repression of the recalcitrant, and massive fines for uncooperative landlords. And so he survived the policy reversal brought by the 1673 Test Act in England and the emergence there of a solidly Anglican administration under Lord Treasurer Danby. But the third Anglo-Dutch war, of 1672–74, increased the pressures on the Scottish regime just as the second war had. Younger nobles freer of the traumas of mid-century were by now appearing, and in 1673 the third Duke of Hamilton led some of these to block all business in the Scottish parliament as they protested against rising duties on key imports (brandy, tobacco, malt). Lauderdale found himself increasingly hemmed in, for few Scots trusted him, and landowners were outraged at being held responsible for their tenants' religious choices. In the mid 1670s he enlarged the Scottish army in order to coerce conventiclers, and his promised 20,000-strong exportable militia figured prominently in Andrew Marvell's *Growth of Popery and Arbitrary Government* (1677), England's defining polemic of these years. Lauderdale's practices grew uglier in 1678 with the dispatch of the 'Highland Host'—an 8,000-strong militia largely from the anti-Presbyterian north—to coerce the Presbyterian strongholds of the south-west.

The angry new politics formed in these continental, archipelagic, and national realignments find an epitome in the career of the Earl of Shaftesbury—John Locke's patron, leading crown servant of the early 1670s and plotter and fugitive a decade later. In a famous parliamentary speech of 1673, Shaftesbury urged the destruction of the Netherlands as enemy to England's trade and to monarchy; in an equally famous speech of 1679, he echoed Marvell: not only were popery and arbitrary government growing, but they were subsumed in French designs at home and abroad. The grounds for that judgement lay in the expansion of French power, commercial as well as military. They lay as well in the contradictory policies of a king who for a quieter life at home had allied with the Anglican and anti-French Lord Treasurer Danby—spokesman for many in parliament—while seconding Scottish troops to French service and retaining on foot for his own undisclosed purposes the English troops which parliament voted to fund in 1678 for a war against France, though it was a war that Charles refused to declare. Such dangerous designs were made possible by Danby's campaign of parliamentary bribery—a campaign that had an Irish dimension in his efforts to conceal the corruption of the Irish finances in the 1670s under the Earl of Ranelagh. Shielded from parliamentary investigation by the sizeable private payoffs he sent to the King, Ranelagh lined his own pockets and systematically starved, to the point of its near-collapse in 1676, the Irish army that 'the protestant interest' deemed vital.

Crisis broke in late 1678; it fed on the mutual alertness of the three kingdoms, but it drew most of all on English apprehensions. Not for nothing did Shaftesbury send forty copies of his great 1679 speech to Edinburgh the day he delivered it; not for nothing did Sir John Temple's *Irish Rebellion* of 1646 run through two new editions in 1679 in London but none in Dublin. The English party labels, 'Whig' and 'Tory', that denominated alignments for the best part of two centuries appeared in partisan form during this crisis. The one a Scottish Covenanting rebel and the other an Irish Catholic bandit, the labels claimed the un-Englishness of partisanship, but they originated in the partisan drive to identify the local foe with disreputable Scottish or Irish extremes. Thus, the Whig dramatist Thomas Shadwell worked to tar English loyalists in his vicious stage satire of Irish Catholicism, *The Lancashire Witches* (1681), earning a silencing from which he only recovered with the 1688 Revolution. Contrariwise, Lauderdale's chaplain had Covenanters' scaffold speeches printed in London to expose the extremism of Covenanters and Whigs alike and (aiming at Ulster Presbyterians too) their conjoint 'opposition to our Episcopal Communions within the British Isles'. A Tory print of 1680, *The Committee, or, Popery in Masquerade*, made the Scottish smear explicit with its depiction of the English Whigs as 'a covenanting people'.

'Masquerade' reached deeply into the culture of these years as well as into court politics, where the King masked his intentions and his ministers and mistresses veiled their contempt for each other and perhaps for the King too, and he for them. The great 'Popish Plot' scare that broke in late 1678, dominating politics and consuming lives for the next five years, seems the biggest masquerade of all. Many contemporaries claimed as much, and partisans manufactured evidence, suborned witnesses, and fabricated counter-plots in order to destroy their enemies. The cynicism of the chief English antagonists, Charles himself and Shaftesbury, is undeniable. Equally undeniable is the widespread belief in an apocalyptic struggle. Chronicles of the martyrdoms of Mary Tudor's reign were reinvigorated by Temple's stories of the killings in Ireland in the winter of 1641–42 and as well by allegations that London's great fire of 1666 had been lit by Catholics. But the sensational details of the plots that Titus Oates and his kind manufactured gained their traction not only from fantasies of Jesuitical or Covenanter assassination schemes and traitorous ties to the rising power of France or to Holland. There was also the problem of England's immediate future. In 1673, when the Test Act 'outed' his Catholicism, many found James Duke of York troubling enough as heir to the throne; by 1678, after several years of royal pretences about the size, location, and purpose of royal armies, after the brutalities of the Highland Host, and now with Oates's smears, many found him altogether frightening. The only reassurances lay in the future. James lacked a male heir, his two daughters by his first marriage were protestant, and King Charles was in 1677 persuaded to lessen the anti-French storm by agreeing to the marriage of Mary, James's elder daughter, to the Dutch leader, William of Orange. The next generation might be safe.

The crisis that convulsed England was not just about James. Anger at episcopal repression owed little to him; and while James's secretary was found to have had dealings with French Jesuits—thus substantiating Oates's claims—a higher-profile casualty was Lord Treasurer Danby, impeached for heading an anti-French and aggressively Anglican administration while corruptly furthering Charles's quest for aid from France. But what gave the crisis its staying-power—in three feverish parliaments, in constituencies across the country, in 'pope-burning' bonfires in London's streets—was the drive to exclude James from the succession to the throne. For James, Exclusion was of course unacceptable; ultimately it was for Charles too, and in 1679 he sent his brother first to Brussels and then to Scotland to ride out the storm. James's stay in Scotland, until 1682, highlighted the weaknesses of Exclusion, and as well the difficulty of trying to regulate a shared monarchy within the framework of one kingdom. By going to Scotland, James signalled his intention of disregarding or resisting any success the Exclusionists might have in England. And fearful though English protestants were of a Catholic king, most feared another war even more. To Church Tories, looking back with horror on the killing of a pious king in 1649, non-resistance was as fundamental as lineal descent. There were many others who, when they saw Exclusionists' demonstrations and pamphleteering, remembered the London mob of 1641 and the destruction that followed. The Tories' angry cry, '41 is come again', gave the opportunist Stuart brothers the means not just to rescue but to expand royal power. For it gained the crown eager partisan allies within the traditional elite for a campaign of persecution and proscription.

James's stay in Scotland threatened war because it reminded those Scots who mattered just how much they appreciated Edinburgh as once again a scene for royalty and patronage. Something of an aristocratic reaction had been building, not just against Lauderdale's monopolization of power but perhaps too against the governmental mood apparent in the establishment in 1672 of the justiciary court, a central and nonhereditary criminal tribunal whose members emulated the English assize judges by periodically taking their non-feudal justice on circuit into the localities. But noble discontent evaporated quickly in 1679 when radical Covenanters assassinated that other prime persecutor, Archbishop Sharp; the noble-led military assaults on conventicles that followed provoked a brief Covenanter rising south of Glasgow that was destroyed at Bothwell Brig. The twentieth-century memorial at the bridge commemorates the rebels' stand for 'civil and religious liberty', but if that was the Covenanters' cause the nobles were unimpressed. The Edinburgh parliament promptly granted the King a massive supply of £150,000, and its members raised scant protest during the 'Killing Time' that ensued. Instead, as low-level guerilla warfare flared intermittently in the southwest, they rallied to York as the rising sun. In 1681, forced to choose between defence of the dynasty and of protestantism, the noble constitutionalist Hamilton chose the former, and the Scottish parliament followed him in asserting the sacrosanctity of the royal succession, Scotland's succession. An English effort to exclude James must bring another Anglo-Scottish war. But Charles's control over the meeting of his English parliaments, and the appearance of sizeable blocs of Tory supporters in country, parliament, even London itself by 1681, ensured that that danger would not have to be faced.

The crown's position strengthened in Charles's last years. Rising customs revenues along with the avoidance of war after 1674 enabled the crown at last to pay salaries and even to fund some improvements. The grand new palace that the King began at Winchester, away from London's turbulence, decayed after his death, but he did in the late 1670s undertake significant rebuilding of Windsor Castle and, in Edinburgh, of Holyrood Palace. At Windsor, frescoes celebrated the three kingdoms' tributes, and that of long-lost France, to the imperial monarch, underscoring the role of the multiple kingdom in generating a claim to royal—and surely English—grandeur. At Holyrood, James's presence prompted a lavish new interior in the early 1680s, with portraits of Scotland's legendary line of 110 kings whose monotonously Stuart features made an unmistakable point about lineal succession. And it was around 1682 that Charles prodded Dryden to write the grand celebration of British kingship that was to emerge in very different circumstances as the opera *King Arthur*.

Such royal confidence rested on state forms as well as cultural assertiveness. Throughout its dominions, the Restoration monarchy recognized the role of force—not enough to justify Whig fears perhaps, but enough to suggest these were not wholly irrational. Rising Irish customs revenues, especially after the 1674 famine, enabled Charles by the end of the decade to sidestep some of those fears by beginning what was to become a long-term practice of placing a good part of the English army on the Irish establishment, in effect condemning Irish consumers and tax-payers to fund a state that was for most of them alien. The soldiers were not just for show. At Oxford, Charles famously deployed troops to secure his 1681 parliament. In the Scottish Highlands, Lauderdale had extended the crown's authority in traditional ways, reinforcing the local power of favoured nobles at the expense of others by giving them and their followers commissions in his vaunted militia. But when trouble flared in Scotland in 1678–79, Charles—like his father forty years earlier—thought supranationally; unlike his father, he had troops ready in Ulster and on England's northern borders in case Scottish forces proved insufficient, and at Bothwell Brig that English aid was needed. Ireland provides another register of the relation of power and force. Improved royal finances and a sense of danger at last allowed Ormond, that old if ineffective general, to embark on some serious reforms in his final stint as Ireland's chief governor. Not only did he put the Irish army, at about 7,500-strong the largest Stuart standing force, on an organized regimental footing and house it in barracks as opposed to the usual miserable quartering in private premises; he also built the impressive Kilmainham military hospital in Dublin. And while Charles himself did not take the French threat seriously, Ormond clearly did, for the magnificent if misnamed Charles Fort at Kinsale on the south-western coast dates to his last years in office. But the Kinsale fort was to fall quickly in the

Williamite wars. Apparently its designers had more confidence in Ireland's domestic peace than did Sir Josias Bodley when he designed coastal fortifications in James I's reign, for they chose a site indefensible on the landward side.

Like any lover of the quiet life, Charles II knew that domestic harmony offered more security than fortifications. And the trade increase that yielded him enhanced customs revenues seemed now to promise greater harmony. Even in Scotland, whose trade still centred on its traditional markets in northern Europe, there were signs of reorientation. A statute Lauderdale pushed through the Scottish parliament in 1672 ended the monopoly of the ancient royal burghs on international trade, particularly in the new commodities; and though Scotland was formally excluded by England's Navigation Act there were many interlopers in the colonial trades: in the 1670s Glasgow was already a major tobacco port. The prominence of brandy and tobacco in the nobles' parliamentary protest in 1673 points to the scale of cultural change; the economic change is clear in the customs records of the 1690s, which show 40% of Scottish receipts deriving from cattle exports to England. London, fast becoming Europe's biggest city, even provided models of fashion—a Scottish noblewoman knew enough in 1673 about commercial developments to instruct her husband in London to bring home new styles from the 'Indian shops' there. In Scotland's Western Isles, one of the Macleans lamented that his chief found too much comfort in coffee to exploit the fall in 1685 of the clan's nemesis, Argyll. Clan chiefs and clan gentry with money to make from cattle, timber, and fish, and new goods to buy, had an incentive to treat their followers and their lands as an economic rather than a military resource. Tenants may not have appreciated the new pressure, but peace spread.

The force of 'civility' was felt still more in Ireland, whose population almost doubled in the forty years after 1649. In the countryside, the later seventeenth century saw the peasantry introduced more thoroughly to a money economy and the English language, though it was in a handful of larger towns, and above all Dublin, that change was most visible. England played some part in shaping that change, not least since continuing English immigration—if at a slackening rate as England's own economic and demographic balance shifted and as the New World became more attractive—helped the capital's population to double in size during the Restoration, to nearly 50,000 by 1685. Dublin became a largely protestant city with a Catholic hinterland, the hub of a region whose new landowning elite needed supplies and capital in order to exploit their estates and fashionable commodities to differentiate themselves from their Irish neighbours. Dublin's expansion was driven by English policy too, and especially by the 1671 Navigation Act's insistence that colonial goods enter Ireland from England; that insistence benefited Dublin at the expense of Ireland's south-western ports, even as it pushed prices up. The likely social consequences of new wealth and cosmopolitan tastes were of course unclear: a court society, with Dublin Castle (or, in Scotland, Edinburgh's Holyrood Palace during James Duke of York's residence) as a little Versailles? Or perhaps a different order was signalled by the expanding literacy rates, the markets for print imports from England and Europe, the rise of something like civil society in Dublin and even in the more conservative Edinburgh: Dublin's Smock Alley Theatre and in 1683 the Dublin Philosophical Society, Edinburgh with its short-lived coffee-house in 1673 and in 1680 the Advocates' Library.

But in that protectionist world, trade and power were increasingly hard to disentangle, and power lay increasingly with England. Scots grew anxious as their trade shifted southwards. When James Duke of York established a Scottish Committee for Trade in 1681 it reported that the only ways for Scotland to thrive were either by greater access to English trade or by establishing her own colonies abroad. English interests of course sought to cement English dominance by statute, and tariffs on Scottish salt and live cattle handicapped the major Scottish exports; but they aimed less at the Scots than at the more commercialized Irish economy. There, their heavy-handed attempts to eliminate competition could have unforeseen consequences. Shut out of England's market for live cattle, Ireland—and Cork in particular—quickly developed a lucrative trade in salted, or 'barreled', beef for French as well as English long-distance voyages. Cork, whose population tripled in the later seventeenth century, became one of Europe's major Atlantic ports; other south-western Irish ports maintained a varied trade with France and Spain. As England discouraged Ireland's woollen exports, market-oriented British settlers in Ulster were by the early 1680s developing the flax production and importing the skilled weavers from Flanders that were to make possible the Irish linen industry. With his own textile works faltering, Richard Lawrence in *The Interest of Ireland* (1682) lamented the burdens English protectionism placed on an Irish economy that lacked its own self-sustaining infrastructure.

It was not only in the economy that England's weight was felt. The eyes of Ulster Presbyterians were on their kinsmen across the North Channel as the Scottish government oppressed the south-western Covenanters. Elsewhere in Ireland, Westminster's protectionism eroded assumptions that the 'English interest' was the only identification that mattered. Many in that interest had come to share Lawrence's uncertainty about settler identity, but old loyalties quickly re-emerged once England's upheavals threatened to spread. Despite the warnings of Oates and Shaftesbury, Ireland stayed quiet in the Exclusion Crisis, for protestants knew how much they had to lose by making trouble while Catholics knew how much they had to gain by waiting peacefully for the Catholic James to become king. Hard work too played its part in the peace: Ormond diligently headed off English parliamentary demands to bar Catholics from the towns by pointing to the economic dangers; quieted local protestant fears in 1678 by banishing Roman Catholic bishops, Jesuits, and friars; and then stilled the resentments of the Old English leaders through long card parties. But he could not establish a quarantine: though himself sceptical of the Plot, he was unable to protect the Roman Catholic archbishop of Armagh, Oliver Plunkett, from Shaftesbury's need for victims. Nor could he withstand Whitehall's pressure to extend to Ireland after 1681 the far-reaching purge of Whig sympathizers on which the crown and its Tory supporters embarked in England. All too aware of the shallowness of the governing protestant interest in Ireland, Ormond was reluctant to purge it of old Cromwellians, and as a result his credit at Whitehall began to wane. Although he held on to office until Charles's death in early 1685, army posts were by then going to the Catholic Richard Talbot's friends, supporters of James.

Scotland had begun its own noble-led march towards absolutism, if not to Catholicism, long before the Plot broke, but James's presence in 1679–82 accelerated it. The Scottish parliament of 1681, looking nervously at a turbulent England, worked hard to reinforce the crown fiscally and politically, not least against a Presbyterian opposition that assumed horrifying dimensions with the appearance in 1680 of a truly apocalyptic rebel fringe, the Cameronians. In addition to an Act branding as treasonous any attempt to alter the succession and another bolstering the excise, parliament passed an unprecedented statute vesting control of all legal processes in the king. Charles's government quickly publicized in the London *Gazette* for English contemplation these examples of virtue. But the Scottish parliament learned from England too, and passed a Test Act against divine-right Presbyterians and Whigs. Loosely worded, the required oath soon consigned numbers to summary execution, but its chief victim was not some Cameronian weaver but the 9th Earl of Argyll, whose own royalism had retrieved from the wreck of his father's execution most of the Campbell estates, but not the lineage's reputation. The Campbells' long history as the Stewart crown's hammer in the Highlands had earned them widespread loathing, and this the mid-century Covenanting revolution had intensified. Lesser Highland chiefs victimized by Argyll's judiciary powers and devastated by the Covenanting marquess's exaction of political fines watched for a chance to bring down their oppressor; the ninth earl's own attempts to restore the family fortunes only exacerbated resentments as he waged a semi-formal war against the Macleans to call in their debts. When at the end of 1681 he tried to modify the oath required of him under the Test Act, James and the Scottish council convicted him of treason, and in so doing took a first step to binding the appreciative smaller clans to what was to become the Jacobite cause.[1] The nobles whom James left to govern in Edinburgh when he returned south in 1682 faced few obstacles as they proceeded to expand Stuart power and carve up the fugitive Argyll's lands. Although the greatest Scottish lawyer, Lord President Stair, joined Argyll in exile, Lord Treasurer Queensberry's fiscal devices replenished the crown's coffers, while Lord Advocate McKenzie published *Jus Regium* (1684), one of the greatest of all defences of absolute and hereditary monarchy.

The conservative political and clerical elites were rallying not just to the Stuart crown but to the established Church. Tory Anglicans and Scottish episcopalians harried dissenters, while Tory grand juries in

---

[1] Named after *Jacobus*, the Latin for James.

England and partisans of the Church of Ireland sent fervid loyal addresses to the King, particularly after the government in 1683 energetically exploited the Anglo-Scottish and half-baked Rye House Plot to assassinate the royal brothers outside London. England remained of course the centre of the Stuart calculus, and Charles condescendingly discouraged further Irish addresses, deeming those from Dublin and Cork too far 'out of the road' to be of much worth as propaganda; nevertheless, the coordination of the kingdoms in that crown-and-church alliance is unmistakable. And after Charles's death in February 1685 the alliance held firm. The Catholic James II of England and Ireland—James VII of Scotland—insisted in his first speech to his English council on his respect for the laws and the established Anglican Church. He appointed as lord treasurer in England the Earl of Rochester, one of his staunchly Anglican brothers-in-law by his first wife, and elicited Anglican tributes to his moderate beginning. In the first 1685 session of James's English parliament, Tories could reassure themselves that they had a king if not quite after their own heart then at least one whose political heart was set right. But though he gestured towards that Anglican interest by granting initial political authority in Ireland to protestant lords justices and still more by then sending over as lord lieutenant his other brother-in-law, the firmly Anglican second Earl of Clarendon, he gave oversight of the Irish army to Richard Talbot, whom he soon made Earl of Tyrconnell; Clarendon was not alone in expressing concern. Cracks in the Church-and-King alliance appeared too in Scotland, where James's favourites, the Drummond brothers, earls of Perth and Melfort, quickly converted to Catholicism and used the leverage they gained to diminish and then drive out Queensberry. Loyalist Scottish nobles began to wonder whether repression of dissenters was quite so desirable when directed by Catholics.

Repression was certainly not James's intended approach in his other, less troubled, kingdoms. A devout Catholic and authoritarian by temperament—he systematically suppressed the colonial legislatures of English America—the King imagined that in England his Tory supporters would at his prompting allow Catholics to worship publicly. Once the emptiness of protestant fears was exposed, conversions among the ill-taught people would, he assumed, follow too fast for his successor on the throne to reverse them. The enthusiasm of the protestant majorities in the Scottish and English parliaments that opened his reign did nothing to disabuse him: in Edinburgh he was granted an annual revenue of £60,000 p.a., and in England £1,200,000 p.a. But beyond assuming that in Ireland the religious commitments of the 'protestant interest' were insincere, he had clearly not considered the implications of admitting a blusterer like Tyrconnell to influence over the army there.

Any gradualism in the King's policies was quickly overwhelmed by rebellions in Scotland and England in the summer of 1685. That they happened at all was perhaps surprising, for the English and Scottish exiles in the Low Countries were a mismatched crew. They ranged from anti-absolutist English (like John Locke) and Scottish (like Sir Patrick Hume of Polwarth, one of Hamilton's supporters in the 1670s), to Charles's illegitimate son the Duke of Monmouth, protestant figurehead for most of the Whigs in the Exclusion Crisis, and to Argyll, as strong a monarchist legitimist as he was a Presbyterian. Determined to forestall a Catholic consolidation of power and to regain his own, Argyll prepared to raise his Highland territories; only with difficulty did Polwarth bring him to coordinate with Monmouth. His ill-planned invasion came to a predictable and rapid end on the scaffold, for harassment since 1681 meant that few even of his tenants rallied to him. Monmouth's descent on south-western England was barely more effective, except in multiplying the executions as Lord Chief Justice Jeffreys mopped up the west with the hangman's rope. Yet, for all their futility, the rebellions acknowledged British identifications: at Polwarth's urging, Argyll proclaimed his concern for British liberties, and it was in solidarity with Argyll that Monmouth—who had been living contentedly in exile—determined to embark on what he suspected to be a doomed enterprise.

The rebellions of 1685 at first strengthened but then broke the political alliances Charles had built in his last years. Tories at Westminster alarmed by Monmouth quickly increased James's parliamentary revenues to a massive £2million p.a., and thus freed him from dependence on parliament for the future. But in Ireland Tyrconnell stressed the poor performance of the Somerset militia against Monmouth and urged on James the importance of a reliable regular army. To the dismay of protestants in all three kingdoms, he then began to disarm the Irish militia and to replace protestants in the army with Catholics; in Scotland, the Catholic Earl of Dumbarton went about the same purgative business. The King's interpretation of the rebellions gave these beginnings an ominous application to England: by overthrowing traitors, James insisted, God had approved his regime and endorsed a more forward policy. Citing that divine mandate, in November 1685 he demanded Westminster's retroactive approval of a hundred Catholic officers whom he had dispensed from the provisions of the Test Act so they could fight against Monmouth. His timing was disastrous, since in October Louis XIV capped years of military harassment of French protestants by revoking the Edict of Nantes that had guaranteed them limited toleration. With Huguenot refugees arriving as living testimonials of the meaning of popery and absolutism, fears that papists would gain access to arms in all three Stuart kingdoms preoccupied the Tories at Westminster. James was forced to prorogue—suspend—parliament. He then watched furiously in the New Year as Edinburgh erupted in rioting after the Drummonds declared their Catholicism. Demanding that rioters be interrogated under torture, the King replaced Queensberry as governor of Edinburgh Castle with the Catholic Duke of Gordon.

The developing crisis certainly had some roots in personality: James, unlike his brother, would not learn from his mistakes. But similar crises developed in all three kingdoms, suggesting origins that lay in an imperial as well as an imperious outlook. Rebuffed by the Edinburgh parliament in April 1686 when he tried to secure an Act for the toleration of the few thousand Scottish Catholics—even though he sweetened the bid with a royal offer of free trade with England—James turned to his prerogative to remodel town corporations, and thus electorates, in hopes of securing a tractable parliament by other means. Rebuffed by the Tories in the Westminster parliament when he tried to enlarge the political role of English Catholics, James in the summer of 1686 turned to the law courts for ratification of his power to dispense with the laws, and duly secured it in a test-case (*Godden vs. Hales*) brought with governmental collusion. Ireland was of course in a separate category, since the (protestant) political elite he had inherited there constituted the minority interest; but in his initial use of protestant agents he showed the same intention of using the existing establishment to undermine itself. Lord

Lieutenant Clarendon followed orders, appointing Catholic judges to the Dublin courts and paying salaries to Catholic bishops. But in Ireland, the English crown had never been able to control the agenda, and Tyrconnell rapidly subverted Clarendon by telling tales at court. By September, Tyrconnell had ensured that two-thirds of the soldiers and nearly half the officers in the Irish army were Catholics.

In England as in Scotland the King hoped to advance the Catholic cause by orderly, if accelerating, means. When he had only protestant heirs, and when the Catholic population of those kingdoms constituted a tiny minority, he had few other options. Conversions among the court nobilities remained limited and decorous affairs, and the King's mistress was a protestant. But Tyrconnell's sense of Ireland's future in the event of a protestant succession to the crown was almost certainly more daring than the King's. And in October 1686 Tyrconnell's Catholicized army drew blood as it dispersed protestant Dublin's observance of the anniversary of the outbreak of the 1641 Rising.

CHAPTER 11
A BRITISH ISLES? 1687–1707

For longer than anybody alive could remember, England's footprint had been growing across its region. Most of England's inhabitants probably had not noticed, but in the years following 1687 few in any of the Stuart kingdoms could overlook the accelerating disturbances that accompanied the extension of English power and influence. Ireland dramatically challenged its uneasy subordination, only to face pressures from across the Irish Sea almost as fierce as those that had followed 1649. Scotland was plunged by revolution into a period of ideological re-evaluation more wrenching than anything taking place in England, and found itself rethinking, painfully, the entire 'British' premise. England had to confront these retorts even as the three kingdoms entered the unprecedentedly expensive war with France that was the corollary of revolution—a war whose stresses of state-building were made all the more painful by devastating harvest failures. The outcome was a new synthesis: one that offered at best a working arrangement rather than a solution for the problems of relationship and identity that beset such awkward neighbours. A British state emerged that in its geopolitical—if not constitutional—configuration would have gladdened the heart of James VI and I; and though Ireland continued for another century a distinct kingdom, it was categorically now subject to British imperatives. Geographers found they could more easily replace such awkward locutions as 'Britannia and Hibernia' with 'the British Isles', while historians and natural historians helped inquiring readers to enliven the maps.

In hindsight, the upheavals of the late seventeenth century seem the all-too-predictable death-throes of a multiple kingdom in an age of religious conflict. Co-existence under a shared crown could never be easy when most inhabitants of one kingdom were alienated Roman Catholics, while the most vociferous strand in another consisted of anxious Presbyterians, and in the third Anglicans whose self-consciousness had grown in the previous generation. But religious difference was not the only ailment of that multi-bodied polity. The individual kingdoms had separate spheres of activity; divergence might be overlooked in peacetime, but the war against Louis XIV's France was the early-modern equivalent of total war, and it strained ancient alignments. Complicating such tensions was the new reality of political economy, symbolized by the foundation of England's Board of Trade in 1696. Commerce and empire formed a calculus rarely imagined in 1603 when Tyrone submitted to Elizabeth's dead hand and when James imposed his royal body on England and Ireland as well as Scotland. The separate kingdoms now discovered more forcibly what they had always known, that their individual interests were distinct.

But the end of the multiple kingdom was no more anticipated than that of the House of Stuart itself. Charles II's late posture—deferential alignment with Louis XIV abroad and belligerent Anglicanism at home—would surely have kept his kingdoms quiet indefinitely. His alliance with English Tories and Scottish nobles looked strong enough in 1685 to bear an enhanced executive power that might yet become a novel kind of absolutism, for the crown's remodelling of boroughs and their electorates in all three kingdoms gave promise of parliamentary docility in fiscal as well as religious matters. But the intensity of James II's religious commitment took most of his British supporters by surprise. The speed with which James's position crumbled underscores the centrality of religion in English and Scottish understandings of the kingdoms that were Restored in 1660: the crown may have been the most visible but it was not the sole focus of celebration.

James's position survived a little longer in Ireland, and it did so because there, for once, the English crown served majority interests. Although Irish Catholics were at last to find that the King's purposes were not theirs, there were moments when his Catholicism made it seem otherwise. And so Tyrconnell played on the King's impatience with the militias to hasten the creation of a Catholic army in Ireland; he manipulated James's Catholic sensitivities to put an end to Clarendon's lieutenancy in 1686; and he extracted from him in the summer of 1687 extraordinary powers to issue new charters to towns, and thus to control the composition of future parliaments. Since Tyrconnell hoped, in a way that James surely did not, to re-establish Old English fortunes—he had little concern for 'the O's and the Mac's', as he called the Old Irish—by drastically modifying the Restoration land settlement, a complaisant parliament was essential. In the longer term, he surely aimed at total reversal of that settlement. The emergence of France as superpower gave Tyrconnell's rush to reversal a certain rationality, for in France he probably saw the possibility of a protector for Catholic Ireland in case James's protestant daughters should succeed him on England's throne.

Tyrconnell's Ireland formed an unnerving backdrop for James's practices closer to home. Early in 1687 the King broke England's unspoken compact of 1660 and challenged the Church interest directly. Dismissing his Anglican brothers-in-law, Clarendon and Rochester, from the Irish lieutenancy and the English lord treasurership, he committed himself instead to Tyrconnell and the court convert, the Earl of Sunderland, at home. Finding little support among the English and Scottish elites for his drive to repeal the anti-Catholic legislation and enact statutory toleration, James that spring issued Declarations of Indulgence in all his kingdoms, using his royal prerogative to suspend the laws against Catholics and dissenters altogether; he further jarred nerves in Scotland by using there the language of several recent Scottish statutes about kings' 'absolute power'. Although in the Declarations he trumpeted toleration, and patronized any dissenters who would collaborate with him, few could ignore his Catholic objectives. Nor could they miss his absolutist methods—as when, in his drive to remodel the universities that trained the English clergy, he ejected the fellows of Magdalen College Oxford from what were legally property rights in their fellowships. To the dismay of his moderate supporters, James dissolved his English parliament in the summer of 1687, and late in the year, with his wife unexpectedly pregnant—a sure sign of God's favour and a new future, he concluded—he increased the political pressure.

England's political elite was goaded past the point of alienation by James's domestic campaign. From late 1687 he repeatedly purged parliamentary boroughs to secure majorities of non-Anglicans, whether collaborating dissenters or Roman Catholics; he tendered the so-called 'Three Questions' to local office-holders over the winter, testing their willingness to work for toleration in a new parliament, and dismissed the most recalcitrant; and he appointed his Jesuit confessor, Father Edward Petre, to the privy council in November. James's reissue of his English Declaration of Indulgence in the spring of 1688, and his command to the bishops to secure its endorsement from the pulpits, was surely sufficient to spark a political crisis. James's success in expanding his armies, in bringing the Roman Catholic element in the English officer corps up to 25%, and in placing not just the Irish but the Scottish armies under Catholic command, gave that crisis a more urgent character.

But crisis nowhere meant resistance. In Ireland, the beleaguered protestants fractured; Ulster Presbyterians seized on Tyrconnell's proffered toleration to break the Church of Ireland's monopoly, though more isolated protestants, fearing another popish massacre, began a flight back to England or on to America that by the end of 1688 became a flood. In Scotland, scattered mob violence against known Catholics showed no sign of becoming more organized, for the Cameronian remnant reminded episcopalian nobles how much they had to lose; anyway, Scots had developed a habit of watching England. But England was in no condition to give a lead. The bishops' opposition to James's command that they disseminate the Indulgence earned for some of them trial for seditious libel; their acquittal sparked widespread celebrations, but nothing more threatening from a nation with painful memories of civil war. Instead, 'the immortal seven'—Whig notables plus two Tories to make a case for bipartisanship—wrote in June to William of Orange in the Netherlands, inviting him to preserve the constitution and his wife's right to succeed her father against the claim of James's new-born son, whom they declared 'suppositious'.

The European environment proved more dynamic in the summer of 1688 than James's kingdoms. As the Immortals knew, William was desperate for help in his war against an expansionist France that threatened the very existence of the Netherlands. And France's increasing resort to economic warfare meant that he was now able to call on the financial backing of the normally risk-averse merchant princes of Amsterdam. When Louis XIV turned to pursue territorial gains along the Rhine, the Dutch leader could risk leaving the Netherlands exposed as he shipped 20,000 of his own troops to England and replaced them in the Dutch defensive lines with hired contract soldiers. He took an even greater risk in confronting a royal father-in-law who had 40,000 soldiers of his own, though these were less well-equipped and were scattered across the three kingdoms. The Immortals had assured him of widespread support in England, but though a few thousand did eventually join him after he landed in the south-west on November 5 and others rallied to his sister-in-law Anne when she fled to dissident nobles in the Midlands, the more characteristic English response was quiescence, a waiting on events. From the possible consequences of this, English and Dutch alike were rescued by James's own providentialism. Not for the last time this personally brave man, a tried and tested soldier, experienced nervous collapse when God seemed to cross his purposes. To the despair of his advisors, James fled, leaving his kingdoms to decide what to do next. It was the foreigner, William, who once again set the agenda.

The Church-and-crown focus of so much of Restoration ideology meant that what might have been a revolutionary assembly, England's Convention Parliament that William assisted into being after James's departure, was very much in need of guidance. Whigs urged James's breach of his coronation oath as well as the laws, and the nation's duty to provide anew for itself—in this case, by offering the crown to William, but also by purging government of Tories. The Tories, strong in the Church and in the Lords, claimed to be the party of order, and they clung to the divinity of authority and lineal descent; while they conceded that by fleeing James had abdicated, their preferred solution was some form of regency. The depth of the partisan divisions dictated compromise. The Tories knew they needed government of some kind, and when William insisted on the crown or nothing their obstructionism crumbled: William and Mary as joint sovereigns was the only way to stop James coming home again. Nevertheless, the imprecision of the Declaration of Rights that the Convention proffered along with the crown in February 1689—its Whiggish talk of a 'vacant' throne offset by Tory-ish silence on just how the newly royal pair found themselves on it—reflected the continuing Tory aversion to revolution.

The danger from Ireland did much to help the Tories swallow their distaste for Williamite change. The European context of the British revolution of 1688–89 is unmistakable: those who supported William before he invaded hoped to check France, and the long-term outcome was a century of resistance to France by an expanded British state that was clearly now a composite state and not just a multiple kingdom. It was in 1689 that the English council at last tore up the two-centuries-old papal bull that had underwritten the security and neutrality of the Channel Islands against France. But at the end of 1688 Ireland seemed the immediate danger—certainly one that Tories could see—and it postponed full British involvement in Europe for two years. In September 1688, as the likelihood of Dutch invasion grew, Tyrconnell had sent four regiments of the Irish army to England. When news came on December 11 of James's flight, the Irish soldiery grew to horrific proportions, and rumours of their (imagined) frenzy of rape and pillage on 'Irish Night'— December 11–12—triggered attacks on Roman Catholics' property around London. They also guaranteed William an enthusiastic reception when he entered the city five days later, once James had demonstrably left for France. Irish Night endured as an argument for 'Dutch William's' authority despite the unpopularity his war measures soon earned him.

Ireland played a central role in English thinking about the merits of government and stability in a dangerous world. William's assertion of the rule of law, parliaments, and protestantism not only distinguished England from its imagined opposite, France. More practically, it underscored the challenge to—and from—a Catholic Ireland whose crown was dependent on the English crown. William's threats to go home unless he obtained the crown and the support to go with it conjured up prospects of a leaderless England vulnerable to those papists to the west—and surely too to their French backers. English protestants, Whig or Tory, now had more than the familiar ancestral reasons for alarm at the prospect of an independent and Catholic Ireland. William accordingly got most of what he wanted in 1689 from the Convention and from the parliament that followed, and not just because London was occupied by Dutch troops.

English fears were not unfounded, for while James's nerve had broken, neither Tyrconnell's nor Louis XIV's had. Tyrconnell badgered James in the spring of 1689 to leave his French refuge, to consolidate Catholic Ireland and remove the remaining obstacle of the handful of Ulster protestants who held Londonderry and Enniskillen; Louis made much the same point, for he saw in Ireland a means to obstruct England's entry into William's wars. It was therefore with some French military support that James in May opened the Irish parliament of 1689—the first since 1666—whose constituencies Tyrconnell had energetically remodelled. The heart-burnings that ensued reinforced the lesson of Ormond's efforts to build a royalist Ireland in the 1640s: Irish Catholics' purposes could not be squeezed into a British agenda. Despite the hopes he had aroused in Ireland, James would not create a Catholic state there. Instead, he tried to humour his British subjects, for reports of open divisions in Scotland, and of discontent in England at the presence of Dutch troops and a Dutch king with Dutch servants and Dutch tax demands, gave him hopes of returning. Accordingly, James refused to disestablish the Church of Ireland, though he did pass an Irish Toleration Act. His British priorities appeared even more clearly in his refusal to repeal Poynings' Law, and in his resistance to the overthrow of the 1662 land settlement; only when parliament blocked supply did he give way over the latter. Fighting had already begun in Ulster, and he needed money.

The war that reshaped Ireland for two centuries was a sideshow for its principals. James, who hoped to lead the Irish army to Scotland to exploit rebellion there, had little interest in Irish causes, and soon abandoned them altogether. William's priorities were as firmly fixed on Europe as James's were on Britain, but like the Tories at Westminster he could not ignore the danger from Ireland. With a bridgehead in Ulster preserved for him by the grim determination of Londonderry and Enniskillen, in August 1689 he dispatched a mixed Anglo-Dutch-Huguenot force of 13,000 under the German, Marshal Schomberg. Although reinforced by 6,000 volunteers from Ulster, the aged Schomberg acted firmly only when he tried to restrain his men from anti-Catholic reprisals: over a third of his army wasted away under horrific conditions that winter. William concluded he had no option but himself to lead another, and better prepared, army of 20,000 to Ireland the following summer. The outcome this time was clearer: the four regiments Tyrconnell sent to England in 1688 had been the best in the Irish army, and many of the arms the French had sent over were antiquated. Although Schomberg was killed at the Battle of the Boyne, outside Drogheda, on 1 July 1690, William led the rest of his army to a victory there that was politically if not militarily decisive. It was the last known European battle in which two kings fought each other. Once again James's nerve broke after a reverse, and he left for France—this time for good—abandoning his Irish subjects to their fate. William, to his relief, soon concluded he could turn to more important business, and entrusted the Dutch general Ginkel with the task of mopping up.

Mopping up took longer than William anticipated, since the uncharacteristically harsh terms he offered after the Boyne—the survival of rebellion in the Scottish Highlands perhaps disinclined him to generosity—found few takers. For a moment, Tyrconnell thought of following his king and quitting the struggle, but thousands of Irish Catholics, both soldiers and irregulars—'rapparees'—were eager to fight on: some hoped for better terms, particularly once the French in the spring of 1691 sent over more troops and a talented general in the Marquis de St Ruth; some hoped for little save vengeance. There was plenty of that to go around, and particularly on the ill-supplied but generally victorious Williamite side: one local protestant commander reported nonchalantly that he had himself seen to the execution of 3,000 rapparees. As the war became uglier it could only intensify religious animosities; but William needed to avoid a struggle for religion, for he had to keep Catholic Spain and the Empire in the coalition against France.

England, at least, might seem to have entered a new and non-confessional age as parliament passed the Toleration Act of 1689. The certainty that the enemy was Antichrist had certainly diminished in both William's British kingdoms since mid-century, but political and religious positions still proved inseparable, and a king of multiple kingdoms faced a task at least as complicated as any faced by the leader of an international coalition. The Toleration Act's concessions were limited, for toleration in any guise only intensified the Anglican fears for the Church that had been sparked by the revolution's crisis of allegiance. The exit of nine bishops and four hundred clergy—'non-jurors' who could not bring themselves to break their oaths of allegiance to James by swearing to William—created schism in a Church that was supposed to give spiritual identity to the nation. Ecclesiastical polemic poured from the presses.

The ferment to the north dwarfed that in England. James VI and I had extolled the virtues of episcopacy because of its fit with monarchy, but now the Scottish bishops found the fit too tight. Unlike their colleagues in the Church of England, they had not insisted on the divine origins of their order, and they were thus more vulnerable to political change. In face of the Covenanter challenge during the Restoration the episcopalian clergy had emphasized non-resistance even more than their English counterparts, and in 1688–89 they were impaled on their own arguments. England's Tory-Anglican evasion, the contention that James had abdicated, was closed to them: not since 1603 had a Scottish king been resident, so the argument that James had deserted the kingdom meant little. Churchmen who had preached obedience were now asked to swallow revolution whole; as a result, no Scottish bishop swore allegiance to William. The Scottish episcopal Church faced an existential crisis.

To William's distress—he was not unsympathetic to James VI's conviction of the merits of bishops—the Presbyterians seized the opportunity. While the nobles acknowledged Scotland's realities of power in December 1688 by scrambling to London in droves, the revolutionary cadre that was the hard-liners of the south-west went to work 'rabbling' episcopalian clergy out of their livings. By the spring of 1689, some 200 had gone, with another 200 ejected by more orderly means. The threat of violence hung over Edinburgh when the Scottish Convention met in March, deterring some northerners from attending, and intimidating legitimists of Church and state. Argument within the Convention was therefore one-sided. With the claim that the King had deserted the kingdom foreclosed, the Convention confronted the nature of authority directly. The Claim of Right that accompanied the proffer of the Scottish crown to William and Mary declared flatly and contractually that James had 'forfaulted', or forfeited, his authority; not coincidentally—since the established Church was handicapped by its recent past—the Claim also condemned episcopacy in Scotland. English observers grew nervous. Some of the Scots who had joined English Whigs in exile in the Netherlands had persuaded William of the security and strength that a common cause would bring, and of Scots' history of enthusiasm for a united protestant Britain. With William's backing, they presented this case and the economic arguments too, to the Convention and found considerable support for a British union, as they had predicted; but in England, the usual disdain for Scots' ways and the Scottish economy swelled as the downing of episcopacy revived painful memories of the Covenanters of the 1640s. The new king's hopes of a cooperative British state dwindled further when the Scottish parliament that followed the Convention challenged the lords of the articles, the management committee once again thick with bishops by which the Scottish crown had done its parliamentary business in the Restoration. By the end of 1690, not only were the established Churches of William's British kingdoms firmly at odds; in Scotland, he now lacked the parliamentary tool that might have offset his own absence.

But in the summer of 1689 parliament was not the most urgent of William's Scottish concerns. Although Presbyterians had seized the initiative, they did not speak for most of the nobles, and certainly not for the north. Episcopalian sympathies ran strong, and Williamite loyalties were scarcely fixed. There had been no Scot among the Seven Immortals, and many were the nobles who maintained contact with the two kings. When the Convention upheld William's claim, John Graham of Claverhouse, Viscount Dundee, a professional soldier and a protestant, headed north to raise the Highlands for James. It was indeed on this prospect that James pinned his Irish hopes in the early summer. The Scottish clans were no more firmly aligned than the nobles, but by mid July Dundee had close to 2,000 men, about half as many as those the government sent against him. At Killiecrankie Pass on 27 July the Highlanders smashed the Williamites, though the charismatic Dundee was killed by a lucky shot. Without that, the government might have been hard put to hold Scotland. As it was, Jacobite resistance continued for another year in the Highlands, and many clans held out far longer against swearing allegiance to William.

The 1689–90 rising formed only the first episode in the long history of Highland Jacobitism; the rising's aftermath—the Glencoe massacre of February 1692—provides a window on the progress of 'civility'. A shared dislike of the 9th Earl of Argyll had brought assorted clans and James Stuart together in the early 1680s, but the alliance's persistence after Argyll's death in 1685 points to broader unease in face of governmental and commercial pressures. There were political opportunists too. The combination of royal absolutism and royal absence meant that politics in Restoration Scotland were even more unstable than in England, and Argyll's had not been the only political career that registered massive shifts in alignment. In order to restore the family, Argyll's son, the 10th earl, briefly converted to Catholicism under James II and then, though thriving in 1689 on his father's martyr's reputation and William's favour, maintained ties with James, as did his Campbell cousin the Earl of Breadalbane; and there were many others. If old loyalties loosened from the top, they also eroded lower down with the expansion of a commercial economy into the Highlands. Some clans that suffered at Campbell hands also saw their own leaders making money aggressively from cattle-droving for the London market—though little enough trickled down the ranks. Unease grew as change seemed to spread across a broad front, affecting personal as well as political relations, and now with the Presbyterians' onslaught threatening religious practice too. Dundee's call to old loyalties and honour in 1689 had considerable appeal, and despite the rising's collapse the outlying clans came in but slowly to take the oath of allegiance required of them by 1 January 1692.

However virulent the inter-clan hostilities during Montrose's 1644–45 campaigns, the massacre in Glencoe was an act of state. There were certainly Campbells in the Scottish administration, and among the soldiers at Glencoe, and they may have taken some satisfaction in the dispatch of McDonalds, but the massacre did not originate in their resentments. Hard-pressed in Europe, William himself was eager to make examples in the Highlands, and Glencoe with its thirty-eight clansmen dead—nobody troubled to count the women and children—was not the worst governmental atrocity since 1689. William's Scottish secretary of state, the Lowland lawyer Sir John Dalrymple of Stair—like some latter-day Sir John Davies—saw Highlanders as barbaric and the McDonalds of remote Glencoe the worst of them, 'that thieving tribe', and 'papists' to boot (which they were not), to be 'rooted out'. Although the Scottish parliamentary inquiry of 1695 originated in partisan rivalries, and the complaints against Stair and others centred on 'murder under trust'—breach of the conventions of the feud—rather than anything more universal, the interest the massacre sparked abroad suggests that civility imposed limits on the civil as well as the uncivil. One fairly dispassionate Scottish account published in London in 1695 observed coolly that the right course would have been to make the McDonalds' 'young men soldiers, or to send them to the plantations'. Failing that, the government expanded the fortifications it had began to build at what became Fort William; in the longer term, commercialization and the Highland clearances were to do their remorseless work.

An exodus of the young men as soldiers provided a partial solution to the Irish crisis, though James's collapse of will helped too. He had hoped to lead his Irish army to Scotland, but even though resistance continued in the Highlands in the summer of 1690 Dundee's death had robbed his cause there of steam, and James in Ireland of hope. He responded to defeat at the Boyne—which was scarcely a Jacobite graveyard—by flight, and by blaming the Irish for behaving 'basely'. No wonder his reputation in Ireland became that of 'James the shit'. William, on the other hand, won for himself that remarkable designation, William III (of England), II (of Scotland), and—if anyone was counting the honours for the subordinate kingdom—I of Ireland. As Ginkel took his motley army westwards across Ireland, his Irish opponents could not help but consider their own value as fighting forces on the European market. They fought hard—for one thing, market-values depended on reputations—and held the Shannon crossing at Athlone for eleven days in June 1691 before regrouping under St Ruth at Aughrim nearby. The battle there on 12 July was Ireland's bloodiest. The Jacobites, in a strong position, inflicted heavy casualties until St Ruth was killed and ammunition ran low. The Williamite charge then left 7,000 Irish dead, many of them officers; Limerick, the last—and formidable—strongpoint, surrendered two months later. With Tyrconnell dead, the Old English general Patrick Sarsfield extracted honourable terms for his men, and then led the so-called 'flight of the wild geese' to wars abroad. The departure of up to 20,000 fighting men from Ireland's wars, perhaps 10% of the adult male population—with another 10,000 family members—was not just a human drama; it also helped to pacify Ireland, as the Cromwellian exodus had done.

The 1691 Treaty of Limerick expressed William's desire to get his forces out of Ireland and back onto the European stage as fast as possible. Not only did Ginkel allow the Irish still in arms to take their arms where they would; gentry in territory still held by the Jacobites willing to swear allegiance to William and Mary were to be protected in their property, and noblemen in their right to bear arms; and conditions of worship would be as in Charles II's reign. These were not the terms Ireland's returning protestants had expected. Probably few thought King William's War was fought simply for religion. It was a war for power, fought in the interests of groups defined by religion and memory, and for Irish protestants James's reign—a Catholic army, mass flight, the imminent reversal of the land settlement—replicated the disasters of the 1640s. The forces under Sarsfield had withdrawn, uncrushed, to fight on in France. Protestants were now determined to destroy their ability to threaten them again.

William called his first, and entirely protestant, Irish parliament in 1692 to restore normality and vote the supply he badly needed—Irish governmental revenues had collapsed in the war. He was under no compulsion to call a parliament in Dublin for, as English parliament-men had insisted in 1641, English statutes could claim superiority there. William probably soon wished that he had let them, for the new normality proved fractious. The Commons' attack on civilian officials, including the Irish chancellor, who had assisted Ginkel in drafting and then administering the Limerick treaty's relatively generous terms, brought the 1692 parliament to an unhappy close, and the attack continued throughout the decade. More notoriously, the protestant elite also sought to fortify its position in the country with what became known as the penal laws: a series of major disqualifications placed on Ireland's majority Catholics. Among other restraints, these barred them from going abroad for education (1695), banished Catholic bishops and members of religious orders (1697), disinherited protestant heiresses who married Catholics (1697), prevented Catholics inheriting or purchasing land (1704), and secured enforcement by entitling informers to proceeds of confiscations under these laws (1709).

The penal laws emerged from bargaining between Dublin and Westminster, for Poynings' Law was in force. At some level, therefore, English administrations participated in the construction in Ireland of anti-Catholic measures in which their records within England might suggest most members had diminishing interest. Surely most importantly, English governments and MPs were usually ready to let Ireland's governors go their own way provided taxes were paid and quiet was maintained—and Britain's Jacobite crises of the early eighteenth century duly left Ireland unscathed. There were sometimes extraneous reasons too for English politicians to fall in with the desires of the protestant establishment in Dublin: in Anne's reign, English Tories who by then distrusted Scottish Presbyterians even more than they did Irish Catholics expanded Ireland's 1704 'Popery Act' to reinforce barriers against Ulster Presbyterians taking local office. But there was in the processes of English state-formation another, and perhaps not quite conscious, significance to the anti-Catholic measures. In face of English opposition—to himself as a Dutchman, to the financial costs of his policies, to their threat to English ways and liberties – William laboriously built a state capable of resisting the overweening appetite of Louis XIV. In his last years, in the breathing-space formed by the 1697 Peace of Ryswick, William's efforts nearly collapsed as he attempted to maintain an army, much of it in Ireland and formally off the English books, despite the peace. However distasteful he found it to break the terms of the Treaty of Limerick—as his government in Ireland did in 1695 in order to gain supply and again in 1697 when it finally secured statutory ratification of the Treaty by retreating from some of its promises—William may have appreciated the larger pay-off. In the high-stakes environment formed by French aggression, the penal measures helped to remind insular English opinion that there was a popish and therefore fundamental enemy in this expensive struggle, and it was close to home.

More obviously, the penal laws secured the 'Protestant Ascendancy' of eighteenth-century Ireland. Protestants had of course already become ascendant. As a result of the piecemeal confiscations following 1691, Catholic landownership had dropped from 22% in James's reign to 14%

in 1703, on the eve of 1704's debilitating 'Popery Act'; by the later eighteenth century, little was left. Discrimination and coercion were certainly standard fare throughout the *Ancien Régime*, and the Austrian Habsburgs turned protestant Bohemia Catholic; what was unusual and eventually provocative was the cohabitation in Ireland of discrimination and coercion with the assertive Englishman's, or Anglo-Irishman's, rhetoric of liberty under law that gained new definition with the 1688–89 revolution. The consequences of the penal laws were commercially as well as politically debilitating for Catholics and indeed for Ireland too. Land was the chief source of capital for those setting up in trade, and eighteenth-century Ireland is renowned for the number of its absentee English landowners who repatriated their shares of the seventeenth-century's confiscations to the comforts of English country-houses, and so drained the Irish economy of specie.

The Irish Church protestants were not to enjoy their supremacy without effort. Most important of all, immigrants failed to arrive from England in sufficient numbers to work the confiscated lands and fill the empty churches. True, the protestant establishment was spared the discomforts of English and Scottish episcopalians who had to reconcile revolution with non-resistance: William providentially appeared in Ireland to do the fighting himself, so there was no revolution and hence no non-jurors. But as Irish protestants buttressed their position against the Catholics who surrounded them and worked for them, and whose ancestral lands they occupied, they shared the typical anxieties and insecurities of settler elites. They also watched jealously the Ulster Presbyterians who spoke the same scriptural language but with very different accents, and whose numbers doubled in the later 1690s as the famine-struck Scottish economy unleashed a new wave of emigration even as migrant flows from England dried up. The Irish churchmen did what they could to antagonize and sometimes humiliate the Presbyterians who by 1700 matched them in numbers, insisting they must pay tithes to and marry (and thus pay fees) in the established parish churches. The settler establishment had to deal as well with an English government eager to extract what revenue it could from Ireland. The disastrous Irish parliament of 1692 set the tone for the settlers' long campaign to establish that despite their distance they were true heirs to English liberties.

Good parliamentarians that they were, many in the Commons insisted that they—not the distant council at Whitehall as Poynings' Law required—had the 'sole right' to originate supply bills. As parliaments became a fixture of the war-burdened post-Stuart world, such claims repeatedly irritated the crown. By the later 1690s both sides had learned to make face-saving gestures to avoid breakdowns like that of 1692, but each resented what it saw as assertiveness in the other.

Such assertiveness only increased as war against France transformed the political environment. The need for taxation inexorably tilted England's own balance of power towards Westminster, the source of supply, at the expense of Whitehall. Coordination of crown and Irish parliament had proved difficult enough ever since Poynings' day, but the task was further complicated by the intrusion now of the English parliament. The House of Commons was particularly responsive to local interests; economic adversity made those interests outspoken, as it had over Irish cattle imports in the 1660s. The conjunction of high wartime taxes and bad harvests in the mid 1690s drew angry protests from the over-represented clothing districts of England's south-west against low-cost, because low-wage, Irish competition. The result was the Irish Woollen Act of 1699, which banned the export of Irish wool or woollen cloth to anywhere other than England—where tariffs already discriminated against both commodities. In the economic field, the increasing prominence of the English parliament in and after the war-torn 1690s thus introduced an aggressively protectionist element into a relationship that the Irish protestant establishment wanted to imagine—once it had itself been preserved from overthrow—in mutually respectful two-kingdoms terms.

The Irish Woollen Act proved a mixed blessing for Ireland's economy. Just as the 1667 Irish Cattle Act had pushed Irish interests towards the more labour-intensive and therefore more profitable food-processing trades and away from droving, so the Woollen Act diverted Irish manufacturing towards linens, where there was much less competition and ultimately—since the rising culture of politeness prized table-linens—steady demand. But the ideological repercussions were more immediate. From the Woollen Act controversy emerged William Molyneux's *The Case of Ireland's Being Bound by Acts of Parliament in England* (1698), the classic argument for the legislative autonomy of the kingdom of Ireland.

Molyneux's argument dramatized a new self-consciousness on both sides of the Irish Sea. In some ways, *The Case of Ireland's Being Bound* put forward an undiluted English constitutionalist claim. Molyneux's preferred outcome would, he said, have been an incorporating union of Ireland with England on the Welsh model; failing that ('a happiness not to be hoped for,' he lamented), there was just one other way to secure the universal good of government by consent—which England's rule in Ireland had been from its outset, he argued. That far-fetched historical contention provoked English writers to run over the history of Ireland's conquest, and to reflect sourly on the utter and repeated dependence of protestant settlers on England's military support. Since Molyneux's book coincided with a 1698 confrontation (in a Londonderry plantation case) between the Irish and the English Houses of Lords over final jurisdiction for appeals in Irish cases—the English Lords more or less won—English senses were primed to smell an Irish drive for independence, a challenge not just to the sovereignty of Westminster's statutes but to the English imperial crown. The Commons condemned *The Case of Ireland's Being Bound* in just those terms.

What gave the Molyneux controversy such lasting notoriety, and a life in the American colonies, was the burgeoning of empire's other and now more familiar meaning, compounded of domination, commercial exploitation, and territorial control. The decade of the 1690s proved crucial in filling out what had been largely a political and religious construction. The later seventeenth century's hugely remunerative trade expansion coincided with and fed the Anglo-Dutch struggle for primacy with France—a fact that escaped neither politicians nor pamphleteers. Increasingly sophisticated addresses to the political economy of England's empire proliferated from across the political spectrum in the last years of the century, above all in the work of the Tory Charles Davenant, with the Bristol Whig John Cary not far behind. The application to Ireland appeared in the anonymous *An Answer to Mr Molyneux* (1698). This offered on behalf of the Woollen Act a strikingly imperialist justification: 'it is incumbent upon a mother nation or supreme government, to regulate all her colonies or members, so as that the tranquility of the whole empire may be best conserv'd'.

Empire was by no means a stable and agreed category of political analysis. It comprehended not just modern colonies but ancient conquerors. Preaching in 1692 to a Channel Islands garrison at last freed from the constraints of neutrality, its chaplain heralded the revival of 'English empire to its former bounds on this side'—a wishful salute to Henry V's gains on the French mainland. And empire was not always a positive force. Whatever ancient Rome's imperial culture and conquests, there had also been Rome's corruptions; 'empire' as a geopolitical term was tainted too by Spanish and (more recently) French tyranny and aspirations to world domination. So while most English people subscribed readily enough to the nation's historic myth of entitlement and domination in an archipelagic hinterland, they were less ready than the author of the *Answer to Mr Molyneux* to define what such domination meant. Revealingly, William's reconquest of Ireland prompted a minor flurry of Arthurianism—its high-point was that ironizing opera *King Arthur* (1691), by John Dryden and Henry Purcell—while one of the most successful literary works of the moment, Daniel Defoe's *True-Born Englishman* (1700), celebrated the absorbent, ambiguous, mongrel qualities of the English and their ways.

Relations between the new Britain and Ireland subsided apace into their ambiguous eighteenth-century pattern: an Irish economy whose informal south-western links with Europe and the Caribbean strained the mould of empire and colony; a two-kingdoms politics in which England's parliamentary spoils-system periodically disturbed a defensive Irish establishment; and a dominant metropolitan culture which drew from the provinces enterprising Anglo-Irishmen like the Deist philosopher John Toland, while Ulster Scots and Catholic Irish added America and the Caribbean as well as London to their itineraries. And, as *Love and a Bottle* (1698) by that relocated Ulster Scot George Farquhar showed, the caricature of the stage Irishman had already begun its rapid and reassuring climb.

The formation of that new Britain entailed the resolution of England's relations with Scotland, a task that proved politically more traumatic than the post-1691 pacification of Ireland. A major destabilizing factor was Scotland's prolonged economic depression throughout the 1690s. Only with England, thanks to cattle, linen, and salt, did Scotland have a trading surplus, and Scottish linens were likely to be threatened by the Irish product-line. The war with France that followed William's acquisition of the Stuart thrones ended any chance that Louis XIV might re-open French ports to Scotland's limited and uncompetitive range of products, while the insult of Scotland's exclusion from England's oceanic trades under the navigation laws meant there was little prospect of extending that list. The devastating series of four harvest failures in 1695–98 killed somewhere in excess of 5% of the population and considerably more in some regions. It was not the worst calamity of the 'Little Ice Age' that peaked in the seventeenth century, but it was the first to be reported in the press. It reminded Scotland's new breed of political economists of the dangers of economic isolation, the more so since—unlike France—the great trading nations, England and the Netherlands, emerged relatively unscathed. Trade and overseas settlement seemed to most Scots not just the way to prosperity but indeed the only path to survival.

The Darien Scheme, touted by the brilliant Scottish projector William Paterson, for a remarkable moment convinced almost the entire Scottish political nation that the solution had been found. The discovery proved disastrous for polity and economy alike. Paterson had, beside the gift of the gab and remarkable skill with the press, a persuasive track-record, for in 1694 he parlayed a fortune made trading between London and the Caribbean into a directorship of the brand-new Bank of England. He had long argued that a trading settlement on the Isthmus of Panama would allow easy exchange of the goods of the two oceans, Atlantic and Pacific, and a way for the Scots to find the prosperity that would enable them to meet England on equal terms in a mutually respectful union. He returned to Scotland in 1695 at an opportune moment. That year the Scottish parliament responded to economic blight by founding the Bank of Scotland, by establishing the framework for a national system of parochial schools, and by giving Paterson a charter for the Company of Scotland trading to Africa and the Indies. By 1698 he had raised in Scotland a capital of £400,000, almost a quarter of Scotland's total monetary stock, and he and his associates busily fitted out five ships to take 1,200 settlers to Panama. The backing was entirely Scottish because the English East India Company's protests about the challenge to its monopoly of Far Eastern trade had closed London and north European capital markets to Paterson, and because William, infuriated by the venture's challenge to Spain, his ally against France, voiced his displeasure far and near. The Darien Scheme was also badly planned, above all in its assumption that the merchants of the world would come calling as soon as a settlement was built. They did not, and meanwhile the settlers died in their hundreds. By 1700, when the settlement was abandoned after the failure of a second voyage, the money was gone along with the dreams of a trading empire, to be replaced by fierce resentment at the English and at a king who had commanded his colonial officials in the Caribbean not to help the settlers in any way.

It was a bad moment for a royal succession crisis. With the childlessness of William and Mary compounded by the death in 1700 of the last surviving child of Mary's sister Anne, who was to succeed on William's death (Mary herself having died in 1694), Westminster moved fast to avert a dynastic storm by passing the Act of Settlement in June 1701. This directed the succession to the heirs of the nearest protestant claimant, the Electress Sophia of Hanover, daughter of Elizabeth, that 'Winter Queen' who had been daughter to James VI and I; various Catholics nearer in descent, including of course 'the Pretender' James II and his 'suppositious' son, were passed over. Parliament's haste is understandable—Louis XIV was unfriendly and James II was still alive. Nevertheless, its failure to consult only confirmed what the Scots already thought they knew: that England saw in Scotland merely a province.

Accordingly, the matter of Britain and the relative of status of its parts reverberated unnervingly at the end of the Stuart century. The ecclesiastical controversies of the Restoration had renewed the old English legend, stretching back to the twelfth-century Geoffrey of Monmouth if not before, of superiority over Scotland: energetic Scottish claims to ancient British proto-Presbyterian purity were countered by Anglican insistence on the pan-British primacy of the apostolically descended English archbishops. These antiquarian labours threatened to open sores that others were working at. In the cause of monarchy as well as good scholarship, the Tory Robert Brady late in Charles II's reign had, by exploring the advent of Norman feudalism, frontally challenged the Whig myth of a fundamental English constitution stretching back unbroken into the mists of antiquity. When Scottish Presbyterians in 1695 published as *Scotland's Sovereignty Asserted* the manuscript researches of Sir Thomas Craig, one of James VI and I's union commissioners, on the meaning of feudal history for English (and Anglicans') claims to primacy, the wider implications were not lost on Brady's main antagonist, the Whig lawyer and antiquarian William Atwood. On behalf of the imperial English crown-in-parliament, Atwood rushed into print against Molyneux and Ireland's autonomy in 1698; his views sharpened by an unhappy stint as lord chief justice of an insufficiently subordinate colonial New York in 1700, he then marshalled all the feudal and the legendary arguments for *The Superiority and Direct Dominion of the Imperial Crown of England over the Crown and Kingdom of Scotland* (1704). The Scottish parliament promptly burned his book.

William's death in 1702 occasioned a heartfelt invitation to escape from such fears. The King's last public wish, which became one of Queen Anne's first, was for an Anglo-Scottish union, and commissioners were duly appointed on both sides. English politicians were readier now to talk to the Scots, for their local dynastic crisis was merging with a much larger one, and indeed with a major European war. Louis XIV in September 1701 provocatively and in breach of the Treaty of Ryswick recognized the young 'James III' (and VIII) as king on the death of his father; Louis quickly followed by breaking the international treaties of 1698 and 1700 which had provided for the partition of the Spanish Empire as the solution to Spain's own approaching dynastic crisis. His decision to pursue the whole Spanish inheritance for the Bourbon candidate seemed to confirm the fears of English and Scottish protestants that he sought a universal popish empire, and it plunged Europe into the War of the Spanish Succession.

Security was therefore on the minds of all the union commissioners, but the English and the Scots came with very different assumptions. The English were heirs to the 1533 statute that declared 'this realm of England' an empire unto itself. The Scots, their inheritance of Roman law inclining them to some flexibility over forms, and their Presbyterian past accustoming them to notions of contract, had long floated federal and confederal options. The English insisted that if there was to be a union— and the repeated absences of English commissioners from the negotiations

suggest they had no very strong feelings about this—it must be an incorporating union, on the Welsh model: the option, that is, which had so
offended James VI and I. The Scots commissioners, some of whom were
genuine enthusiasts for union, did not walk away, but they did demand
compensation for the Company of Scotland's losses. With so much of
Scotland's circulating currency gone the demand is less surprising, but
the English saw no reason for it.

The failure of the 1702 negotiations led to parliamentary retaliations.
These were made more intense by the volatility of a fractious Scottish
parliament unfettered by lords of the articles and by the partisan determination of an English parliament with a short-lived Whig majority in
1705. Scotland had been drawn unconsulted into the War of the Spanish
Succession, so the Scottish parliament's Act Anent Peace and War of
1703 stipulated that after Anne's death involvement in any war would
require the explicit consent of the Scottish parliament; more confronta-
tionally, the 1704 Act of Security required a separate protestant succession to the Scottish throne unless Scotland's commercial and other
interests were provided for. The English Whigs of 1705 replied with the
Alien Act, declaring forfeit all Scots' landholdings in England and bar-
ring key imports from Scotland unless negotiations on union began
within nine months. Since half of all their trade went to England, the
Scots would quickly face economic breakdown; for their part, the
English would be likely to face French trouble-making. The British
kingdoms had been able to indulge their very public falling-out without
suffering French intervention thanks to the Duke of Marlborough's
massive victory at Blenheim in 1704, but Scottish Jacobites might yet
persuade other resentful Scottish patriots to join them in reviving the
'auld alliance' that had so long visited English nightmares. English troop
movements in Ulster and on the northern borders hinted at a military
counter.

Most Whigs and former partisans of King William in both England
and Scotland believed that Louis XIV's drive to empire would eliminate
liberty and protestantism in Europe, and were now ready to contemplate union. Others had to be persuaded. In the autumn of 1706 the
English lord treasurer Robert Harley therefore sent the journalist and
pamphleteer Daniel Defoe to Edinburgh, in the guise of an English

merchant with business north of the border, to report on but also to shape opinion. The disguise itself pointed to underlying change, since none would have thought such a pilgrim plausible a century earlier. Defoe the propagandist faced two audiences. He had to persuade his compatriots—even the Queen, the most English of the Stuart sovereigns and devoutly Anglican to boot, thought her northern subjects 'strange people'—that the Scots would not endanger the polity; and he needed to mollify the Scots. His approach was scarcely even-handed. In Edinburgh, he stressed how much Scots stood to gain economically from access to the English market, but when he reassured English readers that Scottish woollens would not threaten the more developed English industry, he heralded the 'one united English empire' that would emerge from union.

The treaty of union that took effect on 1 May 1707 created a British state of which Defoe surely approved. In addition to instituting the United Kingdom of Great Britain, the treaty put an end to the Scottish parliament, and to the (alleged) thousands of years of Scottish kingship that had defined that nation. The same fate of course met the English parliament and crown, but though there were lamentations in Edinburgh—as there had been at Westminster in 1604 and 1607 when union was discussed—this time there was complacency at Westminster and in the London press. In 1707 there could be no doubt that the monarch was English, and that Anne's successor would not be Scottish. The parliament of the United Kingdom would meet at Westminster as had the English parliament before it, and the Scots were to send a mere forty-five members to the House of Commons, and sixteen peers to the Lords. And the English East India Company stayed, as chartered, firmly English for several decades more. No wonder the English were not alarmed in 1707: few could have thought, as some had a century earlier, that the nation's identity was in danger. It was, after all, in a well-reported mood of national crisis that the Scots entered this union.

Yet the treaty was a treaty, and the work of two separate polities: the old argument that Scotland was a mere province was quietly rejected. And Scotland retained many marks of nationhood within the new British state. Scottish law, Scottish justice, the Scottish courts, even the heritable offices of the Scottish nobles' feudalities that had so appalled the English conquerors in 1652, all were to survive. Law was one pillar of Scottish identity; another was the Kirk, and there lay a rub. The Presbyterian church re-established in Scotland's revolutionary moment of 1690 had been entrusted, in southern Scotland at least, to elderly purists, living memorials of the imperial vision of Presbyterianism's past; the currency in certain Anglican circles of a parallel imperialism based in pan-British claims for England's archbishops boded ill for cohabitation. Indeed, the increasingly virulent Toryism of Anne's English parliaments, with its 'Church in danger' cry, suggests how difficult agreement would have been if the Scots had come to the bargaining-table in militantly Presbyterian mood. But in Scotland, the triumph of south-western intransigence in 1689–90 bred its own reaction: if not quite a resurgence of Scottish episcopalianism, at least an increasing pragmatism, and a readiness to recognize that protestant nations should be left to their protestant ways. From that mood emerged two statutes of 1706, one from each parliament and accompanying the union treaty, providing for the security of the two distinct national Churches.

The Scottish economy, and more particularly the residue of Darien, remained as the major stumbling-block. In this first age of political economy, an age shaped not just by imperial protectionism on the French model but by more adventurous schemes descended from William Petty the political arithmetician, material and political health seemed inseparable. The fiercest non-Jacobite critic of union in the Scottish parliament was the universally respected Andrew Fletcher of Saltoun, a republican former exile who in 1689 had supported Anglo-Scottish union for Whiggish reasons. Since then he had become alarmed by the rise of London's trading empire as the rival to the French territorial empire: only a Europe-wide devolution to a series of city republics could ensure both liberty and a general well-being, he argued. While support for Fletcher's strenuous civic republicanism was limited, many in the Edinburgh parliament warmed to his denunciations of London's monopolizing tendencies. Defoe's arguments about the gains Scots would make if admitted on equal terms to the larger English economy and its oceanic extensions certainly found an audience—indeed, the Union was to buck Europe's protectionist trend and eventually create an economically significant free-trade zone. Nevertheless, the anger in the streets of Edinburgh and Glasgow over the failure of Darien, and the doubts in some of the other burghs about their prospects within a British union, were such that without the hard bargaining of 1706 it is doubtful whether the treaty would have passed. Opponents then, and nationalists since, have levelled the charge of corruption. Individuals were paid off and did profit, but there is no doubt that the £400,000 England offered, partly as 'Equivalent' for the Company of Scotland's losses and partly as compensation for the higher taxes Scots would pay towards England's national debt, salved the nation's pride almost as much as its pocket. And unlike the similarly large sums England had promised the Scots in the 1640s, this one was eventually paid.

***

Conclusions to narrative histories of unfinished processes ought to be tentative. This book could end on a climactic note with one of the more famous farewell-lines of history: the Earl of Seafield's salute to his nation's past when, as Scotland's chancellor, he signed the union treaty—'There's ane end of ane auld sang.' But Seafield attributed too much power to the pen, as the tangled implementation and effects of the Union after 1707 were to show. The Scots managed to preserve nationhood within a British state. Perhaps a more telling motif with which to close would be Welsh, for the Welsh actually discovered nationhood within the same British-state frame. The demands of war accelerated the mining industries, binding Wales more tightly to the larger market, and more frequent parliamentary elections during the wars had a parallel political effect. Meanwhile, an explosion of print followed the lapse of the Licensing Act in 1695, reinvigorating the Welsh language: a flood of Welsh almanacs and hymnals quickly reinforced new patterns of learned taste that emerged with the establishment of the bardic *eisteddfod* in 1700. Far into the modern period, the most thoroughly integrated of the non-English nations of the British Isles—its offspring from Elizabeth's Burghley to James II's 'Bloody Judge' Jeffreys had a signal record of serving the crown—thus remained the most thoroughly non-Anglophone. The capstone of such an integrationist history might be the publication in that watershed year 1707 of *Archaeologia Britannica*, the massive and seminal inquiry by Edward Lhuyd, naturalist, Fellow of the Royal

Society, curator of Oxford University's Ashmolean Museum, and one of the greatest of all Celtic linguists and scholars.

Yet Scots' elegies for nationhood, no less than newly contrived Welsh bardic crowns or even the Irish penal laws, argue a dramatic pitch inappropriate to the close of this story. The union treaty laid the basis for a British state, not a British nation—that would come, if it ever did, over time. The Scots nation survived, the Welsh created a national culture, 'the Irish' were fractured by the 1690s as they had so long been fractured; the English remained untroubled—some would say unthinking—in their confidence of Englishness. Although the London printer Nathaniel Crouch pumped out cheap histories of Ireland—'this stupid people', the first page declared of the Gael—in 1693, Wales (1695), and Scotland (1696), even those who read his books remained oblivious to the archipelagic implications of the recent upheavals. They returned after 1707 to their squabbles over the Church and the costs of war. The notorious readiness of the English into the present to speak of Britain when they mean England properly recapitulates the essence of the treaty of union, with its imperial parliament of the United Kingdom—in a fiction that manifestly deceived few in England at the time—masquerading in the old English parliament-chamber at Westminster. No wonder the Irish have found 'the British Isles' a provocative term for the islands they too inhabit.

PART III

BIBLIOGRAPHIC ESSAY

Scholarship on the histories of the early-modern Tudor and Stewart/ Stuart kingdoms is vast and full of insight. But until very recently it tended to be framed overwhelmingly in national terms, and surely not only because historical archives are often housed in national repositories. The strong survival into the present of that misleading term, 'the English Civil War', is a case in point.

Indictment of the 'little England-ism' of so much of the writing of English history came in two seminal essays by the uprooted New Zealander, J.G.A. Pocock: 'British History: a plea for a new subject', *Journal of Modern History* 47 (1975), and 'The Limits and Divisions of British History: in search of the unknown subject', *American Historical Review* 87 (1982). He was fortunate in his timing, for revisionist English historians were eager to explain the massive upheaval that was 'the English Civil War' without conceding to sub-Marxists the existence of long-term stresses in the English polity. The outstanding response to Pocock's charge was Conrad Russell's *Fall of the British Monarchies 1637–1642* (Oxford, 1991), which assiduously folded Scottish and Irish aspirations and challenges into its brilliant narrative of the onset of what remained for him England's civil war. The approach, characterized by some of its practitioners as 'the New British History', was criticized elsewhere and with some justice for the way it at first seemed to yield merely an enriched English history: the focus remained the same, though there was more depth of field.

Such criticism found justification too in the context, for while Pocock's challenge reverberated among historians of England, particularly those working on the seventeenth century, it came as old news to historians of Ireland. It was after all in the 1960s that the Irish historian J.C. Beckett coined the now-dominant phrase 'the war of the three kingdoms' for the 1640s upheavals; in 1966 the Irish and Atlantic-world historian D.B. Quinn published *The Elizabethans and the Irish* (Ithaca, NY), a classic of historical vision, while in the same year Aidan Clarke produced the quintessential study of identity crisis, *The Old English in Ireland 1625–1642* (London); and Nicholas Canny, the leading early-modern Irish scholar of the last forty years, was readying for publication *The Elizabethan Conquest of Ireland: A Pattern Established 1565–1576* (Hassocks, 1976) just as Pocock published his *J.M.H.* essay.

If these were the beginnings of the new transnational wave in historiography, it proved to be a wavelet rather than a breaker. While so many substantive problems in Irish history are necessarily transnational, English and Scottish historians see a few discrete episodes of undeniably transnational encounter that have to be addressed in transnational terms if they are to be properly understood within the parameters of the national histories: the wars of the 1540s, the regal union of 1603, the wars of the 1640s, the revolution of 1688–89 (though there the most likely transnational element is Dutch), and the Union of 1707 (not insignificantly, of far more concern to Scottish historians than English). Transnational approaches are therefore more likely in essays and essay collections than in monographs, and there as chapters rather than the main story. A few outstanding monographs analyse themes that transcend a single country. As so often, medievalists provide chastening examples: Robin Frame, *The Political Development of the British Isles, 1100–1400* (Oxford, 1990); R.R. Davies, *The First English Empire: Power and Identities in the British Isles, 1093–1343* (Oxford, 2000) and *Lords and Lordship in the British Isles in the Late Middle Ages*, ed. Brendan Smith (Oxford, 2009). If the lesson of those works is the variety and range of individual careers and connections, a breathtakingly archipelagian early-modern parallel would be Jane E.A. Dawson, *The Politics of Religion in the Age of Mary, Queen of Scots: The Earl of Argyll and the Struggle for Britain and Ireland* (Cambridge, 2002); another far-flung career, not coincidentally from the same unconfinable borderlands of the North Channel, is reconstructed in Jane Ohlmeyer, *Civil War and Restoration in the Three Stuart Kingdoms: The Career of Randal McDonnell, Marquis of Antrim, 1609–1683* (Cambridge, 1993).

But if empire, not individuality, is to be the medievalists' lesson, that theme in the early modern period has been developed most forcefully by David Armitage, *Ideological Origins of the British Empire* (Cambridge, 2000), and Allan Macinnes, *Union and Empire: The Making of the United Kingdom in 1707* (Cambridge, 2007), which takes a wider geographic and chronological approach than its subtitle suggests. See also Colin Kidd, *British Identities before Nationalism: Ethnicity and Nationhood in the Atlantic World, 1600–1800* (Cambridge, 1999). But the starting-point for any inquiry into empire must be the tightly focused volume edited by Nicholas Canny, *The Origins of Empire to 1689* (Oxford, 1998). Canny has long been interested in the Irish experience as an opening to larger currents of development: see his *Kingdom and Colony: Ireland in the Atlantic World* (Baltimore, 1988) and more recently his brilliant study of colonization, *Making Ireland British, 1580–1650* (Oxford, 2003). For a very different approach, emphasizing the aristocratic and the military, to the wider meaning of Henrician Ireland's history, see Steven G. Ellis, *Tudor Frontiers and Noble Power: the Making of the British State* (Oxford, 1995). A useful introduction to the diplomatic context is William Palmer, *The Problem of Ireland in Tudor Foreign Policy 1485–1603* (Woodbridge, 1994). Perhaps surprisingly, the most systematic studies of state-building as a process turn insistently towards England (we might note as well that they form an antidote to some of the looser usages of the term 'state' in the essay collections listed below): Michael J. Braddick, *State Formation in Early Modern England, c.1550–1700* (Cambridge, 2000), and John Brewer, *Sinews of Power: War, Money, and the English State 1688–1783* (New York, 1989).

Several other works stand out for the seriousness of their engagement with three-kingdom or even four-nation themes. Allan Macinnes has advanced an insistently British account of *The British Revolution, 1629–1660* (Basingstoke, 2005), while Tim Harris has turned in still more comprehensive fashion to the second revolution in *Restoration:*

Charles II and his Kingdoms, 1660–1685 (London, 2005), and
Revolution: The Great Crisis of the British Monarchy, 1685–1720
(London, 2006). John Kerrigan, *Archipelagic English: Literature,
History, and Politics 1603–1707* (Oxford, 2008), deserves a special
mention for the originality of its address to the cultural interplay of
all four nations through the medium of 'English' literature in the
seventeenth century. Felicity Heal, *Reformation in Britain and Ireland*
(Oxford, 2003), is a remarkably thorough study of religious reform in
all three kingdoms in the sixteenth century (though stronger on
protestant than on Roman Catholic movements), while the essays in
Jenny Wormald, ed., *The Seventeenth Century* (Oxford, 2008), wrestle
seriously and suggestively with the complexity of the four-nation
frame.

But what really catch the eye are the many broadly British–Irish essay
collections (more focused volumes appear in their place in the
individual sections that follow). These are listed in chronological
order of publication: L.M. Cullen and T.C. Smout, ed., *Comparative
Aspects of Scottish and Irish Social and Economic History 1600–1900*
(Edinburgh, 1977); Roger A. Mason, ed., *Scotland and England
1286–1815* (Edinburgh, 1987); Rosalind Mitchison and Peter Roebuck,
eds, *Economy and Society in Scotland and Ireland 1500–1939*
(Edinburgh, 1988); Brendan Bradshaw, Andrew Hadfield, and Willy
Maley, eds, *Representing Ireland: Literature and the Origins of Conflict
1534–1660* (Cambridge, 1993); Anthony Fletcher and Peter Roberts,
eds, *Religion, Culture, and Society in Early Modern Britain: Essays in
Honour of Patrick Collinson* (Cambridge, 1994); Steven Ellis and Sarah
Barber, *Conquest and Union: Fashioning a British State 1485–1725*
(London, 1995); Brendan Bradshaw and John Morrill, eds, *The British
Problem c.1534–1707: State Formation in the Atlantic Archipelago*
(Basingstoke, 1996); Brendan Bradshaw and Peter Roberts, eds,
British Consciousness and Identity: The Making of Britain 1533–1707
(Cambridge, 1998); Glenn Burgess, ed., *The New British History:
Founding a Modern State 1603–1715* (London, 1999); Allan Macinnes
and Jane Ohlmeyer, eds, *The Stuart Kingdoms in the Seventeenth
Century: Awkward Neighbours* (Cambridge, 2002); Thomas Cogswell,
Richard Cust, and Peter Lake, eds, *Politics, Religion and Popularity in*

Early Stuart Britain: Essays in Honour of Conrad Russell (Cambridge, 2002); Allan Macinnes and Arthur H. Williamson, eds, *Shaping the Stuart World 1603–1714: The Atlantic Connection* (Leiden, 2005); David Armitage, ed., *British Political Thought in History, Literature and Theory, 1500–1800* (Cambridge, 2006).

Monographs that have a bearing on the topics of this book, and have contributed to it, are legion—far too many to list. Some of the most salient are grouped below, in rough chronological order of topic within the separate national categories:

England

The outline of the early Tudor saga can be pieced together with the help of John Guy, *Tudor England* (Oxford, 1988), David M. Loades, *Power in Tudor England* (London, 1997), and Steven J. Gunn, *Early Tudor Government 1485–1558* (London, 1995). The early shock to Henry VII's system is detailed in Ian Arthurson, *The Perkin Warbeck Conspiracy 1491–1499* (Stroud, 1994). Detailed coverage of the mainstream is to be found in Sean Cunningham, *Henry VII* (London, 2007), Steven Gunn and Phillip G. Lindley, eds, *Cardinal Wolsey: Church, State and Art* (Cambridge, 1991), G.W. Bernard, *The King's Reformation: Henry VIII and the Remaking of the English Church* (New Haven, 2005), and Diarmaid MacCulloch, ed., *The Reign of Henry VIII: Politics, Policy, and Piety* (Basingstoke, 1995). The essays in G.W. Bernard, ed., *The Tudor Nobility* (Manchester, 1992) are central to any work on that theme; see also Helen Miller, *Henry VIII and the English Nobility* (Oxford, 1986). For the wars of the 1540s, see Gervase Phillips, *The Anglo-Scots Wars 1513–1550: A Military History* (Woodbridge, 1999), Michael L. Bush, *The Government Policy of Protector Somerset* (Montreal, 1975), and David M. Loades, *John Dudley, Duke of Northumberland, 1504–1553* (Oxford, 1996). On England's social crisis, Andy Wood, *The 1549 Rebellions and the Making of Early Modern England* (Cambridge, 2007) is essential; see also Anthony Fletcher and Diarmaid MacCulloch, *Tudor Rebellions* (5th edn., Basingstoke, 2008), and Ralph Robson, *The Rise and Fall of the English Highland Clans: Tudor Responses to a Medieval Problem* (Edinburgh, 1989).

The difficult transitional years are well-covered in David M. Loades, *The Mid-Tudor Crisis 1547–1563* (New York, 1992); the narrative is extended in Penry Williams, *The Later Tudors, 1547–1603* (Oxford, 1995), and given the crucial military turn in Paul E.J. Hammer, *Elizabeth's Wars: War, Government, and Society in Tudor England, 1544–1603* (Basingstoke, 2003). The three key figures of the second half of the century are analyzed in Stephen Alford, *Burghley: William Cecil at the Court of Elizabeth I* (New Haven, 2008), and also his *The Early Elizabethan Polity: William Cecil and the British Succession Crisis 1558–1569* (Cambridge, 1998); and Wallace T. MacCaffrey, *Elizabeth I* (London, 1993) and Simon L. Adams, *Leicester and the Court: Essays on Elizabethan Politics* (Manchester, 2002). The essays in John Guy, ed., *The Reign of Elizabeth I: Court and Culture in the Last Decade* (Cambridge, 1995), give a fine sense of the straitened mood of the last fifteen years of the reign; and for a focus on the military burden, J. McGurk, *The Elizabethan Conquest of Ireland: The 1590s Crisis* (Manchester, 2005). The best introduction to the religious changes of the period is Diarmaid MacCulloch, *The Later Reformation in England 1547–1603* (2nd edn., Basingstoke, 2001); for a study of resistance, see Krista Kesselring, *The Northern Rebellion of 1569: Faith, Politics, and Protest in Elizabethan England* (Basingstoke, 2007). Susan Doran, *Elizabeth I and Foreign Policy 1558–1603* (London, 2000), is a valuable guide to the European (and Scottish) entanglements.

The relation of national identity to a wider world has become a lively field: see especially Richard Helgerson, *Forms of Nationhood: The Elizabethan Writing of England* (Chicago, 1992); Andrew Hadfield, *Shakespeare, Spenser, and the Matter of Britain* (Basingstoke, 2004); Claire McEachern, *The Poetics of English Nationhood 1590–1612* (Cambridge, 1996). The essential work on English cartography is now the second volume of David Woodward, ed., *Cartography in the European Renaissance* (Chicago, 2007). The practical application of civility is grimly demonstrated in Ken MacMillan, *Sovereignty and Possession in the English New World: The Legal Foundations of Empire 1576–1640* (Cambridge, 2006). For the material pressures or incentives to leave home, see David H. Sacks, *The Widening Gate: Bristol and the Atlantic Economy 1450–1700* (Berkeley, 1991) and Keith Wrightson,

Earthly Necessities: Economic Lives in Early Modern Britain (New Haven, 2000). The economics of improvement are explored in Joan Thirsk, *Economic Policies and Projects: The Development of a Consumer Society in Early Modern England* (Oxford, 1978). Material identities, the delights of commodities, and the marketplace, are explored in Lena Cowen Orlin, *Material London c.1600* (Philadelphia, 2000). The most helpful general account of seventeenth-century English history for present purposes is probably Jonathan Scott, *England's Troubles: Seventeenth-Century English Political Instability in European Context* (Cambridge, 2000), since its determinedly European focus challenges conventional English or even British perspectives. Pauline Croft, *King James* (Basingstoke, 2003) is now the best study of that great Briton, though Maurice Lee, *Great Britain's Solomon: James VI and I in his Three Kingdoms* (Urbana, 1990), is stronger on the Scottish career. The essays in Glenn Burgess, Rowland Wymer and Jason Lawrence, eds, *The Accession of James I: Cultural and Historical Consequences* (Basingstoke, 2006), are wide-ranging, and share some ground with Linda Peck, ed., *The Mental World of the Jacobean Court* (Cambridge, 1991). J.G.A. Pocock, *The Ancient Constitution and the Feudal Law: A Study of English Historical Thought in the Seventeenth Century: a Reissue with a Retrospect* (Cambridge, 1987) lays bare the historical outlook of the common lawyers. Glenn Burgess, *Absolute Monarchy and the Stuart Constitution* (New Haven, 1996) argues that the world was not so sharply differentiated as Pocock and many others have thought. But one who did see a differentiated world was King James's son, for whom see Richard Cust, *Charles I: A Political Life* (Harlow, 2005). For the complicated question of ecclesiastical objectives, see the essay by John Morrill, 'A British Patriarchy? Ecclesiastical Imperialism under the Early Stuarts', in the 1994 collection edited by Anthony Fletcher and Peter Roberts (above). Further on the Church, see John Spurr, *The Post-Reformation: Religion, Politics, and Society in Britain, 1603–1714* (Harlow, 2006), Ken Fincham, ed., *The Early Stuart Church 1603–1642* (Basingstoke, 1993), and Anthony Milton, *Catholic and Reformed: Roman and Protestant Churches in English 1600–1640* (Cambridge, 1994). On English apocalypticism, William M. Lamont, *Godly Rule: Politics and Religion 1603–1660* (London,

1969) is still good; see also Alexandra Walsham, *Providence in Early Modern England* (Oxford, 1999), and John Spurr, *English Puritanism, 1603–1689* (Basingstoke, 1998). For the strains war imposed on the early Stuart polity, see Conrad Russell, *Parliaments and English Politics 1621–1629* (Cambridge, 1979). An important collection on one of Charles's few officials with a three-kingdoms vision (however flawed) is Julia Merritt, ed., *The Political World of Thomas Wentworth, Earl of Strafford, 1621–1641* (Cambridge, 1996).

The best recent work on the English [*sic*] Civil Wars is Michael Braddick, *God's Fury, England's Fire* (London, 2008). A geopolitically more balanced account is David A. Scott, *Politics and War in the Three Stuart Kingdoms 1637–1649* (Basingstoke, 2004), and also (a longer work) Ian Gentles, *The English Revolution and the Wars in the Three Kingdoms, 1637–1652* (Harlow, 2007). Mark Stoyle, *Soldiers and Strangers: An Ethnic History of the English Civil War* (New Haven, 2005), argues the presence of ethnic animosities. A work to be read alongside Conrad Russell's *Fall of the British Monarchies* for what it says of the interdependence of Charles's kingdoms in 1640 is John S.A. Adamson, *The Noble Revolt: The Downfall of Charles I* (London, 2007). On the same theme more generally in the 1640s, see Adamson, ed., *The English Civil War: Conflict and Contexts* (Basingstoke, 2009). Ian Gentles, *The New Model Army in England, Ireland, and Scotland, 1645–1653* (Oxford, 1992) is the best work on that army's organization; more generally, see also Barbara Donagan, *War in England, 1642–1649* (Oxford, 2008), Mark Fissel, *English Warfare 1511–1642* (London, 2001), and John P. Kenyon and Jane Ohlmeyer, ed., *The Civil War: A Military History of England, Scotland, and Ireland, 1638–1660* (Oxford, 1998), which broaden the scene. Ann Hughes, *Gangraena and the Struggle for the English Revolution* (Oxford, 2004) brilliantly illuminates the Scots' London sympathizers. David Underdown, *Pride's Purge* (Oxford, 1971), and Blair Worden, *The Rump Parliament* (Cambridge, 1974), remain classics. The best work on Cromwell is John Morrill's entry in the *Oxford Dictionary of National Biography* (available online); see also Morrill, ed., *Oliver Cromwell and the English Revolution* (London, 1990). Patrick Little, ed., *The Cromwellian Protectorate* (Woodbridge, 2007), extends the story valuably. Ronald Hutton, *The British Republic, 1649–1660* (2nd edn., Basingstoke, 2000) does more justice to the geopolitics.

Paul Seaward, *The Restoration 1660–1688* (Basingstoke, 1991), is the best introduction to its theme, while Ronald Hutton's *Charles II, King of England, Scotland, and Ireland* (Oxford, 1989), is impressively concerned to set its subject in a three-kingdom frame. For a comparison of one-kingdom and three-kingdom work, contrast John Miller, *After the Civil Wars: English Politics and Government in the Reign of Charles II* (Harlow, 2000), with George Southcombe and Grant Tapsell, *Restoration Politics, Religion and Culture: Britain and Ireland, 1660–1714* (Basingstoke, 2010). For the increasing episcopal confidence of the Church of England, see John Spurr, *The Restoration Church of England, 1646–1689* (New Haven, 1991). The cultural politics of the Restoration are well caught in N.H. Keeble, *The Restoration: England in the 1660s* (Oxford, 2002), and John Spurr, *England in the 1670s: 'This Masquerading Age'* (Oxford, 2000). Geoffrey Holmes, *The Making of a Great Power: Late Stuart and Early Georgian Britain 1660–1722* (London, 1993), is invaluable for the later years of its coverage. For the king at the centre of the storm, see John Miller, *James II* (New Haven, 2000). The revolutions are variously and incisively handled in Robert Beddard, ed., *The Revolutions of 1688* (Oxford, 1991); Jonathan I. Israel, ed., *The Anglo-Dutch Moment: Essays on the Glorious Revolution and its World Impact* (Cambridge, 1991), and Steven C.A. Pincus, *1688: The First Modern Revolution* (New Haven, 2009): the last, while important, is, as the year chosen for the title suggests, largely English in focus. Craig Rose, *England in the 1690s* (Blackwell, 1999), provides a helpful guide through the choppy waters of the 1690s. Lorna Weatherill, *Consumer Behaviour and Material Culture in Britain 1660–1760* (London, 1988), covers a hugely important subject, and though 'Britain' often reads as 'England' that assumption is here argumentatively important.

Ireland

Irish historiography of the last generation has been remarkably sophisticated, and even the surveys have boldly argued as well as narrated. For fine scene-setting, see K.W. Nicholls, *Gaelic and Gaelicized Ireland in the Later Middle Ages* (2nd edn., Dublin, 2003). At the risk of making invidious distinctions, the following are especially noteworthy: Steven G. Ellis, *Ireland in the Age of the Tudors 1447–1603: English Expansion and the End of Gaelic Rule* (London, 1996); Sean Connolly, *Contested Island: Ireland 1430–1630* (Oxford, 2007) and *Divided Kingdom: Ireland 1630–1800* (Oxford, 2008); Colm Lennon, *Sixteenth Century Ireland: The Incomplete Conquest* (2nd edn., Dublin, 2005); and Raymond Gillespie, *Seventeenth Century Ireland: Making Ireland Modern* (Dublin, 2006). Standing behind those are two major collaborative volumes in *The New History of Ireland*, volume 2: *Medieval Ireland 1169–1534* (Oxford, 1987), ed. Art Cosgrove, and volume 3: *Early Modern Ireland 1534–1691* (Oxford, 1976), eds T.W. Moody, F.X. Martin, and F.J. Byrne.

Among a number of excellent broadly focused essay collections, see: Jane Ohlmeyer, eds, *Political Thought in Seventeenth Century Ireland: Kingdom or Colony?* (Cambridge, 2000); Vincent Carey and Ute Lotz-Heumann, eds, *Taking Sides: Colonial and Confessional Mentalities in Early Modern Ireland* (Dublin, 2003); Ciaran Brady and Jane Ohlmeyer, eds, *British Interventions in Early Modern Ireland* (Cambridge, 2005); Robert Armstrong and Tadgh O hAnnrachainn, eds, *Community in Early Modern Ireland* (Dublin, 2006); David Edwards, Padraig Lenihan, and Clodagh Tait, eds, *Age of Atrocity: Violence and Political Conflict in Early Modern Ireland* (Dublin, 2007); Brian Mac Cuarta, ed., *Reshaping Ireland 1550–1700: Colonization and its Consequences* (Dublin, 2011).

A series of monographs have unfolded stages of the Tudors' absorption of Ireland: Steven G. Ellis, *Reform and Revival: English Government in Ireland, 1470–1534* (Woodbridge, 1986); Brendan Bradshaw, *The Irish Constitutional Revolution of the Sixteenth Century* (Cambridge, 1979); Canny's *Elizabethan Conquest of Ireland, 1565–1576*; Ciaran Brady, *The Chief Governors: The Rise and Fall of Reform Government in Ireland, 1536–1588* (Cambridge, 1996); Hiram Morgan's remarkable *Tyrone's Rebellion: The Outbreak of the Nine Years War in Tudor Ireland 1594–1603* (Woodbridge, 1993); and then at the end of the line, John McCavitt, *Sir Arthur Chichester, Lord Deputy of Ireland, 1605–1616*

(Belfast, 1998). Hiram Morgan, ed., *The Battle of Kinsale* (Bray, Wicklow, 2004), offers some excellent essays on the decisive battle. Several recent individual or lineage studies have done much to refocus debate: Colm Lennon, *Richard Stanihurst The Dubliner 1547–1618: A Biography, with a Stanihurst Text, On Ireland's Past* (Blackrock, Dublin, 1981); Nicholas Canny, *The Upstart Earl: A Study of the Mental and Social World of Richard Boyle, First Earl of Cork, 1566–1643* (Cambridge, 1982); Vincent Carey, *Surviving the Tudors: The 'Wizard' Earl of Kildare and English Rule in Ireland, 1537–1586* (Dublin, 2002); David Edwards, *The Ormond Lordship in County Kilkenny, 1515–1642: The Rise and Fall of Butler Feudal Power* (Dublin, 2003); Anthony McCormack, *The Earldom of Desmond: The Decline and Crisis of a Feudal Lordship* (Dublin, 2005). And for an entry-point into the Spenser industry, see Willy Maley, *Salvaging Spenser: Colonialism, Culture, and Identity* (Basingstoke, 1997).

Attempts to import religious reform to Ireland can be tracked in: Brendan Bradshaw, *The Dissolution of the Religious Orders in Ireland under Henry VIII* (Cambridge, 1974); Colm Lennon, *The Lords of Dublin in the Age of Reformation* (Blackrock, Dublin, 1989); Alan Ford, *The Protestant Reformation in Ireland 1590–1641* (2nd edn., Dublin, 1997); Elizabethanne Boran and Crawford Gribben, *Enforcing Reformation in Ireland and Scotland 1550–1700* (Aldershot, 2006). The best study of language, civility, and power is Tony Crowley, *Wars of Words: The Politics of Language in Ireland, 1537–2004* (Oxford, 2005).

Attempts to reorient the landscape, visually and by colonization, are surveyed in Michael McCarthy-Morrogh, *The Munster Plantation: English Migration to Southern Ireland, 1583–1641* (Oxford, 1986); Philip S. Robinson, *The Plantation of Ulster: British Settlement in an Irish Landscape, 1600–1670* (Dublin, 1984), and of course in Canny's *Making Ireland British*; for the legal spadework in Ulster, see Hans Pawlisch, *Sir John Davies and the Conquest of Ireland: A Study in Legal Imperialism* (Cambridge, 1985). For a landmark of a book on intersecting systems of categorizing the landscape, see William J. Smyth, *Map-making, Landscapes and Memory: A Geography of Colonial and Early Modern Ireland, c.1530–1750* (Cork, 2006). For the societies

so (re-)formed, see Ciaran Brady and Raymond Gillespie, eds,
Natives and Newcomers: Essays on the Making of Irish Colonial Society,
1536–1641 (Dublin, 1986); and Peter Clark and Raymond Gillespie,
eds, *Two Capitals: London and Dublin 1500–1840* (Oxford, 2001), and
James Lyttelton and Colin Rynne, eds, *Plantation Ireland: Settlement*
and Material Culture c.1550–c.1700 (Dublin, 2009).

For the great drama of the early seventeenth century, see John McCavitt,
The Flight of the Earls (Dublin, 2002). Bernadette Cunningham, *The*
World of Geoffrey Keating (Dublin, 2000), outlines a new Catholic
sense of identity. For courtly politics and takings, Victor Treadwell,
Buckingham and Ireland, 1616–1628: A Study in Anglo-Irish Politics
(Dublin, 1998), is important. Divergent and conflicted Anglo-Irish
identities are explored in Alan Ford, *James Ussher: Theology, History,*
and Politics in Early Modern Ireland and England (Oxford, 2007), and
in Aidan Clarke's *The Old English in Ireland*. Hugh F. Kearney,
Strafford in Ireland, 1633–1641 (Manchester, 1960), is still valuable,
though it must be supplemented with Merritt, *Political World of*
Thomas Wentworth.

On the opening and course of wars of the 1640s, see Brian Mac Cuarta,
ed., *Ulster 1641: Aspects of the Rising* (Belfast, 1993); Michael Perceval-
Maxwell, *The Outbreak of the Irish Rebellion of 1641* (Dublin, 1991);
Jerrold Casway, *Owen Roe O'Neill and the Struggle for Catholic Ireland*
(Philadelphia, 1984); Jane Ohlmeyer, ed., *Ireland from Independence to*
Occupation (Cambridge, 1995); John R. Young, ed., *Celtic Dimensions*
of the British Civil Wars (Edinburgh, 1997); Micheal O Siochru,
Confederate Ireland 1642–1649: A Constitutional and Political Analysis
(Dublin, 1998); Tadhg O hAnnrachain, *Catholic Reformation in*
Ireland: The Mission of Rinuccini, 1645–1649 (Oxford, 2002); Scott
Wheeler, *Cromwell in Ireland* (Dublin, 1999) and *The Irish and British*
Wars, 1637–1654: Triumph, Tragedy, and Failure (London, 2002); at
times rather more polemically, Micheal O Siochru, *God's Executioner:*
Oliver Cromwell and the Conquest of Ireland (London, 2008); Robert
Armstrong, *Protestant War: 'The British' of Ireland and the Wars of the*
Three Kingdoms (Manchester, 2005); Patrick Little, *Lord Broghill and*
the Cromwellian Union with Ireland and Scotland (Woodbridge,
2004). On the English context of Ireland's wars, see Karl S.

Bottigheimer, *English Money and Irish Land: The Adventurers in the Cromwellian Settlement of Ireland* (Oxford, 1971), and Toby Barnard, *Cromwellian Ireland: English Government and Reform in Ireland 1649–1660* (Oxford, 1975). Aidan Clarke, *Prelude to Restoration in Ireland: The End of the Commonwealth, 1659–1660* (Cambridge, 1999), tells the end of that part of the story.

Ireland beyond the violence is some of the concern of Toby Barnard and Jane Fenlon, eds, *The Dukes of Ormonde 1610–1745* (Woodbridge, 2000); Toby Barnard, *Making the Grand Figure: Lives and Possessions in Ireland, 1641–1770* (New Haven, 2004), and *Improving Ireland? Projectors, Prophets and Profiteers 1641–1786* (Dublin, 2008); also Raymond Gillespie, *The Transformation of the Irish Economy, 1550–1700* (Dundalk, 1991) and David Dickson, *Old World Colony: Cork and South Munster, 1630–1830* (Madison, 2005). See too Coleman A. Dennehy, ed., *Restoration Ireland: Always Settling and Never Settled* (Aldershot, 2008). And for the renewed violence at the end of the century, see J.G. Simms, *War and Politics in Ireland, 1649–1730* (London, 1986), and William A. Maguire, ed., *Kings in Conflict: The Revolutionary War in Ireland and its Aftermath, 1689–1750* (Belfast, 1990).

Scotland

It is a measure of the richness of its narrative that Gordon Donaldson's *Scotland: James V to James VII* (Edinburgh, 1965) is still in print, but that fact points as well to the shortage of competition at the high end of the survey range. The gap is now half-way filled with Jane E.A. Dawson's *Scotland Re-formed, 1488–1587* (Edinburgh, 2007), a work altogether sensitive to the complexities of nationhood; see also Jenny Wormald, *Court, Kirk, and Community: Scotland 1470–1625* (London, 1981), and Rosalind Mitchison, *Lordship to Patronage: Scotland 1603–1745* (London, 1983). And for an overview of the workings of the polity, see Julian Goodare, *State and Society in Early Modern Scotland* (Oxford, 1999).

The Scottish monarchs of the sixteenth century are well covered: Norman Macdougall, *James IV* (Edinburgh, 1989); Jamie Cameron,

James V: The Personal Rule, 1528–1542, ed. Norman Macdougall (East Linton, 1998); Jenny Wormald, *Mary Queen of Scots: Politics, Passion and a Kingdom Lost* (London, 2001), and Michael Lynch, ed., *Mary Stewart: Queen in Three Kingdoms* (Oxford, 1988); and then Pauline Croft and/or Maurice Lee on James VI. For some of the high-points and low-points of the century, see Marcus Merriman, *The Rough Wooings: Mary Queen of Scots, 1542–1551* (East Linton, 2000); Norman Macdougall, *An Antidote to the English: The Auld Alliance 1295–1560* (East Linton, 2001); I.B. Cowan, *The Scottish Reformation* (London, 1982). Some of the binding ties of the early-modern polity are uncovered in Margo Todd, *The Culture of Protestantism in Early Modern Scotland* (New Haven, 2002); Jenny Wormald, *Lords and Men in Scotland: Bonds of Manrent 1442–1603* (Edinburgh, 1985); Keith M. Brown, *Bloodfeud in Scotland, 1573–1625: Violence, Justice, and Politics in an Early Modern Society* (Edinburgh, 1986).

The seventeenth-century kingdom's dilemmas of union are variously explored in Keith M. Brown, *Kingdom or Province? Scotland and the Regal Union, 1603–1715* (Basingstoke, 1992), the essential starting-point, along with Brian Levack, *The Formation of the British State: England, Scotland, and the Union 1603–1707* (Oxford, 1987), Colin Kidd, *Unions and Unionisms: Political Thought in Scotland 1500–2000* (Cambridge, 2010), and Roger Mason, ed., *Scots and Britons: Scottish Political Thought and the Union of 1603* (Cambridge, 1994); see also Bruce Galloway, *The Union of England and Scotland, 1603–1608* (Edinburgh, 1986), and Arthur H. Williams, *Scottish National Consciousness in the Age of James VI: The Apocalypse, the Union, and the Shaping of Scotland's Public Culture* (Edinburgh, 1979). A different alignment is explored in Steve Murdoch, *Britain, Denmark-Norway, and the House of Stuart 1603–1660* (East Linton, 2000). The descent/ascent into revolution can be tracked in Allan Macinnes's *British Revolution*; Maurice Lee, *The Road to Revolution: Scotland under Charles I, 1625–1637* (Urbana, 1985); Peter Donald, *An Uncounselled King? Charles I and the Scottish Troubles 1637–1641* (Cambridge, 1990); John Morrill, ed., *The Scottish National Covenant in its British Context* (Edinburgh, 1990); and in a remarkable series of books by David Stevenson that take the story across the North Channel: *The Scottish*

Revolution, 1637–1644: The Triumph of the Covenanters (Newton Abbot, 1973), *Revolution and Counter-Revolution in Scotland, 1644–1651* (London, 1977), *Alasdair MacColla and the Highland Problem in the Seventeenth Century* (Edinburgh, 1980), *Scottish Covenanters and Irish Confederates: Scottish-Irish Relations in the Mid-seventeenth Century* (Belfast, 1981). Allan Macinnes takes the story of civility and revolution deeper into the Highlands in *Clanship, Commerce and the House of Stuart, 1603–1788* (East Linton, 1996). E.J. Cowan, *Montrose: For Covenant and King* (London, 1977), crosses the partisan divide, as—in no less style—did the subject of Patrick Little's *Lord Broghill*. For the world Broghill was dealing with, see Frances Dow, *Cromwellian Scotland* (2nd edn., Edinburgh, 2000).

The world of kings and its second fall is the territory of Clare Jackson, *Restoration Scotland, 1660–1690: Royalist Politics, Religion and Ideas* (Cambridge, 2003); Julia Buckroyd, *Church and State in Scotland 1660–1681* (Edinburgh, 1980); Maurice Lee, *'Dearest Brother': Lauderdale, Tweeddale and Scottish Politics 1660–1674* (Edinburgh, 2010); and Tim Harris's *Restoration* and *Revolution* sequence. Paul Hopkins's *Glencoe and the End of the Highland War* (Edinburgh, 1986), and Paul Monod, Murray Pittock, and Daniel Szechi, eds, *Loyalty and Identity: Jacobites at Home and Abroad* (Basingstoke, 2010), sensitively study the losers in the British wars.

And then the Union: in addition to Macinnes's *Union and Empire*, see Christopher A. Whatley, *The Scots and the Union* (Edinburgh, 2006), which sees the Scottish economy as distinctly less robust, and John Robertson, ed., *A Union for Empire: Political Thought and the British Union of 1707* (Cambridge, 1995).

Wales

The size of the market for books obviously limits what can be published, and recent monographs on Welsh history have largely been limited to high-level surveys. Glanmor Williams has dominated the field, in particular with *Recovery, Reorientation and Reform: Wales 1415–1642* (Oxford, 1987); but see also Geraint H. Jenkins, *The Foundations of Modern Wales, 1642–1780* (Oxford, 1987), J. Gwynfor Jones, *Early*

Modern Wales, c.1525–1640 (London, 1994), and Philip Jenkins, *A History of Modern Wales 1536–1990* (London, 1992). More specialized are Glanmor Williams, *Wales and the Reformation* (Cardiff, 1997); J. Gwynfor Jones, *Wales and the Tudor State: Government, Religious Change, and the Social Order, 1534–1603* (Cardiff, 1989); and Lloyd Bowen, *The Politics of the Principality: Wales, c.1603–1642* (Cardiff, 2007).

But perhaps the market shapes production in another way. Could it be that, as Tolstoy argued, happy families are all alike and it's only the unhappy ones that are interesting?—a version of course of the journalists' truism that good-news stories don't sell. The relative thinness of the monographic output in Welsh history would then testify to the success of the Tudor union; for the market might only bear one such excellent study of integration as Philip Jenkins's *The Making of a Ruling Class: The Glamorgan Gentry, 1640–1790* (Cambridge, 1983). But there are two studies of overmighty subjects, from either end of the period: Ralph A. Griffiths, *Sir Rhys ap Thomas and his Family: A Study in the Wars of the Roses and Early Tudor Politics* (Cardiff, 1993), and Molly McClain, *Beaufort: The Duke and his Duchess, 1657–1715* (New Haven, 2001).

General Surveys

In the last few years several detailed histories have appeared that go beyond the frontiers of one kingdom and combine narrative with thematic analysis. They overlap chronologically, and all have different approaches from the present work: Steven G. Ellis and Christopher Maginn, *The Making of the British Isles: The State of Britain and Ireland 1450–1660* (Harlow, 2007); David L. Smith, *A History of the Modern British Isles 1603–1707: The Double Crown* (Oxford, 1998); Jim Smyth, *The Making of the United Kingdom: State, Religion, and Identity in Britain and Ireland 1660–1800* (London, 2001). Much more detailed, and Anglocentric, is Mark Nicholls, *A History of the Modern British Isles 1529–1603: The Two Kingdoms* (Oxford, 1999).

INDEX

[Individuals, groups, and places, as well as developments shared among more than one nation, are indexed below in order; developments specific to one country, along with particular institutions and measures, are indexed under the appropriate country.]